Structuring Conflict in the Arab World

Incumbents, Opponents, and Institutions

This book examines how ruling elites manage and manipulate their political opposition in the Middle East. In contrast to discussions of government–opposition relations that focus on how rulers either punish or co-opt opponents, this book focuses on the effect of institutional rules governing the opposition. It argues that rules determining who is and is not allowed to participate in the formal political arena affect not only the relationships between opponents and the state, but also those between various opposition groups. This produces different dynamics of opposition during prolonged economic crises. It also shapes the informal strategies that ruling elites use toward opponents. The argument is presented using a formal model of government–opposition relations. It is demonstrated in the cases of Egypt under Presidents Nasir, Sadat, and Mubarak; Jordan under King Husayn; and Morocco under King Hasan II.

Ellen Lust-Okar is an assistant professor in the Department of Political Science at Yale University. She received her M.A. in Middle Eastern studies and her Ph.D. in political science from the University of Michigan. She has studied and conducted research in Jordan, Morocco, Israel, Palestine, and Syria, and her work examining the relationships between states and opposition has appeared in *Comparative Politics*, *Comparative Political Studies*, the *International Journal of Middle East Studies*, *Middle Eastern Studies*, and other volumes. She is currently working on a second manuscript, *Linking Domestic and International Conflict: The Case of Middle East Rivalries*, with Paul Huth at the University of Michigan.

Politics, as a practice, whatever its professions, has always been the systematic organization of hatreds.

– Henry Brooks Adams

Structuring Conflict in the Arab World

Incumbents, Opponents, and Institutions

ELLEN LUST-OKAR

Yale University

CAMBRIDGE
UNIVERSITY PRESS

PUBLISHED BY THE PRESS SYNDICATE OF THE UNIVERSITY OF CAMBRIDGE
The Pitt Building, Trumpington Street, Cambridge, United Kingdom

CAMBRIDGE UNIVERSITY PRESS
The Edinburgh Building, Cambridge CB2 2RU, UK
40 West 20th Street, New York, NY 10011-4211, USA
477 Williamstown Road, Port Melbourne, VIC 3207, Australia
Ruiz de Alarcón 13, 28014 Madrid, Spain
Dock House, The Waterfront, Cape Town 8001, South Africa

http://www.cambridge.org

First published 2005

Printed in the United States of America

Typeface Sabon 10/13 pt.   *System* LaTeX 2_ε [TB]

A catalog record for this book is available from the British Library.

Library of Congress Cataloging in Publication Data

Lust-Okar, Ellen, 1966–
Structuring conflict in the Arab world : incumbents, opponents, and institutions /
Ellen Lust-Okar.
    p. cm.
Includes bibliographical references and index.
ISBN 0-521-83818-5
1. Opposition (Political science) – Arab countries – Case studies.
2. Elite (Social science) – Arab countries – Case studies.   3. Political participation – Arab
countries – Case studies.   4. Arab countries – Politics and government – Case studies.
5. Egypt – Politics and government – 1970–   6. Jordan – Politics and government –
1952–1999.   7. Morocco – Politics and government – 1961–1999. I. Title.
JQ1850.A792O65 2005
320.917′4927–dc22   2004051803

ISBN 0 521 83818 5 hardback

Contents

Figures and Tables

Acknowledgments

This book, which has been a decade in the making, would never have been possible without the help of a large and diverse community of support. I hope all will be pleased by the ways in which their insights are reflected here. I also hope that the following remarks reflect fully the enormous gratitude I feel for their support.

For first introducing me to the politics and history of the Middle East and then helping me shape early versions of this project, I thank Jill Crystal and Juan Cole. I also thank Christopher Achen, Doug Dion, Robert Pahre, and Carl Simon for their careful attention and thoughtful comments in the early stages of this project.

The fieldwork itself was made productive and more pleasant with the assistance of a great number of people. I cannot adequately express my gratitude for all of the individuals in Morocco and Jordan who patiently entered into discussions with me; from the *bawwab* on the street to the party leaders, I learned from them all. The staff and fellow researchers at the American Center for Oriental Research (ACOR) in Amman, Jordan, the Center for Strategic Studies (CSS) at the University of Jordan, and the Tangier American Legation Museum (TALM) in Tangier, Morocco, were also extremely helpful. I particularly thank the directors, Pierre Bikai of ACOR, Mustafa Hamarneh of CSS, and Thor Kuniholm of TALM, for their patient support and assistance. In Morocco I also had the good fortune of meeting Laurie Brand, and I am extremely grateful to her for her insights and queries on both Morocco and Jordan, as well as her friendship and support.

In later iterations of this work, I received help and comments from a great number of friends and colleagues. I thank Betty Anderson, Glenn

Beamer, Eva Bellin, David Brown, Barbara Geddes, Noura Hamladj, Bahgat Korany, Vickie Langohr, Kelly McMann, Michele Penner Angrist, Marsha Pripstein Posusney, Andrew Schrank, Randy Stevenson, Meredith Weiss, Carrie Rosefsky Wickham, and Mike Wolf, who offered valuable feedback on parts of the manuscript. I am particularly grateful in this respect to Robert Dahl for his enthusiastic support of what is, in many ways, an extension of his work. I thank Anne Sartori, Alastair Smith, and Jana Kunicova, who gave me helpful feedback on the formal model, and Simon Samoeil for his wonderful assistance in checking my transliteration. For their editorial and research assistance at critical points in this work, I extend my appreciation to Kellianne Farnham, Lilach Gilady, Sara Hirschhorn, Alexandra Kobishyn, Adria Lawrence, Tarek Masoud, Naysan Rafati, Raja Shamas, and Emily Wills.

I am particularly grateful to those who have read the entire manuscript, in some cases multiple times. Amaney Jamal, Fiona McGillivary, Pauline Jones Luong, Glenn Robinson, Mark Tessler, and two anonymous reviewers have shared extremely valuable comments. Lewis Bateman, my editor at Cambridge University Press, not only provided support and insights but was also enormously patient.

The project would never have been possible without significant financial support. I received early support for language study from the Foreign Language and Area Studies Fellowships, administered through the Center for Middle Eastern and North African Studies at the University of Michigan. The International Institute for Peace and Security Studies, also at the University of Michigan, the Council of American Overseas Research Centers, the Social Science Research Council, and the James A. Baker III Institute at Rice University supported subsequent fieldwork.

Of course, nothing is possible without the support of family. I am particularly fortunate, for I am "at home" on both sides of the ocean. My own family is a constant source of inspiration and support. As the youngest of five children, I was always able to look ahead of me and know that anything is possible and nothing is required. My family in Syria has also been enormously supportive. I am still amazed at how readily they accepted me, how patiently they worked to help me learn Arabic, how sincerely they have engaged in my interests, and how cheerfully they have helped with child care. I could not have asked for more.

I am also deeply grateful to my husband, Nazih, and our sons, Stephan and Gibran. Nazih has never doubted this could be done, even if he sometimes has questioned our sanity in doing it. For his willingness to traipse across the world with me, and to share the ups and downs of the work,

I thank him. In contrast to Nazih, Stephan and Gibran have been fairly oblivious to this whole project. That, too, has been a wonderful gift.

Finally, I dedicate this book to two men who were so very different and yet were both fundamental to this work: my father, Robert M. Lust, and my mentor, A. F. K. Organski. My father was a Midwestern truck driver and farmer with an insatiable sense of curiosity. My advisor was an Italian Russian immigrant who never ceased trying to convince me that I should give up working on the Middle East and turn to Italy, where I could sip cappuccinos and have easy access to data sets. Both taught me that while work is deadly serious, it can be done with laughter and joy. Both helped foster my interest in how the world worked and, moreover, were absolutely confident that I could succeed in my desire to push our understandings of it just a little bit further. I am so grateful for the lessons they taught and hope that this work would have made them proud.

A Note on the Use of Language

To make the text more accessible to non-Arabic and non-French readers, I have used the English names of parties and organizations. I have also used traditional spellings of words commonly found in English (e.g., *ulema*, Alawite) and of the names of cities and states. Those who are interested can find the Arabic and French names in the appendix, endnotes, and index. The Arabic is transliterated using a simplified version of the Library of Congress system, including the use of ' for 'ayn and ' for a hamzah. Where individuals have consistently adopted a somewhat different form of transliteration, I have followed their spellings. Thus, the careful reader will note small inconsistencies in the text, but the language fulfills its ultimate purpose: the transmission of information and ideas.

Abbreviations

ASO	Arab Socialist Organization, Egypt
ASU	Arab Socialist Union (Egypt)
Ba'th	Arab Resurrection (Ba'th) Party (Jordan and Syria)
CAPMAS	Central Agency for Public Mobilization and Statistics (Egypt)
CDT	Democratic Confederation of Labor (Morocco)
CHRLA	Center for Human Rights Legal Aid (Egypt)
CNJA	National Council of the Youth and the Future (Morocco)
CSS	Center for Strategic Studies (Jordan)
DFLP	Democratic Front for the Liberation of Palestine
ETUF	Egyptian Trade Union Federation (Egypt)
FBIS	Foreign Broadcast Information Service
FDIC	Front for the Defense of Constitutional Institutions (Morocco)
GDP	gross domestic product
IAF	Islamic Action Front (Jordan)
IMF	International Monetary Fund
LR	Liberation Rally (Egypt)
MAJD	Democratic Front Organization in Jordan (Jordan)
MEED	*Middle East Economic Digest*
MP	Popular Movement (Morocco)
NCC	National Consultative Council (Jordan)
NDP	National Democratic Party (Egypt)
NPF	National Progressive Front (Syria)
NPUP	National Progressive Unionist Party (Egypt)
NU	National Union (Egypt)

OADP	Organization of Democratic and Popular Action (Morocco)
PDI	Democratic Party of Independence (Morocco)
PFLP	Popular Front for the Liberation of Palestine
PLO	Palestinian Liberation Organization
PND	National Democratic Party (Morocco)
PPS	Party of Progress and Socialism (Morocco)
RCC	Revolutionary Command Council (Egypt)
RNI	National Assembly of Independents (Morocco)
SLO	Socialist Liberal Organization (Egypt)
SLP	Socialist Labor Party (Egypt)
SoC	structures of contestation
UC	Constitutional Union (Morocco)
UGTM	General Union for Workers in Morocco (Morocco)
UMT	Moroccan Labor Union (Morocco)
UNEM	National Union of Moroccan Students (Morocco)
UNFP	National Union of Popular Forces (Morocco)
USFP	Socialist Union of Popular Forces (Morocco)

Introduction

Authoritarian leaders are seldom expected to play by the rules. In the prevailing wisdom, autocracies are characterized by unique leaders with different agendas, supported by slightly broader or narrower coalitions and justified through varied institutional façades. Thus, to understand authoritarian politics, we focus on the leaders – distinguishing the personalities and backgrounds of Stalin, Mao, Peron, and Castro; we contrast the foreign and domestic policies of Nasir and Sadat, Stalin and Khruschev; and we examine the differences between personalistic dictators, military juntas, and various forms of one-party states. However, in marked contrast to studies of democracies, which carefully distinguish parliamentary and presidential systems, analyze electoral rules and even sometimes the finer points of voter registration, we largely ignore formal institutions in authoritarian regimes. Even those turning their attention once again to competitive authoritarianism or "hybrid regimes" have dismissed formal institutions, arguing that institutions "are often weak and therefore easily manipulated or changed by autocratic incumbents."[1]

Yet, formal institutions matter in authoritarian regimes. They do so independently of the larger "rules of the game" that characterize "regime types." They do so with regard to political participation, and they do so even in the Middle East, a region in which institutions are perhaps voted least likely to count. Authoritarian elites use institutional rules to create and maintain very different relationships between the state and political opponents and among various opposition groups themselves. In some cases, incumbents foster a "divided Structure of Contestation" (divided SoC), allowing some groups to participate legally in the formal political system while excluding others. In other cases, they allow all opposition groups to participate in the formal political system, creating a unified Structure of Contestation (unified SoC).

ECONOMIC CRISES, POLITICAL DEMANDS

This book examines the importance of SoCs in the context of prolonged economic crises. Doing so allows us to see how these structures influence the relationships between opposition groups as well as the ruling elites. It also allows us to revise our understanding of the politics of economic reform.

Conventional wisdom holds that economic crises create increased discontent, which opponents exploit to demand both political and economic reform. In many cases, authoritarian elites legitimize their rule with promises of economic growth and stabilize their regimes through the distribution of patronage; the economic failure and loss of distributive goods thus strike at the very basis of these regimes.[2] In addition, economic crises and reforms create new winners and losers among political elites and lead to widespread discontent among the masses. According to conventional wisdom, new coalitions of political opponents then form, capitalize on the masses' suffering, and mobilize popular frustration to make political demands.[3] Political change should follow. In some cases, these demands overwhelm the existing regimes, leading to dramatic changes through replacement. In other cases, incumbents hold on to power long enough to foster the formation of new, more open regimes. In general, however, it was the belief that economic crises provided catalysts for political opponents that led scholars and policy makers alike to predict in the 1990s that political liberalization, and perhaps even democratization, would spread from Latin America, Eastern Europe, and the former Soviet Union through much of Africa, the Middle East, and Asia.

Indeed, so ingrained was the expectation that economic crises lead to increased political unrest that much of the literature on economic reform did not address the assumption at all. Rather, it focused on how economic characteristics (e.g., the level of urbanization, the ability of exporting industries to react to currency devaluations, the types of reforms implemented, and the order of their implementation) and political factors (e.g., the level of state resources, structures of political institution, and the size and nature of the ruling coalition) determine when incumbent elites are best able to implement reforms.[4] The studies took for granted that economic decline leads to greater political unrest. The fundamental underlying notion that opposition elites will take advantage of prolonged economic decline to press their political agenda generally went unquestioned.

Yet, not only has liberalization stalled and sometimes reversed since the early 1990s, but also a close examination of cases reveals that economic crises have not always led to sustained demands for political change. Although the so-called bread riots associated with International Monetary Fund (IMF) reforms appear prominent, often dramatic price increases led neither to spontaneous nor to planned political mobilization. In Africa, only about half of the countries with severe economic crises experienced protest movements by the early 1990s, and there was no clear relationship between the intensity of unrest and the severity of austerity measures or economic conditions.[5] More importantly, the economic crises and discontent far preceded any political unrest in the region. Some countries had experienced economic crisis since 1973, but no major unrest occurred until 1990.[6]

That the impact of economic crises on popular protest takes substantial time to become apparent or varies across cases does not necessarily contradict the fundamental assumption that prolonged crises increase the *likelihood* of unrest. Differences in the effectiveness of political repression or the domestic and international support of opposition groups can explain why protest occurs in some places but not others. However, underlying the conventional wisdom is the expectation that when the regime is weakened or opposition groups are strengthened, political demands and the potential for unrest increase. Opposition elites always *want* to mobilize unrest and demand political change; it is their *capabilities* that determine whether or not they do so. The easier it is for political opponents to demand political change and to mobilize the opposition, the more likely they are to do so. In short, opposition elites are more than ready to take advantage of economic crises and heightened mass discontent, using the threat or reality of mobilizing the masses to pressure incumbents into granting political change.

Yet, this is not always true. Sometimes, prolonged economic crises have made political opponents more likely to press their demands, just as the conventional wisdom suggests. However, at others, opposition elites have become increasingly unwilling to mobilize the masses, *even though they are more able to do so*. Such was the case in Morocco and Egypt during the 1990s. Initially, opposition leaders took advantage of the increased popular discontent to demand political change. Yet, by the mid-1990s, party and union leaders no longer wanted to mobilize the masses to demand political change. Even though the economic crises had continued and the masses were highly volatile, the opposition actually became *less* willing to mobilize strikes, protests, or demonstrations to demand political reform.

That economic crises do not always lead opposition elites to demand political reform contradicts a fundamental assumption, and it forces us to reframe the question of how economic crises affect political reform. Rather than asking how governments can manage the increased unrest that accompanies mounting popular dissatisfaction, scholars must ask under what conditions opponents take advantage of increased dissatisfaction to press political demands.[7] While accepting the assumption that increased popular dissatisfaction improves the prospects for protest, research needs to move away from the expectation that this alone makes opponents more likely to challenge incumbent elites. To do so, as we shall see in Chapter 1, requires that we return to the question of when political opponents use an increase in mass discontent to demand political reform in authoritarian regimes.

In addition, these cases suggest that political liberalization is not inherently unstable. The assumption that liberalization is a transient state, through which states move toward democracy or authoritarianism, was prevalent in the literature emerging after World War II.[8] Although scholars examining the Third Wave were no longer as convinced as the early modernization theorists that democracy is inevitable, they nonetheless continued to see political liberalization as a unilinear and progressive process – wherein either regimes move toward greater democratization or revert to a more closed system of authoritarianism. Liberalization was not an equilibrium state. Przeworski argued, for instance, that although incumbents choose liberalization in the attempt to maintain their regime, such contingent or partial liberalization is usually unstable because of the "thaw" principle: "a melting of the iceberg of civil society that overflows the dams of the authoritarian regime."[9] Similarly, although Lucian Pye called for the study of "part free and part authoritarian" regimes in his 1990 Presidential Address to the American Political Science Association, he too believed that "the two polar authoritarian and democratic extremes probably have a higher potential for stable equilibrium than any of the stages in between."[10] Since the majority of transitions from authoritarian rule in Latin America and Southern Europe began with "glasnost"-like liberalization,[11] it is not surprising that partial liberalization was perceived as unstable. Consequently, until very recently, scholars spent more time considering what factors smooth the transition from authoritarianism to democracy[12] than considering the mechanisms by which such part-free, part-authoritarian systems are maintained.

Yet, Morocco and Egypt in the 1990s were excellent examples of "liberalized authoritarianism," wherein the regime remains intact and retains "its capacity to control outcomes ex post."[13] Parties were allowed to participate openly in the political system, and indeed, in Morocco, opposition parties held a significant proportion of seats in the legislature. Yet, neither the parties nor the leaders were under the illusion that the parties held real political power. Despite the prolonged economic crisis and mounting popular discontent, partial liberalization had not "broken the dam." Not only did the opposition fail to overthrow the regimes, but also, precisely when incumbents became weakest, opposition elites were more timid in using popular pressure to make demands. Indeed, in both states, the partial liberalization established in the mid-1970s continued nearly 30 years later.

SoCs help explain both the dynamics of government–opposition relations and when liberalization is more and less likely to be stable. In unified SoCs, opponents become increasingly willing to demand reforms during political and economic crises, when the increased public discontent and the weakened state make it both easier for opposition elites to mobilize and more likely that they will succeed. By contrast, in divided SoCs, moderate political opposition elites may become less likely to mobilize during prolonged crises. In this case, included opposition groups may want to demand greater political freedom if they know that, at the end of the struggle, they will be the victors. However, in the divided environment, included opposition elites have two fears. First, they fear that they will lose what privileges they have if they exploit discontent to cause serious regime instability. In addition, where the division of included and excluded political opponents is based, at least in part, on ideological divisions, they fear that the excluded groups may take advantage of unrest, mobilizing to make their own demands. If prolonged political crises make it more likely that excluded groups will join in any ongoing political unrest to press their own demands, the moderate opposition will refrain from mobilizing against the government. Although it may be easier for opposition elites to demand political change, they prefer not to do so. They prefer to maintain the status quo to either losing the privileges they have achieved or affording currently excluded groups greater influence. In short, the opposition elites' choices to mobilize political opposition in divided and unified SoCs are strikingly different

Once SoCs are established, these structures also influence incumbent elites' strategies in choosing whether or not to repress different opposition groups. Even under the same institutional rules, state elites often treat political opponents differently; they may harshly repress some groups while allowing other groups to operate nearly unfettered. Incumbent elites respond systematically to opposition groups, depending on the structures they have created. In unified SoCs, incumbent elites are likely to support the growth of moderate opposition groups at the expense of radical groups. In divided SoCs, incumbents attempt to balance the strength of included and excluded opposition groups. Contrary to what one may initially expect, state elites in divided SoCs do not have incentives to eliminate their radical opposition. The existence of radical opposition groups, and the threat that they may take advantage of political unrest to demand their own policies, serves to repress the included opposition groups. Incumbent elites thus aim to keep a reasonable balance between the threat of radical, excluded opposition groups and included opponents.

Finally, these structures help determine when partial liberalization is and is not stable. In divided SoCs, where incumbent elites allow some opponents the chance to participate in the formal political system while excluding others, political liberalization may be long-lasting and stable. Indeed, in this case, allowing opposition groups to make some demands actually helps to *preserve* the regime. In contrast, in the unified case, when incumbents liberalize by permitting all significant opposition elites to have limited participation in the political system, liberalization creates demands for even more political change.

SoCs IN JORDAN, MOROCCO, AND EGYPT

Jordan, Morocco, and Egypt are particularly useful cases in which to explore how incumbent elites use different strategies to structure contestation, and how these strategies affect the relationships both among opposition groups, and between these groups and the state, during prolonged economic crises. As we shall see in the remaining chapters, ruling elites created different SoCs. In Jordan, King Husayn created a unified SoC, while in Morocco, King Hasan II had established a divided SoC before the economic crises of the 1980s. In Egypt, Presidents Nasir and Sadat had instituted a unified SoC, but in the early 1980s, Mubarak fostered a divided environment. Thus, Egypt had a very different SoC when it faced its economic crisis in the late 1980s and 1990s than it did when it faced a similar crisis in the late 1960s and 1970s. As a result, the dynamics of opposition varied across these cases. In Jordan and in Egypt under Nasir and Sadat, opponents continued to put pressure on the state, leading to increased repression. In Morocco and in Egypt under Mubarak,

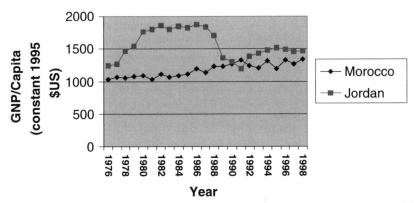

FIGURE I.1. GNP Per Capita – Morocco and Jordan, 1976–1998. *Source:* World Bank tables.

the moderate forces who initially sought to use economic discontent to demand reforms became nearly silent by the mid-1990s, just as the crises escalated.

This divergence is not explained by the nature of the economic crises. Generally, scholars have argued that where crises are short-lived or minor, the masses are unlikely to put significant pressure on incumbent elites. Furthermore, when reform policies are piecemeal, hurting different segments of the population at different points in time, regimes are more insulated from opposition pressures. Finally, not all groups are affected equally, and not all have an equal desire to demand economic and political change.[14]

Yet, it is simply not the case that the crisis in Morocco was less profound than that in Jordan or, similarly, that the crisis Egypt experienced under Mubarak was less significant than the previous crisis under Nasir and Sadat. As shown in Figure I.1, both monarchies, Morocco and Jordan, experienced economic crises in the 1980s that contrasted sharply with the boom years of the 1970s. Morocco's crisis began first. After 1975, two international price changes affected the Kingdom's earnings: the price of phosphate, Morocco's primary export, declined, while the price of oil, one of Morocco's imports, rose. Indeed, expenditures on petroleum increased from 3.6 percent of total imports in 1970 to 13.6 percent in 1973 and to 27.46 percent in 1983,[15] putting a squeeze on the Kingdom's balance of payments. Initially, Jordan was insulated from this shock by worker remittances, increased foreign aid, and the influx of people and money due to the Lebanese and Iran–Iraq wars; In 1981 Arab aid, merchandise exports, and remittances were 17 times higher than they had been in 1973, and they accounted for 84 percent of Jordan's gross domestic product (GDP).[16] By 1983, however, Jordan's fortunes had also changed. As the Iran–Iraq war in the Gulf turned against Iraq, Jordan found itself subsidizing its neighbor's efforts. When Iraq, which had previously received 25 percent of Jordan's exports, could no longer pay for Jordanian goods, Jordan made available $65 million in credit to Iraq to cover outstanding debts.[17] In addition, the Gulf states diverted aid from Jordan to Iraq, and by 1988, Arab aid had dropped from a high of $1.2 billion in 1981 to $450 million.[18] Adding to Jordan's troubles, the King chose to relinquish the West Bank in July of that year. In response, the Palestinian Liberation Organization (PLO) and many in the Palestinian population transferred significant amounts of capital out of the country.

The economic slowdown, as well as subsequent reforms, exacerbated unemployment and underemployment problems. In Morocco, hiring freezes and an expanding population led to an increasing number of unemployed. Public employment decreased from a yearly 40,000 to 50,000 new employees before 1983 to an average of 10,000 new employees per year between 1983 and 1987.[19] Official urban unemployment rates rose from 11.3 percent in 1980 to 18.4 percent in 1984 and declined slightly to 16 percent in 1992. Unofficial estimates were much higher, however, reaching 30 percent in 1984.[20] Educated youth suffered as well as their uneducated counterparts. The unemployment rate among those with secondary education grew from 27.6 percent in 1984 to 43.4 percent in 1990.[21] In Jordan, the official unemployment rate stood at 9 percent[22] by the end of the 1980s, an alarming rate in a country that began the decade with a labor shortage. The situation worsened further following the first Gulf War, when, partially in response to an influx of refugees, the unemployment rate reached an estimated 20 percent.[23]

The unemployment problem was coupled with high inflation. Inflation rates were consistently high during the 1980s, skyrocketing in some cases to more than 30 percent per year. Imported goods became particularly expensive, as local currencies declined in value. In Jordan, for instance, the dinar lost 50 percent of its value between 1988 and 1989.[24] At the same time, most employed found their wages frozen or rising at rates much lower than the rate of inflation. Real wages fell, and the middle classes in particular found their standard of living declining sharply.[25] They joined an already large, discontented populace living below the poverty line.

The crises eventually forced states to turn to the international community for assistance. In 1978, the Moroccan government had announced a new three-year stabilization plan intended to decrease public spending and investment. Implementation was hesitant, however, and the crisis deepened. By 1983, the Kingdom had to turn to the World Bank, and a new program of stabilization and structural adjustment was implemented: restraining government spending and investment, changing the international trade regime, altering the tax system, and reforming the banking systems.[26] Similarly, in Jordan, the government attempted to ease domestic problems, going so far as to sell off part of its gold reserves.[27] In February 1989, however, Jordan agreed to an IMF structural adjustment program. After the Gulf War further exacerbated the state's economic problems,[28] the King entered into controversial international agreements with Israel, partly in the hope of attaining economic benefits.

These reforms increased mass discontent.[29] When these states instituted structural adjustment programs, their immediate task was to solve the balance of payments problem. The initial stabilization programs focused primarily on reductions in government spending (i.e., wage and hiring freezes in the public sector, decreased subsidies on foodstuffs and other basic goods, reduced government investment). For the masses, this meant that prices rose, unemployment increased, and real wages fell. Even where the programs were successful on the macroeconomic level, the results for the masses were disastrous. Throughout the 1980s, mass discontent increased.

In Egypt, the economic crises after the 1967 war and again after the mid-1980s were equally painful, and both provided important catalysts for the political opposition. The first economic crisis actually preceded the 1967 war, although it was also exacerbated by it. Economic growth, which had averaged 6 percent per year from 1960 to 1965, slowed to 1 percent in 1966–1967. The decline was even steeper after the war. Egypt lost foreign exchange it had previously gained from shipping through the Suez Canal, which provided an annual $164 million in revenue from 1960 to 1967; it no longer benefited from oil deposits in the Sinai; and it suffered a decline in investment from about 17.2 percent of GDP in 1964–1965 to about 13 percent in 1967–1975. At the same time, military expenditures increased given Egypt's stalemate in the Yemeni civil war and during the ensuing War of Attrition against Israel, and the largest cities faced increased social pressures as nearly 1 million inhabitants from the towns in the Suez Canal region migrated. These pressures were only partially offset by aid, primarily from the USSR, and the Egyptian deficit increased 86 percent, from $202 million in 1959–1966 to $375 million in 1967–1972. Egypt turned to external borrowing, and by 1975 the external debt reached $6.3 billion, more than triple its size in 1970.[30]

The economic decline was a major blow to the social contract between the regime and the people. The revolutionary regime, which had taken power in July 1952, had been justified in part by its ability to promote economic growth and provide employment. In the face of the growing crisis, unemployment rose from 2.2 percent in 1969 to 7.7 percent in 1976.[31] Equally important, Egyptian salaries failed to keep pace with inflation, and the earning power, particularly of degree holders, declined. As a result, as we shall see, Egyptians became willing to mobilize against the regime, with political involvement extending beyond the few Marxist or Islamist cells that existed prior to 1967 to include increasing numbers of Egyptians.[32]

Economic conditions improved after 1974, but at the cost of painful economic policies, a turn toward the West, and eventually a peace treaty with Israel that further heightened Egyptians' ire. Oil revenues increased; workers' remittances from the Gulf countries rose; and revenue flowed once again from transit through the Suez Canal. In addition, in 1981 Egypt received significant U.S. aid. As a result, the economy grew an average of 9.1 percent annually from 1974 to 1983, and per capita incomes doubled from $334 to $700.[33]

By the late 1980s, this tide was once again changing.[34] Growth declined to 2.6 percent annually from 1986 to 1988, and per capita growth was negative. Mubarak at first attempted to alleviate the economic decline through increased borrowing. By 1988 Egypt's debt had reached more than 115 percent of GDP, an increase of more than 26 percent over 1981 levels,[35] and debt service payments were 60 percent of exports. Consequently, external donors put pressure on the regime to cut public spending, from 63.5 percent of GDP in 1982 to 41.1 percent in 1989.[36]

These reforms hurt Egyptians significantly. The standard of living fell as GDP growth rates slowed to nearly 1 percent in 1989–1990 and the population growth rate remained nearly triple that size. Unemployment reached 1.46 million persons, according to a Central Agency for Public Mobilisation and Statistics (CAPMAS) Labor Force Sample Survey, with 78 percent of the unemployed having at least an intermediate degree.[37] U.S. Embassy officials put the total unemployment at nearly double official figures, estimating in 1991 that between 2.5 and 3 million Egyptians were out of work.[38] Those who were employed fared poorly as well. The Egyptian government tried to reduce unemployment, in part, by dividing the wage bill among an expanding workforce; by 1987 the salaries of government employees had reached only 55 percent of their 1973 level.[39]

Poverty was deep as well as widespread: The consumption level of the average poor was 20.1 percent below the poverty level.[40]

The crisis continued through the 1990s. By the end of the decade macroeconomic indicators had improved dramatically, with foreign debt cut in half, increased foreign reserves, and inflation under control. Yet, in the meantime, a large segment of lower- and middle-class Egyptians had become disillusioned with the regime. This provided opportunities for political opponents to demand not only economic welfare but political reform as well.[41]

In short, the different dynamics of opposition in Morocco and Jordan, as well as those in Egypt over time, cannot be explained by differences in their economic crises. As we shall see in more detail in Chapter 5, although Moroccan and Egyptian political elites were extremely reluctant to mobilize the masses in order to press for political change, the masses *were* willing to mobilize. The failure of these political elites to take the economic crisis as an opportunity to press for political reform cannot be understood by looking for reform strategies that minimized political discontent. Morocco, and Egypt under Mubarak, perhaps even more than Jordan had populations willing to take to the streets and express their demands. Unfortunately, conventional understandings about the depth of economic crises or the structure of reforms simply do not help us understand why elites chose not to exploit this opportunity fully, pressing for fundamental change in the regime.

Civil Society

The difference is also not explained by a difference in the nature of civil society in Jordan, Morocco, and Egypt. Debates over the definition of civil society, as well as the exact nature of the relationship between civil society and regime change, abound. However, civil society can be thought of as the "arena where manifold social movements . . . and civic organizations from all classes . . . attempt to constitute themselves in an ensemble of arrangements so that they can express themselves and advance their interests."[42]

Two sets of theoretical literature predict that where civil society is stronger and networks between social organizations are denser, opposition should be able to use mass discontent to demand political change. The first body of literature examines civil society directly, arguing that civic organizations can help to press for liberalization. The dominant hypothesis is that strong civic organizations are more likely to facilitate demands for political change and, where liberalization begins, to promote a relatively stable transition to democratization.[43] A similar hypothesis emerges from the literature on social mobilization. A dominant argument in this literature is that regardless of how angry the masses become, they will engage in political action only when they are part of organized groups with access to resources.[44] In light of this, one may expect that opposition elites embedded in stronger professional associations, trade unions, civic organizations, and political parties are more likely to demand political change, especially where these groups have significant resources and are highly interconnected.[45] Given this, the Jordanian opposition should have been more adequately organized, and therefore more capable of exploiting economic crises and making political demands, than was the Moroccan opposition.

However, the evidence is quite the contrary. Jordanian opposition elites had much weaker organizational structures than Moroccan opposition movements. In Jordan, all political parties were driven underground in 1957, and the trade unions were effectively depoliticized in the early 1970s. Human rights organizations, women's groups, and other social organizations were also very limited and generally under the direct patronage of the royal Hashemites. Thus, the professional associations and the Muslim Brotherhood, operating as a charitable society, became the most important outlets for political expression both during and following the period of martial law.[46] Although underground, political parties remained particularly active in these associations. Elections of association boards, as well as their activities, reflected political as well as professional concerns.

In Morocco civil society was more developed. Political parties were allowed to operate openly from the early 1970s, and the two main opposition parties, the Socialist Union of Popular Forces (USFP) and Istiqlal, had particularly close ties with two of the three large umbrella unions. The USFP had ties with the Democratic Labor Confederation* (CDT); many in the union's executive bureau were members of the USFP's political bureau, including the CDT's Secretary General, Nubir Amaoui. The Istiqlal Party was intricately linked to the General Union of Moroccan Workers† (UGTM); All members in the UGTM executive bureau were important members of the Istiqlal Party. Through the unions, the parties were able to mobilize popular protests, demanding political as well as

---

* Confédération Démocratique du Travail.
† Union Générale des Travailleurs au Maroc.

economic reforms. By the early 1980s, Morocco had also developed nearly 3,000 relatively independent associations for human rights, women's issues, and other social groups.[47] In short, the organizational structure in Morocco was *more* developed than that in Jordan.

Similarly, civil society in Egypt under Mubarak was more developed than that in Jordan, and it was also more developed by the 1990s than it had been under Nasir and Sadat. Upon assuming power in 1952, Nasir attempted to dominate civil society. For instance, labor unions were organized under a single union, the Egyptian Trade Union Federation, which the government controlled tightly. The government also brought other voluntary organizations under strict regulation through a series of decrees in the 1950s and early 1960s. Thus, although the number of voluntary organizations in Egypt rose from approximately 800 in 1950 to 2,000 in 1970, the organizations lacked autonomy. Although this situation was not completely reversed by the 1990s, Egyptian civil society had grown considerably stronger by 1990. New legislation passed through the 1980s gave organizations greater latitude. In addition, the sheer number of civic organizations in Egypt grew from 7,593 to 10,731 between 1976 and 1981 alone, totaling nearly 27,000 by 1998.[48] The unwillingness of political parties to demand greater reforms in the mid-1990s, then, is explained neither by the autonomy nor the size of Egypt's civil society. Both were greater in the 1990s than they had been in the 1960s and 1970s.

There is also no evidence that Moroccan organizations became less capable of mobilizing over time. One explanation would be that unions, an important part of the support for Moroccan opposition parties, become less capable of mobilizing during economic crises. Joan Nelson argues, for instance, that union membership dropped in most of the nations simultaneously experiencing economic and political liberalization. In addition, high unemployment and trade liberalization reduced union bargaining power vis-à-vis private management.[49] Similarly, Barbara Geddes argues that labor unions' power declines over the periods of economic crises. This is a partial explanation of why labor has not been "able to translate its opposition to adjustment policies into credible threats to punish the initiators of adjustment."[50]

Although this is perhaps the most compelling explanation of why political unrest may decline during a period of economic crisis, it is not wholly satisfying. It explains why opponents may become less capable of pressing demands, not why they may become less willing to do so. Yet, it is not an inability to make demands that has led to the declining political activity of Morocco's opposition parties. Interviews with members of the opposition as well as with foreign officials close to the scene suggest that the opposition parties could quite easily have mobilized mass opposition. Rather, it appears that they did not want to do so. Even in the cases that Geddes examines, it is not clear whether the opposition's failure to successfully challenge the government came from an inability to do so or a refusal to try. She notes that "Labor has not lacked the capacity to mount opposition; there have been numerous strikes and demonstrations. But this opposition has not routinely led to threats of regime breakdown, the defeat of incumbents at the polls, or the wholesale abandonment of market-oriented policies."[51] The reasons she gives for this focus on the opposition's ability to challenge, but we will see that there are important reasons why political opponents may not be willing to mount serious challenges even when they are capable of doing so.

State Institutions

Significant differences in the strength and arrangements of political institutions could also explain the divergence in these cases. Perhaps the most common explanation for divergence in the ability of governments to withstand economic crises is regime type. For instance, Linz and Stepan distinguish between several types of authoritarian rule: civilianized authoritarianism, hierarchical military rule, sultanism (personalized dictatorship), totalitarianism, and post-totalitarianism, arguing that the likelihood of democratization and consolidation depends on the nature of the incumbent regimes.[52] Similarly, Geddes finds that the nature of authoritarianism – and particularly whether a regime is personalistic, a military dictatorship, or single-party – affects whether or not regimes can withstand economic hardship.[53] Jennifer Gandhi and Adam Przeworski also argue that institutional arrangements in authoritarian regimes (i.e., civilian, military, or monarchical structures) affect economic development and regime stability.[54]

However, these typologies of authoritarian regimes do not explain the different outcomes in these cases. Both Morocco and Jordan were monarchies; the King and the palace were the center of power. Former Prime Minister Zayd al-Rifaʿi summarized Jordan's political system:

Jordan has a highly personalized governmental system in which decisions are made by the king, by the influence of the king's advisors, and in some cases, by the prime minister and his cabinet. It is a fact of political life in Jordan that we do not have an institutionalized process of decision-making.[55]

The same could be said of Morocco.[56] In both kingdoms, the monarch was the supreme authority, making the final decisions in public policy and controlling the distribution of both political and economic resources.

Similarly, Egypt under Nasir, Sadat, and Mubarak had fundamentally the same regime type. The Free Officers' Revolution ushered in a dominant-party, authoritarian regime governed by a ruling elite closely tied to the military. The fundamental bases of the regime, and even leading figures in the government, remained the same through the Mubarak period.

Furthermore, there is no need to believe that the divergence existed because the regimes had significant structural differences. Some have argued, for instance, that the level of economic ties between the state and society affects the likelihood of collective action. Where the state is responsible for distributing basic necessities and jobs to the masses, mobilized opposition is less likely. Similarly, the level of decentralization in the economic system can affect the likelihood that reforms result in economic inefficiency, high redistribution, and political unrest.[57] Morocco did not have greater control over the masses than Jordan, however. Both states had long officially accepted the private sector, allowing for private ownership and arguing in favor of a laissez faire economy, but both had also established large state sectors. In Jordan, more than 70 percent of the populace was employed by the state.[58] More importantly, even were such differences across these states present, they would explain the different levels of mobilization in each state; they would not explain why Moroccan elites became less willing to mobilize over time, while Jordanian elites did not.

Finally, one could question whether repression in Morocco is simply higher than that in Jordan, or whether repression in Egypt under Mubarak has been higher than that under Nasir and Sadat. Christian Davenport has argued, for instance, that where national constitutions grant civil liberties and restrict the granting of emergency powers, repression is less likely and mobilization increases.[59] In both Jordan and Morocco, however, constitutional liberties were strictly proscribed, and both King Husayn and King Hasan II had invoked emergency rule. In Egypt, civil liberties were more tightly restricted under Nasir and Sadat than under Mubarak.[60] Greater repression does not explain the divergent patterns across these regimes. Indeed, we will see in both Morocco and Egypt that the masses were willing to mobilize against the regime, but their opposition elites were not.

Satisfied Elites

Finally, the diverging dynamics are not simply due to the fact that elites' demands had been met in Morocco or Egypt under Mubarak. The parties' demands and the level of state repression had not changed significantly.[61] By the mid-1990s, King Hasan II had not responded to the oppositions' demands; internal security organs had not stepped up their activities against the parties; and the masses could be even more easily mobilized than they were previously. The same held true in Egypt, where mass discontent increased and opposition parties saw their modest gains of the 1980s slipping away. According to conventional wisdom, then, once these states experienced unrest and partial liberalization, we should have expected their opposition to remain mobilized until either they pushed successfully toward democratization or were repressed soundly in a return to authoritarianism. Yet, this was simply not the case.

Rather, to understand the divergent dynamics of unrest during economic crises, we need to deepen our understanding of government–opposition relations. We need not only to take into account how incumbents alter the rules of political participation, thereby making it easier or more costly for opposition groups to voice demands, but also to examine how these changes in the rules governing political participation alter the relationships *between* various opposition groups. In political liberalization, incumbents can create structures that allow all opponents access to the political system, or they can create rules that allow some groups to participate while continuing to prohibit others. These rules not only regulate the level of opposition that the incumbents face, but also influence the strategic interactions between competing opposition groups. This, in turn, has a dynamic effect on the opposition's willingness to challenge the incumbent elites.

THE METHODOLOGY

This work uses the method of structured comparison to examine the role that institutions governing participation play in authoritarian regimes. It uses a simple formal model of opposition–government interactions to derive hypotheses about when opposition elites exploit increasing discontent to demand political change. It extends this model to determine whether incumbent elites, after creating different SoCs, choose to repress some opposition groups and not others. The hypotheses derived from the model are then examined through case studies of Morocco, Jordan, and Egypt.

The study focuses on whether or not moderate opposition elites use the threat of unrest to make political demands, not on whether or not such protest occurs. The study examines the opponents' threats to mobilize protest rather than their actual mobilization because these demands are necessary for political liberalization; protest itself need not be. When incumbent elites negotiate with the opposition in order to avoid overt confrontation, political liberalization may take place without protest.

The study focuses on the decisions of moderate opposition groups and incumbents for two reasons. First, examining moderate political opponents is more feasible than examining radicals. Incumbent elites generally prefer moderate opposition groups to radical groups, and they are thus likely to permit them greater political freedoms, including freedom of speech. This makes it easier to obtain information on moderates that can support or refute the model's predictions than it is to obtain similar information about radicals. In addition, there is a compelling theoretical reason to focus on the moderates. Regime changes tend to occur when moderates join in anti-regime activities. Splits within ruling coalitions are the most extreme example of this, but any opposition in which moderates join with radicals is particularly threatening. Examining the moderates' strategies is therefore critical to understanding the likelihood of regime change.

The Model

Although the components of the model will be described in subsequent chapters, it is important to be explicit about the ways in which the model and case studies have informed each other. Formal models are useful tools for developing hypotheses, particularly when combined with the case studies for validation and interpretation. Models force scholars to present hypotheses with mathematical rigor, and they demonstrate the logical limitations of arguments. In addition, they can yield hypotheses that previously were not considered, and these can cast new light on empirical evidence.

This work has benefited from the formal model in both of these ways. My understanding of included and illegal opposition, and the constraints operating on both, was largely developed during fieldwork in Morocco and Jordan during 1994–1995. As I sought to understand the divisions both within and between opposition groups, it became apparent how the incentive structures for various actors differed, largely depending on their different relations with the state. The insight that state elites created divided and unified SoCs, and the relative costs to mobilizing for elites in various groups, came directly from this fieldwork. The initial model, then, formalized some of what I learned during nearly two years in Jordan and Morocco.

The model, however, is not a mere formality. I subsequently derived three important lessons from it that, returning to the data, appear well founded. The first hypothesis, as demonstrated in Chapters 4 and 5, is that state elites will have very different incentives to strengthen different types of opposition groups, depending on SoC they maintain. The second is that political liberalization is more likely to be stable in divided SoCs. When some political opposition groups are allowed to participate in the system, while others are barred, incumbent elites may be able to continue to provide limited rights while thwarting further demands. The final hypothesis derived from the model is that we are likely to find cycles of opposition demands in divided SoCs. It is in the very nature of these regimes to have waves of opposition demands. Initially, moderate opponents make demands, other groups threaten to join in, and moderate demands are weakened. These three hypotheses, which we will discuss in subsequent chapters, were derived through the development of the model itself.

Case Studies

Case studies are equally important in this work. The studies of Morocco and Jordan are based on fieldwork, which was critical for developing a more nuanced understanding of government–opposition relations. The assumptions set forth in the model are based upon in-depth interviews with members of the opposition elite, the government elite, informal observers, and the general public, many of whom pounded into me patiently but forcefully the difference between being *capable* of mobilizing and being *willing* to do so. Subsequent fieldwork in the West Bank, Gaza, and Syria, as well as the congruence between these findings and secondary case studies, has convinced me of the validity of the assumptions underlying the model, as well as the hypotheses derived. In short, fieldwork helped convince me that I have gotten the process right.

The nature of monarchies made Jordan and Morocco extremely useful for this study. Management of the political system is a legitimate role for the king. Monarchs are political arbitrators and directors, and they are expected to intervene actively in politics to promote political stability.[62] As Brynen, Korany, and Noble argue: "What is interesting about the monarchies is that they appear to be in a position to establish many of these rules (during liberalization) and to thereby act simultaneously as both interested players and far-from-impartial umpires in the political reform process."[63] Given this role, the different strategies monarchs use to incorporate opposition groups into or exclude them from the political system were quite apparent. For the purposes of theory formation, the relatively transparent nature of the ruling coalition and the king's ability to manage explicitly the relations between different opposition groups rather openly was particularly helpful.

The value of closely examined case studies is that they can be used not only in theory building, but also in testing hypotheses. In this study, returning to the cases of Morocco and Jordan has helped test auxiliary hypotheses from the model. The secondary study of Egypt under Nasir, Sadat, and Mubarak, conducted entirely after the theory was developed, demonstrates that state-created structures of contestation (SoCs) influence government–opposition dynamics independently of regime type. Both Morocco and Jordan are constitutional monarchies. As this work will show, King Husayn of Jordan and King Hasan II of Morocco chose to use very different rules and formed distinct political environments. The likelihood and timing of the unrest in these two states as they experienced economic difficulties was thus quite different. Similarly, Egypt is a dominant-party state, but it has had different political environments at different points in time. Egypt under Nasir and Sadat had an undivided political system, while under Mubarak it had a divided one. In short, in all types of regimes, incumbent elites can manipulate the relationships among various opposition groups and between these groups and the state. How they do this – the SoCs that they form – influences the difficulties these incumbents face in the future.

It should be noted that, for the study at hand, these secondary case studies are a more appropriate test of external validity (i.e., generalizability) than a large-*n* study of political unrest would be. This theory is fundamentally concerned with understanding when political opponents make demands for political change, threatening to mobilize popular discontent in an attempt to obtain these demands. It is aimed at understanding the level of political stability and opposition demands, not the prevalence of political strikes, demonstrations, or other measures of unrest. Certainly, opposition elites may choose to make demands, and have these demands granted, without ever seeing the escalation and mobilization of the masses. At the same time, in some regimes unrest is quite common, and yet such demonstrations are characteristics of the nature of the regime and society rather than signals of regime instability. The prevalence of demonstrations and work stoppages in France is an excellent example. In contrast, strong government–opposition contestation in Jordan often takes the form of national conferences, hardly the type of event that in other states would raise much concern. Consequently, comparative case studies are an appropriate test of when opposition elites *make demands, threatening political unrest.*

OUTLINE OF THE WORK

The goal of this work is to examine cases of political crises to determine how state-created SoCs affect the dynamics of opposition. In doing so, it demonstrates that authoritarianism need not sustain itself primarily through repression, even during prolonged economic crises. In Morocco, for instance, King Hasan II's rule was sustained in part because opposition elites became less willing to demand reforms. This work also takes an important step toward examining how authoritarian regimes work and distinguishing among different types of authoritarianism. Often authoritarianism is distinguished by the nature or size of the ruling coalition. This study shows, however, that the institutional mechanisms put in place to structure government–opposition relations influence opposition elites' willingness to challenge the government, independent of the ruling elites or regime type. Indeed, in some cases, the same ruling elites have created very different SoCs. Finally, the study sheds new light on the classic work of Dahl, who sees two dimensions to the "paths" toward polyarchy.[64] I argue that the extension of suffrage is less important than the extent to which the political system expands to include the participation of competing political tendencies. The work also suggests that opening limited participation may not be a stable path toward polyarchy, but rather an equilibrium state in itself.

This book addresses the question of how state-created institutions shape government–opposition relations as follows. Chapter 1 argues that our inability to predict when opposition elites are willing to push their demands for political reform stems from two related problems in the literature: first, a limited, explicit acknowledgment of and theoretical development regarding competing opposition groups, and second, a failure to develop theories about how incumbent elites actively shape opposition groups and the relationships between them. Chapter 2 sets forth a theoretical framework through which we can understand how incumbent elites create different political environments. Chapter 3 argues that an opposition group's inclusion in or exclusion from the formal political sphere (i.e., its legality or illegality) has an influence on its incentives to mobilize. Chapters 4 and 5 examine how the dynamics of opposition–government relations change in divided and unified SoCs. Chapter 6 examines why incumbent elites use very different strategies in dealing with individual opposition groups in different structures. Finally, the conclusion considers questions remaining in the study of the formal institutions governing participation in authoritarian regimes.

1

The Manipulation of Political Opposition

It hath been always her [Catherine de Medici's] custome, to set in France, one against an other, that in the meane while she might rule in these divisions.

M. Hurault, *Discourse Upon the Present State of France*, 1588

For a prince . . . is a sure axiome, Divide and Rule.

J. Hall, *Meditations I*, 1605

Politics is rarely, if ever, a two-player game. Multiple opponents vie with one another, as well as with the state, over power and resources. They are motivated by competition as well as by the need for cooperation – keeping a careful eye on each other while simultaneously attempting to gain support and assistance through a combination of cajoling and compromise, threats and personal intrigue. This insight is not new; in 1588 Hurault recognized the state's ability to "divide and rule" with respect to Catherine de Medici in France. Similarly, Aristotle wrote that one of the strategies by which a tyrant could preserve his rule was to keep his subjects preoccupied with fighting each other.[1] Clearly, determining when opposition elites are willing to mobilize the masses and make sustained demands for political change requires an examination of three factors: the relationships between opposition groups and the state, the relationships between competing opposition groups, and state elites' ability to manipulate these relations.

Yet, in the wide and disparate literature that examines "contentious politics,"[2] the incumbents' ability to divide and rule, creating competition between the opposition groups, is not examined adequately. The literature fails to consider fully how state elites use different strategies to manipulate the development and strength of various opposition groups, thereby influencing their opponents' willingness to mobilize the masses. Consequently, it often fails to appreciate the strategic interactions among various opponents and particularly the tools by which incumbents shape these interactions.

This chapter examines why limitations in the current conceptions of contentious politics make it difficult to understand why opposition elites who were once willing to mobilize under domestic unrest would choose not to do so even as their ability to do so increased. It argues that the literature has three limitations. First, scholars have tended to overlook important relationships among various opposition groups. Second, they have largely ignored the extent to which state elites influence the relations among various opposition groups, shoring up some while harshly repressing others. Finally, they have paid little attention to the institutional arrangements through which incumbent elites shape relations among opposition groups, thereby affecting when opposition groups will make sustained demands for political change and when they will not. Not all work in this large literature suffers equally from these omissions; however, as this chapter demonstrates, scholars of contentious politics have largely ignored how incumbent elites create institutions through which they actively manipulate the development and strength of opposition groups. As a result, the notion of government–opposition relations that provides the underpinnings for work on economic crises and political stability supports the conventional wisdom that economic crises stimulate political unrest.

ASSUMING A UNIFIED OPPOSITION

In much of the work on government–opposition relations, scholars ignore important divisions among opposition groups. This is most evident in formal models of contentious politics, in which determining the likelihood of political unrest is often posed as a problem of competition between a single challenger group and incumbents.[3] In some cases, these works consider how different types of opponents (e.g., distinctions between leaders and followers, or among activists with different policy preferences, risk-taking propensities, or levels of ideological conviction) affects the likelihood of unrest; yet even here, scholars often focus on a single set of contenders.[4] This conception underlies much of the work on collective action as well, where the central problem is to understand when individuals choose to join in a single movement.[5] Competing opposition groups are simply not taken into account.

Other scholars explicitly consider multiple opposition groups, but they do not fully explore strategic interactions among contenders as they vie with each other as well as with incumbents for power. The driving question for many class-based theorists is "What would allow various classes to join together, mobilizing in concert against the regime?"[6] Social movement theorists take a similar approach, examining how various groups could be brought into a coalition, depending on their level of political discontent, their ability to interact with each other, the extent to which their interests coincided, their organizational structures, and the tactics they used.[7] Yet, while these scholars examine the interactions among these groups, many assume a cooperative relationship. For instance, McAdam, Tilly, and Tarrow argue that the successful mobilization of one opposition group will spur mobilization by other groups.[8] Others argue that there is a contagion effect across opposition groups, leading to the simultaneous mobilization across states or movements.[9] These arguments stand in quite stark contrast to previous arguments of Gamson and Tilly that the repression of some groups may increase the ability of others to mobilize.[10] Importantly, however, they all demonstrate an important limitation: Opposition groups fail to adjust their strategies in response to what they believe other opposition groups may do.

Even recent work that explicitly recognizes competing forces suffers from this limitation. This work seeks to understand how the existence of multiple movements affects the emergence and success of competing contenders.[11] It is significant because it recognizes the importance of competing groups, but it also fails to examine the full range of potential interactions among groups. For both Meyer and Staggenberg, examining movements and countermovements, and Glenn, examining "Competing Challengers," the relationship is by definition competitive. Yet need the relationship among various opposition groups be defined from the outset?

In an important contribution to the literature on political protest, James DeNardo suggests that political conditions can affect the relationship among various opposition groups. Examining the strategic interactions among different factions in movements, DeNardo points out several important divisions among groups that affect the dynamics of their movements: pragmatists versus ideologues, reformists versus revolutionaries, and radicals versus moderates. As the oppositions' "political fortunes" improve (i.e., as opponents become more likely to be successful), the relationships among various opposition groups change. Quite reasonably, DeNardo's analysis applies easily to the problem at hand if one assumes that as economic crises continue, the oppositions' political fortunes improve as well.

DeNardo's distinctions are useful, but they do not fully explain why moderate political elites who previously challenged the government become less willing to do so as crises continue. DeNardo writes:

> Having achieved their goals, the moderates try to arrest the government's rush past their position by preventing any further radicalization of the movement's demands. The radical pragmatists, on the other hand, retreat toward their sincere demand as the incentive to compromise evaporates. Thus, as the movement's political potential increases . . . the moderates and radicals are split.[12]

Yet, this explanation assumes that the government is more likely to meet radical demands than moderate ones, a condition that contradicts DeNardo's own very reasonable assumption that governments prefer moderate positions to radical ones and thus, when making concessions, should satisfy the moderates' demands before they meet those of the radicals. If the moderates have the ability to thwart the radicals' success, they should choose to do so only once their own demands have been fully satisfied. Why would they sacrifice their own potential success before their demands have been met? The answer to this question is critical to determining why moderate opposition elites who were previously willing to challenge the government choose not to do so when the probability of success is increasing.

Although DeNardo's model does not fully explain why opposition groups become unwilling to mobilize precisely at the time that the government is weakening, his work does suggest that examining the strategic interaction among opposition groups can help explain the puzzle at hand. The moderates' decision over whether or not to mobilize is not focused on its relationship with the government alone. Rather, opposition groups consider the effect that their own strategies will have on other groups, as well as on the incumbent elites. In addition, DeNardo recognizes the distinction between an opposition's *ability* to challenge incumbent elites and their *willingness* to do so. Political opponents may become more capable of challenging incumbents as crises continue, but they may not wish to do so. It is thus important to separate cases in which political opponents fail to challenge incumbents because they are unable to do so from cases in which opponents are unwilling to challenge even though they have the resources to do so.

In short, because scholars generally ignore the divisions among opposition groups and focus on behavior to assess the attitudes of opposition elites, they conflate the opposition's desire to mobilize against the government with its ability to do so. The assumption that decreased mobilization costs and increased likelihood of success make opposition elites more able to challenge incumbents is reasonable. However, if one recognizes the existence of multiple opposition groups, it becomes clear that more favorable conditions for protest do not necessarily coincide with a greater willingness of the opposition to protest.

In a formal model, Arich Gavious and Shlomo Mizrahi suggest a potential explanation for this situation. They argue that when multiple opposition groups can independently succeed in achieving a common goal, mobilization is less likely to occur. This corollary of the free rider problem is interesting, but it does not explain the problem at hand. It suggests that opposition elites would be *unable* to mobilize their supporters, not be unwilling to do so.[13] Yet, as we will see in Chapter 5, the existence of multiple opposition elites can actually decrease their willingness to challenge incumbents.

To explain this, we need to consider how simultaneous changes in the power of other groups affect the opposition groups' expected outcomes from challenging incumbents. Specifically, the emergence or strengthening of radical opposition groups may make opposition forces less willing to stimulate popular unrest even if it is easier for them to do so. By recognizing the potential for competition among opposition groups, and in particular how state elites affect the relationships among these groups, we can disentangle an opposition group's willingness to mobilize from its ability to do so. Indeed, we can understand why opposition elites may not choose to mobilize even as their capabilities increase.

THE STATE

The second important lacuna in the literature is the tendency to overlook the role state elites play in shaping the relationships among opposition groups. Despite the wealth of energy that scholars have spent in "bringing the state back in,"[14] they have not fully examined how state elites explicitly shape the dynamics of government–opposition interactions. Rather, understanding when political opponents will challenge the incumbent elite is primarily relegated to a decision-making exercise by which opponents consider the likely costs and benefits of mobilizing to make demands.

That this problem exists is somewhat ironic, since scholars working on contentious politics assume that incumbent elites are stronger than opposition elites. Even in work on democratic polities, opposition elites are considered disadvantaged: They mobilize at the fringes of the political system and possess fewer political resources. Indeed, this assumption is so prevalent that the majority of the literature focuses, either implicitly or explicitly, on the factors that allow opponents to overcome their inhibitions.[15] This book does not question this assumption. Rather, it argues that despite this, scholars have not fully considered one of the most important cards that the incumbents have to play: their ability to create institutions that shape the incentives driving the relationships among various opposition groups.

To determine the likelihood of political unrest, many scholars look at how the state distributes positive and negative incentives for mobilization or how states shape groups' identities and demands. Incumbents can alter the costs of participation by holding out as carrots the prospects of participation, of ministerial seats, or other incentives, or by using sticks such as threats of increased repression, the loss of participation, or the loss of special privileges.[16] They can also provide negative incentives, most notably through the level of repression in response to mobilized opposition and the rapidity of this response. The relationship between repression and mobilization is complex and not fully understood. Generally, the expectation is that the repression of political opponents may reduce their likelihood of mobilizing when their fear of repression is greater than their anger toward the regime. However, when repression only succeeds in further angering the already disgruntled opponents, it may serve to radicalize demands and increase mobilization.[17]

A similar logic underlies work that examines the likelihood of Islamist mobilization in the Middle East. At the center of this debate is the question of when Islamists will become politicized and potentially antidemocratic forces. For many, the answer has tended toward the expectation that Islamist forces, when allowed to participate in the political system, are willing to help maintain a democratic system.[18] For these scholars, the state can play an important role in radicalizing Islamists when it chooses to repress them. In short, the state elites' decision to include or exclude opponents from the political system, and to respond to them with more or less repression, plays an important role in determining the likelihood of individual groups to choose to mobilize.

State elites also shape the responses and strategies of individual opposition groups. Work on the repertoires of collective action demonstrates, for instance, that the means by which different groups choose to mobilize vary. In part, the choices of modes of mobilization are historically determined. As Tarrow notes, "Particular groups have a particular history – and memory – of contentious forms. Workers know how to strike because generations of workers struck before them; Parisians build barricades because barricades are inscribed in the history of Parisian contention; peasants seize the land carrying the symbols that their fathers and grandfathers used in the past."[19] Indeed, as we shall see in the cases examined here, in Jordan political opponents mobilize in part through national conferences, harkening back to the first National Conference of 1928, in which opposition forces presented a united front. In contrast, opposition forces in Morocco turn to general strikes to demand political change, just as they did in the nationalist movement against the French nearly 50 years earlier.

State-created incentives also shape repertoires.[20] In a context where strikes and demonstrations are illegal, political opponents may turn to petitions to express their demands, and where all nonviolent forms of protest are repressed, they may turn to violence. In these cases, the choice to mobilize a demonstration or strike – thereby not only expressing their demands but also challenging the very rules of the game – is a more significant challenge than in the state where this is a legally acceptable strategy.[21] It is thus not surprising that when political constraints are lifted, as they were for instance in Jordan after 1989, opposition groups engage in new forms of action. Similarly, when the regime changed the electoral law in 1993, political contenders altered their strategies.[22] These included not only registration with authorities and the establishment of formal headquarters, but also the expression of demands in the open publication of newspapers and in convening public conferences.

Finally, scholars of both social movements and political protest recognize that the state's ability to withstand such opposition demands also affects the likelihood that opponents choose to mobilize. The extent to which the maintenance of the state overrides individual class interests, and the autonomy of the state from these classes, affects the ability of the state to implement economic reform and to withstand the resulting discontent. As Theda Skocpol argued in her seminal work, the weakening of the state due to fiscal crisis or international vulnerability paves the way to understanding the emergence of major social revolutions.[23]

Recently, scholars have extended this logic to consider how splits within the ruling regime, between hard-liners and soft-liners, affect the likelihood of mobilized opposition and regime change. Most recently, attention has focused on how the divisions between incumbent elites are exacerbated in periods of economic crises and reforms.[24] These scholars thus seek to understand when soft-liner elites will call upon the opposition to join them in their struggle against their hard-liner counterparts, as Gorbachev did when speaking to the Ukrainian opposition in February 1989:

You keep up the pressure. We'll press from the top, and you keep pressing from the bottom. Only in that way can perestroika succeed.[25]

Potential splits between opposition elites into reformist and radical groups are also important for understanding when opposition and incumbent elites can cooperate in a reform process. Scholars have begun to recognize this.[26] Yet, while they consider theoretically how state elites can respond differentially to various opposition groups, they have not explicitly examined the mechanisms state elites use to shape the relationships among the opposition groups and the factors that lead incumbents to be more or less lenient toward different groups. This has been left to the intricacies of history and case studies.

In short, how state elites affect the interaction among various opposition groups has been largely overlooked. Their ability to provide incentives that induce individual groups to mobilize or remain silent, and to choose among various repertoires of action, is recognized. However, the extent to which these incentive structures affect the relative strength of various opposition groups, and the impact of this relationship on opponents' willingness to mobilize, has been overlooked. Yet, as we shall see in Chapters 4 through 6, this relationship has a critical influence on opposition groups' strategies and, subsequently, on the state's choices in repressing or advancing alternative opposition groups.

INSTITUTIONS

The literature suffers from a third difficulty as well: Scholars have largely overlooked the ability of incumbent elites to use different institutional arrangements to shape the relationships between the state and opposition groups and among opposition groups themselves. Since these relationships affect the likelihood of sustained opposition demands during political and economic crises, they need to be examined explicitly. Moreover, they are independent of regime type. Although the institutional and sociopolitical patterns associated with various political regimes have important effects on the ability of opposition groups to mobilize, a full understanding of opposition–government interactions requires a study of the institutional arrangements specifically designed to include and exclude various opposition forces.

Scholars know that institutions matter. Democratic and authoritarian regimes generally differ in the level of repression and therefore in the levels of protest they experience.[27] Gurr has argued further that the level of authoritarianism is, at least in part, determined by the origin of the regime: Those that have come into power through violence are more likely to suppress their opposition.[28]

Grounded in the rational choice approach, new institutionalists recognize that even within democracies or autocracies, rules are important.[29] For instance, many have suggested that electoral rules affect the ability of small opposition parties to gain representation[30] or that presidential and parliamentary systems may have very different prospects for democratic consolidation.[31] In both cases, underlying these theories is the notion that institutions affect the ability of various groups to have their demands met within the formal political system. Where institutions make such accommodation difficult or unlikely, we may be more likely to see opposition groups mobilizing against the state. In addition, Jennifer Widner has argued that where corporatist political structures exist, political unrest emerges earlier in response to economic crises.[32] In this case, the critical difference between corporatist and noncorporatist systems is not the desire of opposition elites to mobilize, but their ability to overcome the collective action problem. Where corporatist organizations exist, mobilization is easier. In short, institutions can structure the political environment, affecting both the likelihood that opposition groups can mobilize and their desire to do so.

The social movement literature also recognizes the importance of institutions. Most notably, these scholars have begun to consider how "political opportunity structures"[33] foster political protest.[34] McAdam defines the political opportunity structure as a "highly consensual list of dimensions of political opportunity: 1) Relative openness or closure of the institutionalized political system, 2) the stability or instability of that broad set of elite alignments that typically undergird a polity, 3) the presence or absence of elite allies, 4) the state's capacity and propensity for repression."[35]

For social movement theorists, political opportunity structures both create opportunities for mobilization and are, in turn, influenced by them. As Tarrow writes:

> people join in social movements in response to political opportunities and then, through collective action, create new ones. As a result, the 'when' of social movement mobilization – when political opportunities are opening up – goes a long way towards explaining its 'why.' ... Even groups with mild grievances and few internal resources may appear in movement, while those with deep grievances and dense resources – but lacking opportunities – may not.[36]

Yet, while this insight is important, this scholarship is far from settled on which institutions are critical in spurring mobilization. As critics have argued, the concept has been stretched to include nearly every conceivable factor that influences mobilization. Gamson and Meyer write that the concept of political opportunity structure "threatens to become an all-encompassing fudge factor for all the conditions and circumstances that form the context for collective action. Used to explain so much, it may ultimately explain nothing at all."[37]

Not only has the concept of the political opportunity structure been stretched to include myriad institutional structures, but these studies tend to focus on how institutions affect the likelihood of mobilization across all groups, not how they influence the *relationships* among groups. Meyer and Staggenberg[38] provide a partial exception, examining how political opportunity structures affect the emergence of countermovements. Even here, however, the extent to which state elites create institutional arrangements that foster competition or cooperation among groups, and the effect of such relations on groups' willingness to protest, is not fully examined.

Yet, through the rules they make and the institutions they create, incumbent elites help determine not only what opposition groups exist and how strong they may be, but also how these groups interact with each other. Incumbents cannot dictate their opponents' actions, but they can influence them. Furthermore, the incentives they offer opponents to influence their decisions go far beyond the sticks and carrots that are typically explored. Coercion and co-optation are obviously important factors. However, equally important but often overlooked are sets of rules (both formal and informal) that shape the relations of opposition groups with each other.

In short, although not all of the literature suffers from these problems to the same extent, scholars have tended to overlook the importance of divisions among opposition groups and the ability of state elites to create institutional mechanisms by which they influence these divisions. The most basic understanding of opposition groups, and one that leads scholars to expect that economic crises increase the likelihood of political unrest, is one in which a single opposition group (or a coalition of like-minded groups) challenge the incumbent regime. From this model, it is reasonable to conclude that economic crises increase the likelihood of unrest.

This model is not only empirically untrue, it is also misleading. A review of the literature not only demonstrates the overall tendency toward this simplified model, but also shows that scholars have at times recognized the limitations of these assumptions. Some scholars have recognized the divisions among opposition groups; others have considered the importance of the state; and still others have examined how incumbents create institutional structures that subsequently shape the mobilization of opposition. Yet, they have failed to put these insights together, considering how state-created institutions affect the relationships among opposition groups, as well as relationships between these groups and the state. These institutional structures, however, are critical in determining when opposition elites are willing to mobilize against the regime.

WHY THESE OVERSIGHTS?

Before examining in more detail how state elites manage the divisions among opposition groups, it is useful to step back and consider why this has been so frequently ignored, to ask, in a sense, why the "dog didn't bark." Understanding why state manipulation of the opposition has not been studied fully sheds light on some important problems in the studies of social movements, political protest, and politics in the non-Western world.

A first explanation for why most studies have failed to examine how incumbent elites manipulate the relationships among political opposition groups is that the majority of the literature on social movements and political protest is developed through studying the West.[39] Kowalewski and Hoover found that of 101 studies of repression and mobilization published between 1965 and 1990, 61 percent examined the First World.[40] Similarly, McAdams, Tarrow, and Tilly conclude,

the core of the current theoretical corpus of work on contentious politics focuses on western reform movements, while specialists outside the domain of recent western democratic experience (e.g., students of previous centuries and/or China, Latin America, Africa, the Middle East or Eastern Europe) have often borrowed ideas and apparatus of social-movement specialists but have not established a genuine dialogue with analysts of contemporary Western European and North

American Movements. Differences inherent in these settings have all too frequently been dealt with by culturalist proclamation – or by assuming the universality of certain models – rather than by parsing differences into variables that can be integrated into systematic comparisons with movements in various parts of the world.[41]

Scholars of non-Western states may see the situation somewhat differently, arguing that their contributions to the literature have often been overlooked.[42] But, in either case, the failure to have such a dialogue has meant that pluralist assumptions have dominated our thinking about state–opposition relations. The dominant view of politics in the West (and in consolidated democracies more generally) is of a government that is a distributor of resources and policies, dealing out repression or accommodation in response to the demands of various groups. The bulk of the work on social movements and protest in these states also examines groups that make demands on the state, but not groups that fundamentally challenge the incumbent regimes. They seek to overturn policies and governments, not to rewrite the rules of the game.

Even studies that have examined how state-created political opportunity structures affect the relationships among various opposition groups focus on institutions that indirectly affect these groups' mobilization. For instance, Meyer and Staggenborg argue that competing social movements are more likely to emerge in federalist structures, since policy advocates on both sides of an issue can receive support or opposition for their demands at various levels of bureaucracy.[43] This view of the state is very much at odds with a conceptualization of incumbent elites as proactive actors, creating incentive structures that alter the relationships among various opposition groups. Yet, students of authoritarian regimes are much more likely to perceive incumbents as manipulating their opponents, intervening in the relationships among them in order to make groups less likely to mobilize against the state. One possibility, then, is that the focus on the West thus explains why the manipulation of opposition groups has been so long overlooked.

However, this raises an important question: How much can we generalize the insights gained from the cases here to the rest of the world? Are these conclusions valid only in Morocco, Jordan, and Egypt, the Middle East, or the non-Western world? Can the lessons learned here help us to understand politics in both democratic and non-democratic states? Can they be generalized to non-Islamic states?

Further empirical work needs to be done, but the study suggests that the model can be generalized, and that we need to question and revise theories of contentious politics accordingly. Although monarchies are particularly useful to examine because the kings are quite straightforward about how they manipulate the rules of the game, the Egyptian case demonstrates that the model extends quite easily to nonmonarchies.

The model extends to non-Islamic states as well. The division between Islamist and secular forces is an important distinction in this work. However, the nature of Islam as a political force does not explain the very different dynamics discussed here. Moreover, similar ideological divisions have existed elsewhere, with the division between nationalist parties and others in the Latin American states, and the resultant attempts by incumbent elites to establish rules prohibiting nationalists from participation in the system during the 1960s, illustrating a close parallel to the cases examined here.[44]

The second enigma is that even in work on cases outside the West, theoretical literature has not gone very far in theorizing about how authoritarian leaders use institutions to influence the relationships among political opponents. Here, perhaps because scholars generally believe that authoritarian leaders are capable of manipulating, vetoing, or ignoring institutional outcomes, they have failed to examine how incumbents use institutional arrangements to influence the relationships among political opponents. Scholars did not completely abandon the examination of formal institutions, but many did turn their focus away from these institutions, and even formal politics, to examine everyday, informal politics.[45]

Informal politics is important, but it does not negate the role of formal institutions. Even within authoritarian regimes, rules constrain actors. They create incentives for elites and the masses to choose different strategies, and they help establish their expectations about how others will act. Elsewhere, I have argued that even in authoritarian regimes, incumbents are aware that the rules they make can influence behavior. Furthermore, they choose to establish rules by which they obtain the outcomes they prefer rather than resorting to extralegal methods to manipulate their opposition.[46] Even authoritarian elites prefer to abide by the rules, when it is possible to do so and still get what they want, because to do so helps preserve the legitimacy of the regime.

ON INCUMBENTS, OPPONENTS, AND INSTITUTIONS

Incumbents cannot dictate their opponents' actions, but they can influence them. Through the rules they make and the institutions they establish, governments help determine which opposition groups exist and how these groups interact with each other. They give opponents incentives that influence the strategies they choose, and these go far beyond repression and accommodation as they are typically explored. Coercion and co-optation are obviously important. However, equally important but often overlooked are institutions that help determine which opposition groups form and how they relate to each other. Ruling elites create institutions that influence when political opponents unite and when they divide, when they emerge and when they dissolve. Opposition groups are in part created, not simply discovered.

Governing elites are also constrained. They are constrained in part by economic conditions and foreign relations. They are also constrained by the very institutions they create. Indeed, as we shall see in Chapter 6, the formal institutions governing the opposition also affect the informal strategies that governments use to manage their opposition. In short, institutions shape the emergence and relationships of various opposition groups, but they also constrain the governing elites. Understanding how incumbents create formal institutions to structure the opposition, and how this affects government–opposition relations, is the goal of this work.

2

Structures of Contestation

Most would agree that authoritarian elites attempt to manage and manipulate their political opponents. They decide whom to appease with ministerial portfolios and whom to throw into prison. In addition to using such sticks and carrots, ruling elites manipulate the opposition through SoCs. Through the establishment of institutions and the selective implementation of policies, they allow some groups to participate in the political system while excluding others. Although this has generally received only passing attention, these SoCs have critical implications for the relationships between state and opposition elites, particularly during prolonged economic crises. SoCs shape relations among different opposition groups, as well as between these groups and the government. In doing so, they help determine when and if opponents challenge governing elites.

Yet, is there a systematic, theoretically coherent way to understand the intrigues of state and opposition elites? Can the potential for incumbents to respond with payoffs or imprisonment, or for opposition elites to compete or cooperate, be defined? This chapter argues that it can be. It focuses on how incumbents create different institutional arrangements through which they influence opposition elites' choices to form coalitions and press for political change. These arrangements vary significantly according to where incumbents draw the line between legal and illegal opposition groups. This chapter will set forth a framework within which to consider government–opposition relations. It will then examine the changing strategies in Jordan, Morocco, and Egypt. The effect of the SoC on the dynamics of opposition movements will be the focus of discussion in the subsequent chapters.

DRAWING THE LINES: ILLEGAL AND LEGAL POLITICAL OPPONENTS

Incumbent elites shape the political environment through the distribution of two types of goods. First, they can grant concrete changes in economic or political policies that respond to the opponents' demands.[1] Assuming that opposition groups hold fixed preferences, the more the government responds to a group's demands, the more moderate that opposition becomes.[2] Incumbent elites can also grant access to the political process. They choose whether or not to permit different groups or elites the right to make their demands legally (e.g., forming political parties and associations, contesting elections, publishing papers). Some groups may be allowed to participate in the formal political system, while others remain excluded.

Incumbents establish the rules of the game through which opposition elites are permitted to, or prohibited from, participating in the formal political system. Returning to Dahl's classic work, his diagram of the paths to polyarchy makes clear what options these leaders have.[3] In his diagram, reproduced in Figure 2.1, leaders in closed hegemonies can choose to increase political contestation, moving to competitive oligarchies. For Dahl, political access in the process of liberalization could be limited by establishing criteria based on gender, race, and income. Alternatively, incumbents could choose to increase participation while maintaining limited competition. Through this process of inclusion, the regime could move from a closed hegemony (at the extreme, a dictatorship) to an inclusive hegemony (a totalitarian or populist authoritarian regime). Finally, the regime could take the most risky path, increasing contestation and inclusion simultaneously, moving from hegemony to polyarchy.

These distinctions remain apt. Today, it is more difficult for incumbent elites to limit political participation based on class, gender, and racial

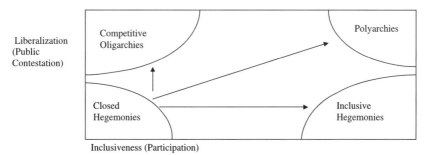

FIGURE 2.1. Paths from Hegemony to Polyarchy.

criteria. International organizations exert considerable pressure on liberalizing states to create inclusive participatory processes. However, while incumbents may not limit political participation based on these criteria, they continue to limit access to the formal political sphere. The expansion of participation in the political system is often moderated through pacts between incumbents and the included opposition in which limits of political competition and participation are explicitly set forth. Furthermore, incumbents continue to establish what Dahl called "mixed" political systems,[4] in which some political groups are explicitly excluded. Yet, instead of basing such exclusion on ascriptive characteristics (e.g., gender, wealth, or race), incumbents exclude opponents based on the forms of support through which they intend to organize (e.g., ideology, religion, geography) and their willingness to accept the established regime.

In the Middle East and North Africa, as in much of Africa, Latin America, Eastern Europe, and the former Soviet Union, the boundaries of participation are the outcome of negotiations between opposition elites and authoritarian rulers. King Hasan II spelled out the rules of the game for Morocco's political opponents in the revised 1972 Constitution; President Hafez al-Asad of Syria negotiated these rules in the formation of the National Progressive Front (al-Jabhah al-Wataniyah); King Husayn of Jordan recently revised the rules governing government–opposition relationships in the National Charter (al-Mithaq al-Watani) of 1991; and the Tunisian liberalization began with a national pact in 1988. Few are under the illusion that these negotiations are between equal partners, but in each case, they determine the boundaries of participation: official issues on which political opposition elites may challenge the government and the strategies they may use to do so. These negotiations also are intended to commit those who are permitted entrance into the formal political sphere to maintaining the rules of the game.

DIVIDED AND UNIFIED SoCs

The outcomes of these negotiations create important distinctions between political systems, and these distinctions are independent of the type of political regime that exists. Even in systems with a low level of political liberalization (or contestation), there are distinctions between the levels of legitimate participation (or inclusion). This variation can be simplified into three ideal types of SoCs within nondemocratic states, as Figure 2.2 illustrates. Here, Dahl's pure (or closed) hegemony is an exclusive, unified

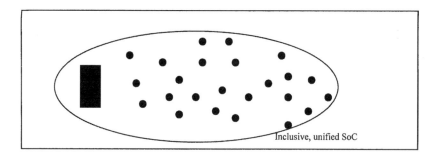

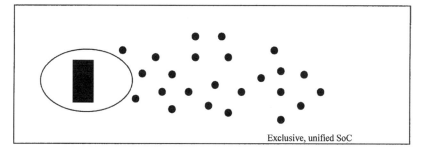

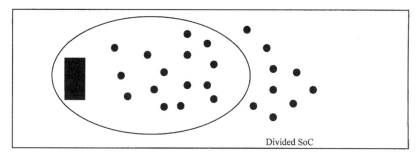

FIGURE 2.2. Structures of Contestation.

SoC. No political opponents are allowed to participate in the formal political sphere. Inclusive hegemony is an inclusive, unified SoC. All political opponents participate in the formal system but the incumbent elites carefully limit their participation. Finally, the middle ground is the divided

SoC. Incumbents allow some political opponents to participate in the political system while continuing to exclude others.[5]

SoCs represent strategies of rule, but they are independent of individual leadership styles. Indeed, because incumbent elites try to maintain political control by manipulating the political system, the same elites may create different SoCs at different points in time. The regimes of former King Husayn of Jordan and former King Hasan II of Morocco illustrate this well. Both are constitutional monarchies in non-oil states with actively reigning monarchs. As we shall see, both reigned over newly independent states and faced significant challenges in consolidating their rule. Yet, by the beginning of their economic crises, King Husayn had established an *exclusive, unified SoC*, while King Hasan II had created a *divided SoC*.

These SoCs were the outcome of strategic decision making by incumbent elites, not simply a reflection of historical and social factors. Important historical differences do exist between Morocco and Jordan, but these are not the reason for the divergence in these states' SoCs. King Husayn and King Hasan II initially used very similar strategies of rule, and it was only in the 1970s that their strategies began to diverge. Similarly, the regimes of Nasir, Sadat, and Mubarak in Egypt all stem from the Free Officers' Revolution of 1952, and yet Nasir and Sadat established *unified SoCs*, while Mubarak institutionalized a *divided SoC*.

A closer look at Jordan, Morocco, and Egypt demonstrates that it is not simply leadership characteristics, historical experience, or regime type that have led to very different government–opposition relations during economic crises. Rather, incumbents use institutions to create different SoCs as part of their ruling strategy. A rather detailed examination of political development in Morocco and Jordan shows why we should view SoCs as the outcomes of incumbents' strategies, not as predetermined by historical experience. The case of Egypt then demonstrates that the manipulation of SoCs is not limited to monarchies.

SOCS IN MONARCHIES: THE CASES OF JORDAN AND MOROCCO

There are several important historical differences between Morocco and Jordan: The Alawite dynasty in Morocco preceded the Hashemite dynasty in Jordan by nearly 300 years; the Alawites came under French colonial rule, while the Hashemites ruled under the British Mandate; and Morocco's first king, Muhammad V, was an integral part of the independence movement against the French, while Jordan's King 'Abdallah remained closely tied to his British allies. Yet, despite these historical differences, Husayn and Hasan II used very similar strategies of rule when they ascended to power. Initially, they both tried to liberalize their political system, creating relatively inclusive, unified systems. When this failed to appease their opponents, both called for martial law, excluding all opposition from the formal political system. Jordan remained an exclusive, unified SoC at the beginning of the 1980s, but in Morocco, King Hasan II reversed his strategy, creating a divided SoC in the early 1970s.

Challenges of Early Rule

King Husayn and King Hasan II would live to become two of the longest-reigning modern monarchs, but to do so they surmounted enormous challenges. Both were very young when they assumed the throne and struggled to assert their authority. More importantly, both had to establish their rule in newly independent states where neither national identities nor institutional structures were well established.

Transjordan. The Hashemite Kingdom of Jordan (initially, Transjordan) was born from two complementary desires: King 'Abdallah's desire to establish Greater Syria and Great Britain's desire to establish control over the area after the fall of the Ottoman Empire. Amir 'Abdallah was the son of Sharif Husayn, who came from the Hijaz and led the Arab Revolt with the support of the British and T. E. Lawrence, the famed "Lawrence of Arabia." In return for his efforts – which were intended to weaken the Ottoman–German alliance in World War I – the British had promised Sharif Husayn support in establishing an "Arab Kingdom." When the war was over, however, the British reneged on their promises. Still hoping to establish a kingdom, Amir 'Abdallah had entered Ma'an (in southern Jordan) in November 1920 and moved toward Amman, gathering the support of local tribes. The British saw an opportunity: By granting 'Abdallah support in establishing his government, they could partially fulfill their promise to Sharif Husayn and, more importantly, create a leadership capable of helping maintain their interest in the region. By July 1921, they gave him their support.

'Abdallah thus created structures governing Transjordanians within the context of his strong relationship with and reliance upon the British. In 1923 'Abdallah and the British signed an agreement in which the Amir promised to develop constitutional, representative institutions, while the British would recognize the "independent government" of Transjordan.

'Abdallah took steps to establish a legislature, but his interest in granting suffrage and privileges to gain political support did not extend to an interest in sharing political power.[6] Initially, 'Abdallah hoped that the legislature would serve to bolster his power, weakening the British influence over him. However, political opponents, and specifically Arab nationalists, used the Legislative Council to demand that the Amir oust the British completely, which would have eliminated critical military and financial support upon which 'Abdallah relied. 'Abdallah and his loyalist supporters responded harshly, threatening to close the parliament. Not surprisingly, the British supported these efforts, and by the early 1930s, Amir 'Abdallah had checked the opposition.[7]

Political tensions rose again after World War II. Palestinians resented 'Abdallah's attempt to annex the West Bank, thereby partially fulfilling his long-held dream of creating a greater kingdom.[8] Tensions between 'Abdallah and Palestinian notables loyal to the Grand Mufti of Jerusalem dated back to the early 1930s, and Palestinian opposition intensified as many blamed 'Abdallah for their defeat in the 1948 Arab–Israeli War. Moreover, the Palestinian population was more urban and educated than the Jordanian population, and they were unwilling to accept living under what they saw as a "traditional" regime.[9] Most Palestinians' ultimate goal was to reclaim their land, and Jordan provided a convenient base from which to carry out their operations. They felt little allegiance to the Hashemite monarch.

'Abdallah hoped to weaken this opposition by expanding political participation to the West Bank. In December 1949 he dissolved parliament in preparation for elections in mid-April 1950.[10] Political participation was high; the parliament was successfully established; and King 'Abdallah unified both sides of the Jordan River, thereby establishing the Hashemite Kingdom of Jordan. However, the King continued to face intense opposition from both Transjordanians and Palestinians.[11] Despite 'Abdallah's promises of further political reform, he was assassinated on July 20, 1951, as he entered the Dome of the Rock Mosque in Jerusalem.

The King's death drew into question the nature of the Jordanian regime.[12] The question of succession led to uncertainty. 'Abdallah's son, Talal, was crowned, but he was a weak and unstable ruler from the outset.[13] In addition, the West Bank had been officially annexed to Jordan, but support for the monarchy was far from secure. Palestinians resented the annexation, and many Transjordanians continued to question the legitimacy of Hashemite rule over the East Bank as well. In the political system that had expanded to include leftists, Islamists, and pro-government centrists, these forces took advantage of the political vacuum left by 'Abdallah's death to step up their political demands.

Initially, pro-monarch loyalists and the opposition compromised on a revised constitution of January 2, 1952. The Prime Minister and each member of his council were now responsible before the House of Deputies (Article 51). The House of Deputies could hold votes of confidence on the Council or its individual members, and withholding confidence by a two-thirds majority would result in the resignation of the council or deputies (Article 53.) However, although these measures strengthened the House of Deputies, the legislature remained subordinate to the executive. The King maintained the right to dissolve parliament and could do so without disbanding the Executive Council. Furthermore, the Cabinet still initiated legislation.

The confrontation between the palace loyalists and the opposition heightened. As before, opposition to Jordan's nonconfrontational stance toward Israel and the Hashemites' dependence upon the British united otherwise ideologically diverse political parties.[14] Unwilling to appease the opposition's demands for fundamental changes in domestic and inter-national policies, loyalists issued a series of emergency laws intended to squelch the opposition.[15] In the midst of this increasing tension, loyalists determined that Talal was unfit to rule and chose the late King 'Abdallah's young grandson, Husayn, to take his place.

Thus, when the 17-year-old King Husayn ascended the throne in May 1953, he faced severe challenges. There was no domestic consensus on the institutional framework of the regime, and a significant proportion of both Palestinians and Transjordanians viewed Hashemite rule as illegitimate. Consequently, Hashemite loyalists relied on significant British support for their rule, but this heightened opposition. King Husayn assumed a difficult position, and few had much hope for his survival.[16]

Morocco

King Hasan II also faced significant opposition and contestation over the role of the monarchy when he ascended the throne in 1962. The Moroccan monarch was in a somewhat better position than his Jordanian counterpart, for Morocco had been a territorial entity under Alawite rule far longer than Transjordan. However, it too had come under colonial rule by the early 20th century. Furthermore, although the Alawite dynasty had a long history, the role of the monarchy after independence and the territorial unity of the country were still highly contested.

The foundations of the current Alawite dynasty in Morocco date back to 1660, when the first Alawite chief, Mawlay Rashid, began to establish control over the territory. His successor, Mawlay Isma'il (1672–1727), further succeeded in driving the Spanish and British from the northern coastal areas and establishing Meknes as his capital. He also brought his subjects under tighter control – if not through loyalty, then through sheer terror. The elite military, formed from slaves brought from the south and known as 'Abd al-Bukhari, or the Buwakhir, included as many as 150,000.[17] Closely related was the extension of the state's institutional structure (the *makhzen*, literally meaning "storehouse"), with both the internal court affairs and the domestic civil administration.

Although civil and military structures existed, the Sultan had not consolidated control over the territory.[18] Tribal divisions remained strong and salient, and challenges both between tribes of the *makhzen*, the dynastic family itself, and the outlying tribes were significant. Sultans engaged in a constant attempt to maintain the "relative monopoly of coercive means"[19] through force and alliance building, while allegiances for most lay outside the palace. Murabitun (i.e., religious leaders) had large followings, and Amazigh[20] (Berber) tribes remained largely autonomous from, and often hostile to, the *makhzen*. Indeed, much of the country remained outside the control of the Alawite sultans.[21]

By the early 20th century, Morocco also came under colonial influence. The French, interested in Morocco for its strategic importance and economic potential,[22] expanded their influence there by the late 1800s, but they did not formally occupy the country until 1912. By then, France and Spain overcame their major obstacle to full occupation of the territory: inter-European competition.[23] At the Algericas Conference on Morocco in 1906, France gained the support of the European states and the United States to share police control over Morocco with Spain, although technically the country remained independent. The Sultan's acceptance of the agreement in June 1906, the outbreak of a civil war in 1908, and continued violence led to the establishment of the French protectorate over much of Morocco four years later. Spain maintained control over the northern coast and the southwestern Sahara.

Like Amir 'Abdallah and the British in Transjordan, the French faced tribal resistance to their control over Morocco.[24] General Louis Lyautey, as French Resident-General, struggled for 22 years to put down tribal insurgency throughout the country, which reached its height in the Rif War of 1924–1926. As General Augustine Léon Guillaume, who served in Morocco during the 1940s and as Resident-General from 1951 to 1954, recounted: " 'Not a single tribe submitted to [the French] without having first exhausted to the bitter end its means of resistance.' "[25] The French also sought to establish control by creating alliances with Moroccan elites. Foremost among them was Sultan Mawlay Yusuf, elected by the Fez ulama as sultan after the forced abdication of his brother in 1912. Upon his death in 1927, the French would arrange the election of Yusuf's third son, the Sultan Muhammad Ben Yusuf (later known as Muhammad V), to the sultanship. Given his young age and shy disposition, they believed he would be an easy leader to control.[26]

They were wrong. Colonialism in Morocco stimulated the development of Moroccan nationalism, and Muhammad V supported the movement. French policies of economic exploitation and the extension of secular French law over juridical domains raised Moroccan opposition. Differential French policies toward the Moroccan Arab and Amazigh populations also increased alarm among Moroccans. Most important was the "Berber Dahir" (Edict) of 1930, by which the French sought to establish separate courts and education systems for Berber and Arab Moroccans. For Moroccans, the Dahir represented the French attempt to engineer the downfall of Islam, separate the Moroccan people, and promote the division of Morocco into Arab and Amazigh states.

The 1930 Berber Dahir provided an important catalyst for the nationalist movement. Two intellectuals from Fez, 'Allal al-Fasi and Ahmad Bellafrej, were at the forefront of the movement, and the Sultan Muhammad V took an active interest in their work.[27] Encouraged by the Sultan's support, the nationalist leaders set about creating a reform plan, demanding political, judicial, social, and economic reforms, which they presented to the French on December 1, 1934. The French rejected the plan and warned the Sultan to be silent, threatening otherwise to arrest the leaders of the movement.[28]

Despite, or perhaps because of, this response, the nationalist movement grew. By 1936, the nationalists had mounted demonstrations in every major area of Morocco. The following year, the announcement of a plan to divert water to the colons (French settlers) led to rioting in Meknes, brutal French suppression, and subsequent demonstrations in Casablanca, Fez, Rabat, Oudja, and Marrakesh. By the middle of 1937, the French had banned the Nationalist Party and an estimated 10,000 nationalist sympathizers were detained; al-Fasi was exiled to the French colony of Gabon.[29]

Repression only strengthened nationalist sentiments. By 1944, al-Fasi and Bellafrej joined with Muhammad Hasan al-Quzayri and Muhammad al-Yazidi in forming the Istiqlal (Independence) Party. Furthermore, the Sultan spoke out on behalf of the nationalist movement. In January, he told then French Resident-General Maréchal Puaux that he could guarantee calm in the streets of Morocco only if leading members of the Istiqlal Party remained free. The French responded by arresting Ahmed Bellafrej, Muhammad al-Yazidi, and 16 other Istiqlali leaders, and Fez and Rabat erupted in rioting. Consequently, the French increasingly turned away from Muhammad V and toward T'Hami al-Glawi, the Amazigh leader of Marrakesh and the Sultan's greatest rival,[30] for collaboration. Three years later, in April 1947, the Sultan made a daring trip to Tangier, speaking of "legitimate rights of the Moroccan people" and calling for strengthening Moroccan ties with the Arab League.[31] Subsequent attempts to split the Sultan and the Istiqlal Party failed, leading instead to increased nationalist demonstrations, strikes, rioting, and boycotts. Finally, the French deposed Muhammad V on August 20, 1953, exiling him to Corsica and, later, to Madagascar.[32]

Although Muhammad V's cooperation with the Istiqlali movement made him subject to French repression, it also gave him legitimacy to return to the throne. Violence escalated after the Sultan's deposition; terrorism and counterterrorism led to almost a quarter of a million French troops pitted against thousands of guerrillas and military occupation of the major Moroccan cities. Inside France, the French government faced rightists who refused to relinquish their control over Morocco; inside Morocco, the French faced not only nationalists' attacks but also the pressure from France's allies (among them, al-Glawi) not to grant independence. When the frustrated French opened Franco–Moroccan talks in Aix-les-Bains in August 1955,[33] the Istiqlal Party and their nationalist supporters refused to accept French reforms without the participation of the exiled Sultan Muhammad V. At last, on October 31, 1955, the Sultan and his family were taken to Paris for negotiations. One week later, the French issued a joint Franco–Moroccan Declaration of La Celle-Saint-Cloud establishing Morocco as a constitutional monarchy,[34] and on November 17, 1955, the Sultan Sidi Muhammad Bin Yusuf returned to the Moroccan throne.

The Sultan's exile gave him legitimacy, but it did not eliminate the power struggle between the monarch and the parties. The issue in contention was how much power a king should have in a "constitutional monarchy." On the one hand, King Muhammad V promised great changes. Speaking in his first throne speech after return from exile, the Sultan argued that the time had come for "a thorough-going transformation of the habits, the institutions and the methods of government, as it will also imply an emancipation of the individual, assuring him the secure enjoyment of all his freedoms."[35] He promised that the development of "a constitutional Arab Muslim democratic monarchy" would be a major priority,[36] but he was as reluctant to establish true power-sharing relationships as Amir 'Abdallah had been. The 1958 Royal Charter proclaimed that the monarch wanted to reinforce individual and collective liberties and to consolidate a multiparty system; in reality, however, it enhanced the King's power. The National Consultative Assembly it created could debate policies and make recommendations but not set policy. The government was at the mercy of the King, as demonstrated in 1960, when the King dissolved the government of 'Abdallah Ibrahim, taking the portfolio of the Prime Minister for himself and naming his son, Crown Prince Hasan II, as Vice-Prime Minister.

The King also used the requirement of multipartyism to fragment political forces. Unlike in Jordan, the independence movement in Morocco had helped foster the development of a large and important opposition party, the Istiqlal. This was King Muhammad V's most significant rival. The Istiqlal hoped to control the rules of the game, excluding other contenders and entering into an exclusive partnership with the monarch. Consequently, it moved to outlaw the Popular Movement, a primarily Amazigh party that mobilized in the Rif and Atlas mountains after independence. However, the King had different incentives; he feared being dominated, or perhaps even ousted, by the Istiqlal, as the Sultan of Tunisia had been. He wanted the division of his opposition, not partnership with it. Thus, he allowed 'Abd al-Karim al-Khatib and al-Mahjubi Ahardan to create the Popular Movement (MP) from the old Army of Liberation.[37] He also promoted natural fissures in the Istiqlal; the broad-based revolutionary party began to split along rural–urban, class, and ideological lines.[38]

The struggle between the King and the parties intensified, as it had in Jordan. Although its dominance was broken, the Istiqlal Party remained the single strongest party. Its membership rose from approximately 100,000 to 1.6 million members in the early months of independence.[39] Its continued challenges to King Muhammad V led him in 1961 to dissolve the National Consultative Assembly. Thus, the power struggle turned, at least for the time being, toward the monarchy when the King died unexpectedly. His son and right-hand man, Hasan II, assumed the throne.

In short, King Husayn and King Hasan II faced similar challenges when they came to power. In both Morocco and Jordan, the regime's institutional structures were still very much contested. The debate over Jordan's constitutional revision demonstrated significant divisions among political contenders over the nature of the constitutional monarchy and the relative power of the King. Conservative tribal forces favoring a traditional monarchy stood in contrast to more liberal, generally urban political forces favoring democratic institutions and modern political parties. The fundamental disagreements underlying this debate had not died down when King Husayn was crowned in 1953. Although the Alawite dynasty in Morocco was much older than the Hashemite Kingdom in Jordan, the French and Spanish occupation and subsequent independence had brought the debate over the nature of the Moroccan monarchy to the fore as well. When King Hasan II ascended to the throne in 1962, the Constitution of Morocco had not yet been written. In short, neither King Husayn nor King Hasan II inherited a consolidated political system.

Facing the Challenges: Bases of Rule

The kings not only faced very similar challenges, but also relied upon similar bases of support to legitimize and strengthen their political control. They reinforced their legitimacy through their historical religious role. They also sought to establish a role as the arbitrator of power among contending forces, the "father" of bickering children.

Legitimacy through Islam. The kings used both rituals and institutions to reinforce their religious legitimacy. King Husayn stressed his role as custodian of Haram al-Sharif in Jerusalem (much to some Palestinians' dismay) and provided royal patronage of Islamic projects including, most notably, the renovation of the Dome of the Rock. King Hasan II also emphasized his sharifian lineage, publishing annually the genealogy linking him directly to the Prophet Muhammad. In addition, he used the demonstration of the *bay'a*, the wearing of traditional white clothing and patronage of Islamic projects (most notably the Hasan II mosque in Casablanca), and used titles such as "Commander of the Faithful" (Amir al-Mu'minin) or "God's deputy on Earth" (Khalifat Allah fi al-'Ard) to emphasize his religious legitimacy.[40]

The unique religious significance of the kings granted them a privileged position, which was incorporated into the institutional frameworks of these states. For instance, Article 19 of the 1962 Moroccan Constitution states, "The King, Amir al-Mouminine, Supreme Representative of the Nation, Symbol of its unity, guarantor of the permanence and continuity of the State, ensures the respect for Islam and the Constitution."[41] The monarch is thus "appointed by God to carry out a mission which can neither be ignored nor questioned"[42] and is granted immunity in Article 23 of the Constitution.[43] Similarly, Article 31 of the Jordanian Constitution granted King Husayn immunity, dictating that "The King is the Head of the State and is immune from any liability and responsibility."

Arbitration. In addition, the kings crafted a role as the arbitrator of contending political forces. They wanted to promote Moroccan and Jordanian national identities, but they also wanted to maintain social divisions, between Amazighs (Berbers) and Arabs in Morocco or between Palestinians and Transjordanians in Jordan, various tribal and regional groups, and competing ideological parties. As John Waterbury and Alan Richards noted:

What the monarchs want is a plethora of interests, tribal, ethnic, professional, class-based, and partisan, whose competition for public patronage they can arbitrate. None of these elements can be allowed to become too powerful or wealthy, and the monarch will police and repress or entice and divide.[44]

Which groups the monarchs would repress or entice, and how they would do so, varied over time.[45]

MANAGING THE OPPOSITION: STRATEGIES OF RULE
IN JORDAN AND MOROCCO

King Hasan II and King Husayn initially used very similar strategies to manage contending forces within the polity. Both sought to liberalize their political systems, fostering competition among political parties. Yet, the early experiments failed. In the heady period following World War II,[46] nationalists in both Jordan and Morocco demanded greater political freedom and a significant reduction of the monarch's power, if not his elimination. The experiments culminated in the closure of elected parliaments, the repression of political parties, and the establishment of martial rule.

Jordan

Although the rivalry between loyalists and opponents continued after Husayn's coronation in May 1953, the new king initially sought to liberalize the Kingdom's politics and change the balance of power between contending forces. King Husayn immediately appointed Fawzi al-Mulqi as Prime Minister to spearhead the liberalization, and in his statement to parliament on May 24, 1953, al-Mulqi promised: " 'The government will at the next meeting refer to the House all regulations and ordinance for the re-examination and revision of the constitution to allow liberty of speech and formation of political parties.' "[47] He suspended emergency regulations, freed political prisoners, removed censorship regulations, and even allowed the Communist newspaper to obtain a license for publication. He also helped usher in constitutional amendments that increased the power of parliament.[48] The young King chose to establish an inclusive, unified SoC, and this strengthened the nationalists at the expense of palace loyalists.

Al-Mulqi came under fire. Loyalists objected, fearing al-Mulqi's measures would permanently isolate them from the political arena. Opposition parties also put pressure on the government, demanding more significant reforms. In their eyes, al-Mulqi voiced anti-British sentiments, but the fundamental dependence on the British had not declined. Moreover, the opposition parties and parliament still remained subordinate to and dependent upon the king. Jordan's continued military and financial reliance on the West seemed unacceptable in the politically charged atmosphere of the early 1950s, and Arab nationalists, leftists, and the extreme right used the limited opening to increase pressure on the regime, apparently hoping to undermine it fully.

The government walked a tightrope between loyalist and opposition demands. In response to loyalist and international pressures, al-Mulqi proposed an Anti-Communist Law in December 1953. It provided that anyone caught donating money to a Communist organization or selling and distributing its literature was liable to one to three years in prison, and any member of a Communist organization was subject to imprisonment with hard labor.[49] While the law could have served to divide the Communists from the remaining political forces, the palace failed to create a significant distinction between the privileges accorded Communist and non-Communist parties. In January, al-Mulqi's government also legislated the 1954 Party Law, officially legalizing political parties and requiring that they obtain a license from the government.[50] Yet, in an attempt to satisfy the loyalists, the government treated opposition parties harshly. The illegal Communist Party could not receive a license, but it operated as the National Front. The secular Ba'thists and Islamic Liberation Party (Hizb al-Tahrir) were also denied licenses. As King Husayn realized that the opposition was not satisfied with limited reforms, he turned to loyalists for support. He called on al-Mulqi to resign and asked a conservative loyalist, Abu al-Huda, to form a new cabinet.

Abu al-Huda's government, formed in May, represented a movement away from liberal politics. He reinforced Jordan's willingness to cooperate with Britain and opposed a Jordanian–Iraqi union. More importantly, he intended to reign in the opposition. Given his previous poor relationship with the opposition and the opposition's strong presence in parliament,[51] he was well aware that his government would be unable to work with the legislature. Thus, on May 18th, the King dissolved parliament before it could vote on Abu al-Huda's government, and new elections were set for October.

As elections approached, tensions mounted. The government repressed the opposition by reviving martial law.[52] In response, opponents marched through the streets of Amman and West Bank cities, shouting slogans against Abu al-Huda. Election day saw widespread violence, and the government called in the Arab Legion to restore order in Amman. At least 10 civilians were killed, but the electoral process continued. A loyal legislature was elected, and on November 8, 1954, Abu al-Huda's government received a vote of confidence.[53]

Abu al-Huda's government reversed al-Mulqi's liberalization and weakened the political parties. The 1955 Press and Publication and Political Party laws strengthened government control. A new Law of Municipalities granted the Council of Ministers the authority to request the resignation of locally elected mayors or presidents of municipal councils when it objected to their decisions, and the Law of Preaching in the Mosques required sheikhs to obtain permits from the Chief Justice, who also had the authority to revoke these permits at any time. In short, within one year, Abu al-Huda reasserted the executive's control over the parliament.

Nevertheless, the opposition continued to challenge domestic and international policies. In the parliament, they attacked Abu al-Huda's policies and refused to ratify the government's budget proposal, arguing that spending on security forces and prisons far outstripped expenditures on social services.[54] In foreign policy, opposition parties expressed their support for Nasr and their opposition to the Baghdad Pact, the Western-oriented, defense pact of the Central Treaty Organization (CENTO). They took their demands to the streets as well, culminating in October in popular demonstrations in Amman, Nablus, and Ramallah. The Arab Legion was called in to restore order, and once again, Abu al-Huda resigned.

King Husayn was in a difficult position. Despite popular opposition, he preferred to remain in alliance with Iraq and Great Britain. Thus, he appointed Sa'id al-Mufti to form a new government and prepared to join the Baghdad Pact. As negotiations over Jordan's entry into the Pact proceeded, the political situation deteriorated. Nasr unleashed a major propaganda machine against the regime and the King; Sa'id al-Mufti's government fell; and leftist political parties and popular opposition mobilized anti-Hashemite demonstrations and riots.[55] After a brief attempt to form a new government under the loyalist Hazza al-Majali, the King dissolved parliament and called for new elections.

Opposition continued to escalate, leading King Husayn, on January 9th, to call on a long-time loyalist, Samir al-Rifa'i, to head the new government. Al-Rifa'i was determined to restore order. He announced that Jordan would not join the Baghdad Pact, and then he imposed a national curfew. Yet, demonstrations continued. Led by the National Socialist, Communist, and Liberation parties, people rallied for new elections, the abrogation of the Anglo–Jordanian Treaty, and a replacement of the British subsidy by Egyptian, Syrian, and Saudi funds. Al-Rifa'i's government clamped down, rounding up opposition leaders and strengthening security.[56] Opposition spread through the army as well, leading to the arrest of two officers and seven others for plotting a military coup.

Seeking some reconciliation with the opposition, King Husayn dismissed Sir John Bagot Glubb in March. Glubb was a British soldier who had served as commander of Jordan's Arab Legion since 1939. By dismissing him, King Husayn could fend off accusations that the Hashemites were pawns of the British and promote the notion that domestic politics were played fairly. It also allowed him to offer Jordanians positions in the officer corps. Husayn immediately promoted 'Ali Abu Nawwar, a military officer whom Glubb had distrusted, to the rank of major general and appointed him the Arab Legion's Chief of General Staff.[57] Abu Nawwar's sympathies lay with the nationalists, but Husayn believed that he could gain Abu Nawwar's loyalty.

King Husayn was wrong. Abu Nawwar used his position as Chief of General Staff to bring nationalists to positions of power. Abu Nawwar and a group of military officers also put pressure on the Prime Minister and the King to grant nationalist leaders government portfolios. The compromises between the King, al-Mufti's government, and the nationalists ultimately failed, and the King again called for new elections.

The elections of October 21, 1956, provided the grounds for the final showdown between the King and the nationalists. The Ba'thists,

National Front (Communists), and National Socialists, united in their anti-British and pro-Egyptian positions, won nearly half of the seats in parliament. King Husayn recognized their success, calling on Sulayman al-Nabulsi, head of the National Socialist Party, to form a new leftist-dominated government on October 29, 1956.[58]

October 29th was a momentous day. In July, Jamal ʿAbd al-Nasir had nationalized the Suez Canal, at the same time stepping up attacks on Israel from Gaza. On the 29th, as al-Nabulsi formed his cabinet, Israel attacked Gaza and French and British forces landed in Port Saʿid. The Nabulsi government's first act, then, was to break off relations with France, voting unanimously to recognize the Soviet Union and China and to abrogate the Anglo–Jordanian Treaty. As the Suez crisis escalated in November, Jordan found itself in a dangerous situation as Iraqi, Saudi Arabian, and Syrian troops moved into Jordan. Ostensibly, their mission was to protect Jordan from Israeli–British attacks, but their presence threatened the Hashemite regime. Husayn was further threatened when al-Nabulsi asked the Hashemite Iraqi troops to withdraw while allowing Saudi and Syrian troops to remain.

Al-Nabulsi's government promised radical changes in foreign policy.[59] It sought to establish friendship with radical Arab states and diplomatic relations with Communist countries.[60] It also welcomed the opportunity to sever ties with the West. Al-Nabulsi purged officials with pro-Western leanings from the government, and he refused to cooperate as Britain and Jordan began negotiating the Anglo–Jordanian Treaty.

Al-Nabulsi was also prepared for radical domestic changes. He liberalized freedom of speech, the press and publication and allowed Communists to act freely despite the continued application of the Anti-Communist Law. Unlike King Husayn, the Prime Minister was not alarmed by the threat of communism. Perhaps more strikingly, he was also not determined to protect Jordanian sovereignty. On the contrary, on December 16th he announced that

the country could not "live forever as Jordan" and it "must be connected militarily, economically and politically" with one or more Arab states.[61]

In short, al-Nabulsi's government threatened King Husayn's regime as leftist sentiment spread through the country, including within the military. Palace loyalists voiced their intense concern that they were being shut out from power and that the monarchy was threatened. The final straw was the government's insistence that Jordan relinquish Western support. Husayn knew that without support from the West,

Jordan was at the mercy of its neighbors. If they then refused to pay, Jordan would collapse, and the King was not confident of his neighbors' intentions.

In an effort to halt the movement toward the left, he sent an open letter to al-Nabulsi on February 2nd, focusing on the Communist threat and asking the government to reverse its positions.[62] The government refused, and in response the palace banned Communist publications. The cabinet could not reverse these decisions, but it could publicize the rift between the King and the cabinet. In the meantime, the King's negotiations with the British over the Anglo–Jordanian Treaty had failed. Despite Husayn's attacks on the Communists, the British decided to cancel the treaty and terminate their subsidy.

The showdown between the palace and the government finally came over the question of the Eisenhower Doctrine. Parliamentary members objected to the Doctrine, in which the United States offered aid and military assistance to Middle Eastern countries willing to join the United States against the Communist bloc. The King favored accepting it. On April 4th, al-Nabulsi announced that the government would accept Soviet aid if offered and would reject American support. Finding this unacceptable, the King dissolved the government on April 10th. Three days later, he faced a military coup attempt organized by his right-hand man, 'Ali Abu Nawwar. In an impressive show of courage, the young King rode out to meet officers near Zarqa, thwarted the coup attempt, confronted Abu Nawwar, and promptly exiled him from Jordan.

The nationalists mounted one last challenge. On April 22nd, nationalists and Communists met in Nablus and drew up a set of demands, asking the government for a federal union with Egypt and Syria, the rejection of the Eisenhower Doctrine, and reinstatement of dismissed officers. That night and the next day, Egyptian Voice of the Arabs broadcast the nationalists' demands throughout Jordan, and the following day, on April 24th, the opposition organized a general strike. Supporters flooded the streets in massive demonstrations throughout the West Bank. Prime Minister Khalidi's government resigned, and Ibrahim Hashim, a loyalist, took control of the government. He announced a curfew, imposed martial law, dissolved political parties, and reestablished the King and loyalists' supremacy over the nationalists.

The opposition had lost this final showdown. As Peter Snow writes:

From April 1957 onwards, there was no pretense made of democracy in Jordan. The country was ruled by a cabinet, appointed by and responsible to the King, not to parliament. The King ruled with the support of the army, and where the army's will differed from that of any portion of the people, the army had its way. From this time on, the welfare of the people depended on the benevolence of Hussein and his army.[63]

Political parties operated underground after 1957. Elections were held in 1962 and 1967, but they were carried out on an independent basis. Leftists could not field candidates openly, although the Muslim Brotherhood – which gained special concessions as a charitable organization and one that had demonstrated its loyalty to the king – did, and won at least one parliamentary seat in 1962.

The period continued to witness some intense conflict between the King and the now illegal opposition, particularly from leftists (including the underground Communists, Ba'thists, and Arab Nationalists). Much of the opposition was centered on the question of the King's control over the West Bank and relationships with Israel, and so it was not surprising that it increased dramatically following the radicalization of the PLO after the 1967 Arab–Israeli War. The violence culminated in the Jordanian civil war of 1970 (Black September). The King also experienced more minor military uprisings in 1974, when the military mutinied at Zarqa in response to increased prices, pay inequities, and alleged corruption.[64] Yet, he did not alter his strategy.[65] When the economic crisis began in the 1980s, Jordan had an exclusive, unified SoC.

Morocco

King Hasan II's first task was to establish the political rules of the game, set forth in the 1962 Constitution. In Article 3, the King established a multiparty system. His interest in multipartyism was clear; the King could increase internal legitimacy, improve Morocco's international image, and break the dominance of the Istiqlal Party in a single stroke. In addition, the Constitution ensured the King's dominance. It gave the King the power to appoint the Prime Minister, dismiss all ministers, preside over government, dissolve the Chamber of Representatives by decree, and go directly to the people with referenda.

The constitution was accepted in a popular referendum by 80 percent of the population. The MP, the Liberal Party, and the Independents supported the document, favoring it because it stressed respect for national sovereignty, the independence of the judiciary, and the prohibition of one party rule. The National Union of Popular Forces (UNFP), the Moroccan Labor Union (UMT)[66] and Moroccan Communist Party opposed it, particularly objecting to the King's dominant position. The Istiqlal accepted, although with reservations. While they objected to the King's dominance and had favored one-party rule, they still hoped to be partners with the young King.

At the 1963 elections, however, it was clear that the King did not see himself in the same partnership as the Istiqlal. Although the palace allowed the opposition to campaign freely, the King and his allies created a strong pro-palace coalition, the Front for the Defense of Constitutional Institutions (FDIC),[67] in an attempt to counter the parties. Then, even though the loyalist FDIC did not win a simple majority of the seats (it obtained 69 seats, while other parties got 75), the King asked its members to form the government.

Opposition parties, including the Istiqlal and UNFP, were strongly opposed, and subsequently they stonewalled the government's policy proposals. With 69 seats, the opposition front created a legislative impasse, and after two years the legislature had passed virtually no legislation. In the meantime, domestic economic conditions worsened. A series of strikes and unrest ensued, culminating in the Casablanca riots of March 9, 1965.

In an attempt to restore calm and shore up his own position, King Hasan II invoked Article 35 of the Constitution and declared a state of emergency. He publicly blamed the political parties for failing to pass legislation and discrediting the democratization process. In terms set forth earlier, he then established an exclusive, unified environment. The parties were not officially banned, but they lost their raison d'être and their ability to operate in the political system. The King reconstituted the government, creating a cabinet filled with only his closest advisors. Political freedoms of speech and association were limited, and all efforts were made to discredit, marginalize, and repress opposition actors. The army was brought in and given increased authority.

The democratization process in Morocco appeared to have been short-lived. After elections in 1969, independents and loyalists dominated the legislature. Of 300 seats, the MP gained 44, Istiqlal 12, and UNFP 1. Independents won the remainder. Domestic violence was also increasing. The King and his opposition had been involved in a cycle of violence and repression since 1966, with intellectuals and students at the forefront of the unrest. On May 4, 1970, it escalated with a general strike of students in Rabat, spreading to the popular quarters.

As violence escalated, the King attempted to promulgate a new "democratic and social" constitution, but the opposition made it clear that they were unwilling to accept his terms. The opposition rejected the

King's widened powers in the 1970 Constitution, written in an attempt to reestablish the constitutional monarchy. The Constitution gave the King wide powers: He had the ability to appoint the prime minister and other ministers, dissolve parliament, declare a state of emergency, and rule by decree. The King also appointed the judges of the Supreme Court and the governors of the country's 19 provinces and two prefectures (Rabat and Casablanca).

None of this was acceptable to the opposition forces, and unrest continued. The Istiqlal Party and UNFP boycotted the referendum in 1970, and in reaction to their intransigence, the government seized the Istiqlali paper, *L'opinion*, five times in the first seven months of 1971. Seeing the parties as intransigent, the King relied more on patronage to obtain support. In turn, however, the national welfare declined, charges of corruption increased, and general discontent rose dramatically.

By 1971, the King had lost the support of the armed forces, his most important allies. On July 10, 1971, the military reacted to the growing national unrest, mounting an attempted coup at Skhirat during a party at the palace. The King, invoking his religious role, asked the dissident troops to join him in praying, and the troops abandoned their cause. On August 16, 1972, King Hasan II faced another challenge when a Moroccan Air Force escort plane attempted to shoot down his plane. This time, the King outsmarted the officers. Pretending to be the pilot, he radioed the military stating that the King had been seriously injured and asking for permission to land.

Spurred by attempted military coups and increased domestic unrest, King Hasan II wrote a new Constitution that gave slightly more limited powers to the palace: The King shared the role of revising the Constitution with the parliament, and some administrative powers were delegated to the prime minister. Yet, the fundamental supremacy of the King was unaffected. The opposition parties, now formed as the National Bloc, still rejected the reforms. The King and the parties were engaged in a stalemate. He was not willing to grant the parties the latitude they desired, and the parties were unwilling to accept his rules of the game.

Consequently, the King turned toward repression. He appointed Ahmad 'Usman, his brother-in-law, as Prime Minister and, after the coup attempt of 1973 in the Atlas Mountains, sought even tighter control over the military. He also increased the restriction of opposition movements, abolishing the National Union of Moroccan Students (UNEM),[68] the student organization, in 1974 and suspending constitutional rights until the plots against the King could be resolved. Furthermore, although the Constitution had been approved in a referendum by 98.1 percent of the voters, the palace did not call for local or national elections. Opposition parties had boycotted the referendum, and it was clear that they still did not accept Hasan II's rules of the game. In reality, the monarch was ruling through exclusive authoritarian rule. Using a combination of repression and economic measures intended to improve conditions for the elite and bourgeoisie,[69] he hoped to save his political neck.

He did, and his luck, or *barakah* (blessings), improved. By 1974 Spain had acquiesced to international pressure to relinquish its remaining colonies, including its control over the Western Sahara (or Spanish Sahara). The territory held only approximately 60,000 persons, but it had significant phosphate deposits, exporting 2–3 million tons annually by 1972. It was also tied historically to the Alawite dynasty; thus Muhammad V had made the initial claim to the territory in 1958, and Hasan II renewed the claim in 1974 before the International Court of Justice. In October, the Court recognized the competing claims of Morocco and Mauritania, arguing that self-determination under the UN Charter would supersede their temporary control. This gave Hasan II a reason to assert control over the territory and provided an opportunity to rally domestic support. In November, as 350,000 Moroccans marched into the territory during the "Green March" intended to stake their claim to the area, Morocco and Mauritania divided the former colony.[70] Popular support for the Moroccan King soared.

Finally, the opposition parties were ready to return to the bargaining table on the King's terms. After almost a decade of violence and repression, and now coupled with the popular support gained from the Green March, the parties realized that they were unable to topple the King. In addition, the attempted military coups had frightened some opposition groups as much as they had the King. Consequently, they established their willingness to accept the Constitution; the King called for new elections; and a political bargain was struck.

Not all political forces were allowed into the system, however. UNEM, the Movement of March 23, and other forces that had shown themselves either too strong or intransigent during the previous decade would be excluded. Others, such as the Communist Party, would be allowed to re-organize in a more moderate form, in this case under the name Party of Progress and Socialism (PPS). More importantly, King Hasan II did not permit Islamic groups such as Ila al-Amam to form legal political parties. Although the Istiqlal claimed some traditional religious legitimacy, the King made it clear that he was the supreme religious leader of Morocco, the Commander of the Faithful. The King's unique role as Commander of the Faithful was to remain unrivaled in the official political sphere. As Korany noted, "The result [was] a clear line of demarcation established by the regime between 'constructive' opposition (i.e., working within the bounds of the regime) and an opposition not permitted by the palace to function, whatever the justification given."[71] A set of opposition groups thus remained ever-present, just outside the realm of formal politics. Although they had no legitimate voice in the political system, both masses and incumbent elites recognized their presence and knew their demands.

UNIFIED AND DIVIDED SoCs IN JORDAN AND MOROCCO

In both Morocco and Jordan, the monarchs consolidated their reign, but by the mid-1970s they did so very differently. In Morocco the King created a division between legal and illegal opposition elites. This division increased as the economic crisis continued, making legal political opponents increasingly reluctant to mobilize popular protests. In contrast, the Jordanian monarch did not foster a division between moderate and radical elites. Consequently, political opponents remained willing to mobilize popular opposition to challenge the government.

Through their different approaches to political opposition, the monarchs created very different government–opposition structures. In Morocco, a large and increasingly fragmented set of political parties was allowed to participate in the formal political system. (See Appendix.)[72] These parties, however, were sharply divided from the illegal opposition groups, mainly religious-based societies, that remained outside the system.[73] Many of these groups questioned the legitimacy of the King and challenged the entire political system, including the role of the included opposition parties. Despite their potential for anti-regime activity, however, King Hasan II allowed the growth of the Islamist opposition in the early 1980s as a counterweight to his secularist opponents. He thus created and fostered divisions among opposition groups.

King Husayn, on the other hand, kept all opposition illegal. As the Appendix shows, a wide range of political forces existed in Jordan, but they were not allowed to participate openly in the formal political sphere. Rather, parties such as the secular Ba'th Party, the Popular Front for the Liberation of Palestine (PFLP), and the Democratic Front for the Liberation of Palestine (DFLP), as well as the Islamist Liberation Party, would be forced to operate underground. Only the Muslim Brotherhood would be permitted to organize openly, and it would do so as a charitable society.

Like King Hasan II, Husayn would promote divisions among opponents. Indeed, he allowed the Muslim Brotherhood to operate as a charitable society in order to counter leftist opponents,[74] and he played upon divisions between Jordanians of Palestinian and Transjordanian origin. However, in the formal political system, he did not separate opponents into legal and illegal factions. All parties were illegal until the early 1990s, when they were all allowed to enter the formal political sphere. In terms of our model, Morocco had a divided SoC after 1975, while Jordan did not.

DISTINCTIONS IN DOMINANT-PARTY REGIMES: EGYPT UNDER NASIR, SADAT, AND MUBARAK

Changes in SoCs are most easily observed in the monarchies, but similar distinctions exist in other hegemonic regimes as well. The regimes of Nasir, Sadat, and Mubarak were all based upon the Free Officers' Revolution of 1952, but the Egyptian leaders used different strategies toward the political opposition. Nasir moved quickly to consolidate power after wresting control from King Faruk. By the 1960s, Nasir had created a unified, exclusive SoC, which Sadat would inherit. Sadat would take steps to include limited political opposition after 1976, but the level of inclusion was so minimal and short-lived that it did not serve to divide the opposition effectively. In contrast, after assuming power in 1981, Mubarak created a divided SoC by allowing a much broader set of political parties to join the formal sphere while at the same time excluding significant opposition.

Consolidation of the Unified SoC Under Nasir

The foundation of a unified SoC in Egypt dates to July 1952, when Jamal 'Abd al-Nasir and a group of approximately 100 coconspirators in the Free Officers' movement mounted a coup against King Faruk. The officers, with significant popular support, sought radical changes in the regime. The Revolutionary Command Council (RCC) moved immediately to expel the King. The RCC did not have a specific, agreed-upon policy agenda, but the officers set about immediately to shore up support and weaken their opponents. By September, they had established Agrarian Reform Laws intended to weaken the landed aristocracy. They also implemented liberal reforms – releasing political prisoners, punishing corruption, lifting censorship, abolishing the secret police, and promising constitutional rule.[75] In what was both a social and a political revolution, the new military junta moved to expand the role of the lower classes, stimulate economic growth, and revive the political and military might of Egypt.

Nasir and his compatriots were less intent, however, on establishing democratic freedoms. Socialism, not democracy, was the call of revolutionary movements of the time, and by the end of the decade, Nasir had quashed civil and political liberties in an attempt to shore up both the movement and his own personal power. The leadership formally abolished the monarchy and dismantled political parties in the new Constitution of 1953.[76] That same year, Nasir established the Liberation Rally (LR) to act as single popular force of the revolution. Yet it was intended more to depoliticize Egypt than to mobilize the polity. As ʿAli Sabri, First Secretary of the subsequent Arab Socialist Union (ASU), stated, "Its primary and basic goal was the destruction of the political organizations opposing the revolution."[77]

Indeed, by 1954, when the debate over whether or not Egypt should return to democratic rule heated up, Nasir was poised to exclude all opposition. The showdown between Nasir and those demanding a return to a parliamentary system – largely found in the trade unions and professional associations – ended in co-optation of willing forces and repression of stalwart opponents.[78] In March, the RCC dismissed all officials who had held high positions before the revolution. Further opposition was excluded through the use of military and "People's Courts" established in November of that year. These courts were first established under the leadership of Jamal Salim, Anwar al-Sadat, and Husayn al-Shafi'i, but all members of RCC helped to "secure the Revolution first."[79]

A series of institutional reforms helped to consolidate Nasir's power. A new constitution, put to a referendum in 1956, created a presidency with vast powers. The 1956 "Law on the Exercise of Political Rights" established state control over all forms of political participation; the 1958 Law No. 162 confirmed the president's right to declare and terminate states of emergency; the 1960 Law No. 156 nationalized the media, effectively eliminating freedom of the press; a 1963 law stipulated that union leaders must be members of the ASU;[80] and the 1964 Law No. 32 allowed the government to prohibit organizations that threatened "morality" and the "interest of the republic."

State-controlled entities replaced pluralist organizations. Trade unions came under the state's control through a series of decrees, consolidated in January 1961 when the unions designated in Law No. 91 were formed and the Egyptian Trade Union Federation[81] (ETUF) was born. The government would have effective veto power over leadership decisions. Other major institutions – universities, professional associations, the media, and mosques – came similarly under the regime's control.[82] Independent political groups were banned, with remaining cells existing only underground. The LR, having done its job, was disbanded and replaced by the National Union (NU) in 1957 and then by the ASU in 1962.

None of these organizations were intended to function as "effective instrument(s) of political actions."[83] They had no significant influence on public policy, and they had no real role in political discipline. As Mark Cooper noted, "The elite was disciplined by Presidential appointment and dismissal; the masses were disciplined by the police."[84] Repression was palpable. Public debates on political issues were strictly prohibited, and the heavy-handed nature of the state ensured that discussions remained limited to close friends and relatives.[85] In terms of our model, Nasir had created an exclusive, unified SoC.

Egypt Under Sadat: Shifting Sentiments, Stable Structures

Sadat, inheriting this SoC upon Nasir's death on September 28, 1970, faced an enormous challenge. He had been part of the Free Officers' movement in 1952, but he lacked Nasir's charisma as well as an independent support base. Indeed, Nasir had appointed him as Vice President largely because he was relatively weak and did not appear to have strongly held, independent preferences. Even after Nasir's death, Sadat signaled his willingness to tread in the tracks of Nasir, assuring Egyptians as late as October 1970 that he would continue Nasir's program.[86] His major rivals, 'Ali Sabri and Shara'wi Goma'a,[87] accepted his ascension to power because they thought they could manipulate him. Sadat received the unanimous endorsement of parliament and won the referendum for President with 90.4 percent of the popular vote, not because he was strong but rather because he was weak.[88]

However, after coming to power, Sadat immediately sought to create his own power base, countering his rivals. He did so through major foreign and domestic policy changes. Indeed, Sadat's policies diverged so much from Nasir's that a joke came to circulate in Egypt:

When the chauffeur of the presidential car reached an important intersection, he asked Anwar es-Sadat for direction.
"But which way did Nasser usually go?" asked Sadat.
"At such times he usually went left, Your Excellency."

"Ah," replied Sadat. "Well, signal that we're going left and then turn sharply to the right."[89]

Sadat's experiment with liberalization began almost immediately after taking power. In his first speech before the National Assembly, he announced the need for "political building."[90] The following spring, he moved against his opponents in a breathtaking flurry of personnel changes and institutional reforms:

Sadat moved with more speed, dexterity and firmness than many had thought him capable of. By the end of May he was firmly seated alone in power. He had re-organized the cabinet (14–16 May); appointed key governors (14–16 May); had parliamentary immunity lifted and eighteen members expelled from the National Assembly (14 May); had street demonstrations in his support (15 May); purged the police, intelligence and information apparatuses (16–17 May); appointed a provisional secretariat of the Arab Socialist Union (17 May); disbanded the ASU Central Committee and replaced it with the National Assembly (20 May); set up a committee to carry out elections to the ASU (20 May) and a committee to write a new constitution (27 May); and had come to terms with the Soviets (25–27 May), whose domestic fellow-travelers were taking the political heat.[91]

This "Corrective Revolution" was intended not only to weaken Sadat's opponents, but also to gain support from a constituency seeking liberal reform. Sadat relaxed state control over the trade unions, released political prisoners, reinstated judges and civil servants who had been dismissed under Nasir, and returned property confiscated for political reasons. He also promised the development of the rule of law, announcing to workers on May Day in 1971, " 'We have begun abolishing [emergency] measures, so as to enable the legislative system to become the source of a legal framework for the Revolution. . . . Everything will be covered by a law, every person and every measure will have a law of its own.' "[92] The new Prime Minister, Mahmud Fawzi, the first civilian to head the government since 1952, echoed these sentiments, assuring parliament " 'that the government would seek to promote democracy, through expanded freedom of expression and national dialogue.' "[93]

Sadat would implement other important changes as well. In contrast to Nasir, who had repressed and imprisoned Islamist groups, Sadat portrayed himself as the "Believer President," released members of the Muslim Brotherhood from prison, announcing a general amnesty in July 1975, and allowed Islamists to publish al-Da'wa after 1976.[94] He also took bold measures in economic policy, announcing the *infitah* (economic opening), which eased restrictions on the private sector, the importation of foreign

goods, and foreign investment. These policies, established first in Law
No. 43 of 1974, were extensions of measures taken since 1971 to gain the
support of the Egyptian business class.[95] In foreign policy, Sadat shifted
Egypt's orientation from East to West, eventually seeking U.S. support
and accommodation with Israel.

Sadat's policies had profound implications for the distribution of political power in Egypt. Liberalization weakened his opponents. The re-
organization of the ASU allowed Sadat to sideline his major rival, 'Ali
Sabri. Returning dismissed bureaucrats and judges also gave him an opportunity to fill positions with his supporters, pushing out those loyal to
his rivals. Even the cabinet saw a significant decline in the presence of the
military; military officers held 26.3 to 65.5 percent of the posts during
Nasir's regime but only 10 percent after 1976.[96] As Bruce Rutherford
concluded:

> by the end of 1971, this combination of tactics and attitudes had enabled Sadat
> to attain a firm grip on power. He had purged the top elite of opponents, defined
> the legal character of his regime in a new constitution, and restaffed the second
> tier of the elite with personnel who would implement his reforms. He had also
> begun to build a base of support among the middle class.[97]

Significant as this restructuring was, however, it did not represent a
fundamental change in Egypt's SoC. Sadat remained the most powerful
actor in Egypt's "presidential state." Indeed, despite his pronouncements
of "freedom" and "democracy," he had, by the time of his assassination in
1981, obtained more titles than Nasir: Elder of the Egyptian Family, President of the Republic, Prime Minister, Supreme Commander of the Armed
Forces, High Chief of the Police Forces, High Chief of the Judiciary, and
Head of the National Democratic Party that succeeded the ASU.[98] Even
more importantly, Sadat made no real attempts to include the political
opposition.

Even after 1976, when Sadat introduced further reforms seemingly
aimed at creating a more liberal system, Egypt's SoC was not divided.
As we will discuss more fully in Chapter 4, he announced the formation
of platforms within the ASU and then, in the Political Parties Law of
1977, legalized political parties. Yet, his inclusion of opposition forces was
minimal, and liberalization remained "tentative, non-uniform, superficial
and occasionally fictitious."[99] It was to be multipartyism in appearance
only, what Zahra al-Sayyid calls "*shekal dayquri*,"[100] and by 1981 it was
clear that Sadat maintained an exclusive, unified SoC.

Divided SoC: Mubarak

In contrast, the decades under Mubarak saw the solidification, or "further institutionalization,"[101] of a divided SoC. Relatively strong included opponents matched strong political forces outside the system. These groups were engaged with each other in a struggle over control of the rules of the game, as well as with the incumbents over political control.

Assuming his position after Sadat's assassination in 1981, President Mubarak faced a crisis. As Mustapha Kamel el-Sayyid writes, state authorities

> found during the 1981 "autumn of fury" that the cost of repressing all political and social forces in the country was not only too high, but counterproductive. Sadat was assassinated among "his soldiers" after having ordered the arrest of 1,500 citizens of all political persuasions. Mubarak, his successor and then the vice-president of the republic, was standing next to Sadat when the assassins' bullets put an end to his life. Such a lesson is not easily forgotten.[102]

To ease the tensions, Mubarak reintroduced the experiment in liberalization that Sadat had initiated in 1976. Elections would be held regularly after 1984, with the number of legal political parties expanding to 13 by the early 1990s.[103] (See Appendix.) The licensing of political parties was restricted, however. The party law established under Sadat remained in effect, banning any parties established on the basis of class, sect, community, geography, race, origin, religion, or creed.[104] Party licenses could be refused or revoked if parties violated more general principles as well: failing to preserve national unity, safeguard social peace, adhere to the Constitution, defend "socialist gains," or protect the "alliance of the working class."[105] Legalization also was at the discretion of the Committee for the Affairs of Political Parties (Lajnah Shu'un al-Ahzab al-Siyasiya), which, containing the Minister of the Interior and three retired judges appointed by the president, acted as "an agency for the regime."[106]

Thus, while the inclusion of opposition groups rose under Mubarak, there remained a large network of opposition groups and institutions outside the formal system. Many were Islamist groups, for while the Muslim Brotherhood was allowed to operate openly (as we will discuss more fully in Chapter 3), it nevertheless remained illegal. Increasing numbers of more militant organizations soon also emerged as "Islamists barred from contesting power within the formal party system diverted their activity to institutional outlets outside the regime's control."[107] Some secularist parties remained barred as well, however, and Egypt's political system was transformed from one of nearly uniform repression of opposition organizations to a much more diverse one of legal and illegal groups.

Indeed, Mubarak's maneuvers underscored the fact that liberalization was aimed at guaranteeing the survival of the authoritarian regime, not at democratization. Mubarak "moved the red lines a little further" in the new arrangement, but "opposition parties acknowledged their role as a permanent opposition who should not seek power."[108] The National Democratic Party (NDP), successor to the ASU, dominated the Popular Assembly throughout Mubarak's rule. In addition, Mubarak maintained military courts and tight control over security services, although the regime's reliance on them varied over time.[109] The goal was "limited" or "restricted" pluralism aimed at promoting unity, not contestation.[110] The means was a divided SoC.

REFINING DISTINCTIONS IN SoCs

Examining changes in SoCs, three points should be clear. First, the distinction between regime types and SoCs is obvious. There is a lot of room within regime types for minor but important shifts in the rules of the political game. These shifts, when they concern which political opponents may participate in the formal system and which may not, can lead to changes in SoCs. Thus, in monarchies and revolutionary authoritarian regimes, SoCs may change. Indeed, even the same leaders – King Hasan II, King Husayn – created different SoCs at different points in time.

The second observation is more problematic. To discuss the theoretical implications of different government–opposition relationships, it is useful to create ideal types of SoCs. In reality, however, the borders between these ideal types are fuzzy. In all regimes, including democracies, some groups or demands are not allowed in the formal political system. The simple existence of excluded political groups in an otherwise open political system does not necessarily signify a divided political system, at least not for the purposes of this work. Similarly, in some political systems, a small number of extremely weak political groups may exist as token opposition. The remaining legal opponents at the end of Sadat's rule and the non-Baʿth members of the National Progressive Front (NPF), which Asad created in Syria, are examples of such legal opponents. Again, however, the existence of a few weak legal opponents in an otherwise exclusive political system does not mean the SoC is divided. Rather, a divided SoC is defined as one in which there are multiple, relatively strong included and excluded opposition groups. That is, both included and excluded oppositions have a reasonable chance of successfully challenging incumbent elites on some issues. How incumbents attempt to manage this balance, and the effect it has on opposition elites, is the subject of subsequent chapters.

Finally, incumbents may create disparities between the political liberties that they grant individual groups and these groups' legal status. For instance, although the Muslim Brotherhood was illegal in Jordan throughout the 1970s and 1980s, as a society it was given latitude that other political organizations were denied. Similarly, although the Egyptian Muslim Brotherhood remained illegal, it was allowed to participate in the political system in conjunction with formally recognized parties. This semilegal status is important, but it does not negate the impact of the formal institutional structures. As we shall see shortly in Egypt's divided SoC, the combined threat of greater repression and fear of the Muslim Brotherhood led moderate opposition elites to weaken their attacks on the state as the crisis continued, despite the fact that the Brotherhood had previously enjoyed a privileged status.

3

Playing by the Rules

The Inclusion and Exclusion of Political Oppositions

An opposition group's inclusion in or exclusion from the formal political sphere, and the SoCs within which a group acts, influence the incentives that opponents face when deciding whether or not to challenge incumbent elites.[1] As part of their role in expressing and relieving popular dissatisfaction, included opponents are allowed to challenge the regime. Thus, they pay lower costs of mobilization than illegal opponents do. However, in return for this privilege, their demands are constrained. Legal opposition groups must balance the restrictions of incumbent elites with the desires of the popular constituencies, moderating their policy demands. They must also mobilize enough opposition to relieve popular pressure while not allowing it to create a significant threat to the incumbent regime. These elites pay a high price if they create unstable situations that political opponents from outside the system can exploit.

In contrast, illegal opponents face higher costs for mobilizing popular protest than their legal counterparts, but they are more capable of capitalizing on the increased discontent that accompanies prolonged economic crises. Unlike included opponents, illegal groups prefer to mobilize in conjunction with legal opposition groups rather than to mobilize independently.[2] The two sets of opposition groups have some important diverging interests. Consequently, opposition elites' decisions to exploit economic crises and press political demands depend as much on the interactions between these two sets of opposition forces as they do on the relationship between each opposition group and the government.

The purpose of this chapter is twofold: It explores the characteristics of included and excluded opponents, and it seeks to demonstrate that it is not the character of the individual opposition groups in Egypt, Jordan, and Morocco that is responsible for the divergent government–opposition relations, but rather the SoCs. The chapter begins by examining the nature of the primary opposition forces existing in Egypt, Morocco, and Jordan. This overview is helpful in examining how the distinction between inclusion and exclusion is related to, and yet separate from, the ideological distinction between moderates and radicals. The chapter then examines the characteristics of illegal and legal opposition, first in their relationships with the state and then in their relationships with the masses. It focuses particularly on how the very different SoCs in Morocco, Jordan, and Egypt affect the opposition. Finally, the chapter sets forth a simple model that takes into account the importance of SoCs.

PRIMARY CONTENDERS IN MOROCCO, JORDAN, AND EGYPT

As discussed in Chapter 2, Jordan, Morocco, and Egypt under Nasir, Sadat, and Mubarak created very different SoCs. Morocco and Egypt under Mubarak had divided SoCs: Moderate secularist parties were allowed to participate legally in the formal political system, while Islamic parties and more radical secularist forces remained outside. In contrast, Jordan after 1957 and Egypt under Nasir and the early years of Sadat banned all opposition parties. Despite these differences, however, the three governments faced very similar political forces contending in the political arena: loyalist supporters, Islamist opposition, and secularist opponents. (The details of the main parties are presented in the Appendix.)

Loyalist Supporters

The governments of Morocco, Jordan, and Egypt under Nasir, Sadat, and Mubarak drew support from loyalists and their clients. The composition and diversity of the loyalists varied, however. This is significant because all governments are in fact coalitions of elites struggling over policies and resources, and the extent to which they experience internal dissension is influenced by the nature of the coalition. As we shall see, however, although the coalitions varied across these cases, there is no reason to believe that this explains the differences we see in the dynamics of opposition.

In Egypt, the governing coalition under Nasir was quite different from that under Sadat and Mubarak. Nasir drew support from the original Free Officers, their relatives, and close associates (e.g., 'Ali Sabri, Mustafa Kamel Murad, Khalid Muhyi al-Din). As discussed in Chapter 2, the composition of the loyalists changed under Sadat as the President sought to sideline his opponents. The open-door economic (*infitah*) policy gained the support of upper-class business elites, and the government gradually included more members of the bourgeoisie and technocrats but fewer military officers.[3] This same composition characterized the Mubarak government. Yet, while Sadat and Mubarak governed with the support of similar coalitions, they had very different government–opposition dynamics.

Morocco and Jordan also had somewhat similar governing coalitions, although they too experienced different opposition dynamics. Neither saw a major social and political revolution. Thus, they continued to draw upon the support of large landowners and the business elite. In Morocco, the King drew support from old rural and urban notables, traditionally from Fez. The coalition gradually expanded to include figures from Rabat and Marrakech, as well as elites who used their ties with the government to establish major business ventures. (Most notable in this regard was Ahmad 'Usman, the King's brother-in-law and the owner of the country's largest holding company.) In Jordan, loyalists were generally associated with the tribal elites from the south of the East Bank, but the King gradually drew support from prominent Jordanians of Palestinian origin as well.[4] The unity and unwavering loyalty of the tribes should not be overstated, however. The kings distributed spoils and rotated government positions with an eye toward balancing tribal and regional divisions.[5] There is no reason, however, to believe that the task was any harder for King Hasan II than it was for King Husayn.

In all cases, loyalists depend on their direct relations with the government to achieve their aims. They advocate conservative policies, and they have very little use for political parties or true democracy.[6] This was true even in Egypt. The government under Nasir created a succession of secular organizations (e.g., the LR, the NU, and then the ASU), and Sadat established the National Democratic Party (NDP) after political parties were legalized in 1976. These parties were intended to counter the potential popularity of the opposition parties and legitimize the political game, however. They were to be vessels for powerful actors, not mechanisms for elite recruitment or enforcement.[7] In Jordan and Morocco, the palace remained out of party politics, but loyalists formed parties such as the National Rally of Independents RNI or the Constitutional Union (UC) in Morocco, or al-Ahd in Jordan, for much the same reason.

Islamist Forces

There is also no reason to believe that the different strength of Islamists explains the divergent experiences in Egypt, Jordan, and Morocco with the opposition during prolonged economic crises. Islamist forces all seek a close link between Islam and politics, but they differ in the extent of the changes they seek, in their use of violence against the regime, and in their willingness to make concessions.[8] More moderate groups such as the Muslim Brotherhood in Jordan and Egypt or later al-Jama'ah al-Islah wa al-Tajdid (al-Islamiyah) in Morocco argued that they did not seek to overturn the regime through violence, but they demanded greater adherence to Islamic law. More extreme groups, such as the Liberation Party in Jordan, Justice and Charity and Islamic Youth in Morocco, and al-Jihad and al-Takfir wa al-Hijrah in Egypt, rejected such accommodation. Such groups reject the legitimacy of the regime, and many (but not all) of them are willing to use violence to achieve these means.[9] Thus, there are important differences among Islamist groups.

There are also differences in the strength of political Islam in Egypt, Morocco, and Jordan. Islamists in Egypt have been stronger and their relationship with the government more conflictual than those in Morocco or Jordan. The Egyptian Muslim Brotherhood was founded by Hasan al-Banna in 1928, and it has remained Egypt's strongest Islamist group. As discussed in Chapter 2, the Muslim Brotherhood had initially supported the Free Officer Revolution, but the relationship between the regime and the Brotherhood shattered by 1954. Sadat proclaimed himself the "Believer President" and sought a closer relationship with Islamist groups, but this relationship, too, was broken. As we shall see in Chapter 5, Islamists were considered the most important opposition forces in Egypt by the time they assassinated Sadat in 1981. In addition to the Muslim Brotherhood, which remained the strongest and most moderate force, Egypt had an estimated 45 militant Islamist groups in 1992.[10]

Islamists appeared to be a less significant threat in Jordan and Morocco. In Jordan, Islamists were the single most important opposition force by the late 1980s, but they were considered more moderate than those in Egypt and Morocco. The government banned Islamist political parties, as well as secularist parties, in the 1950s, but it permitted the Muslim Brotherhood to operate as a charitable society. This additional political space allowed the Jordanian Muslim Brotherhood to gain strength at the expense of other opposition parties, but it did not appear to be as great a threat as its Egyptian counterpart. In Morocco, the King was widely believed to have covertly fostered the growth of Islamist parties, but he kept them at arm's length. He allowed secularist parties a role in the system, but he banned formal Islamist parties. There, too, Islamists remained a power on the fringes of the system, but not one as significant as the Islamist forces in Egypt.

The strength of Islamists does not explain why the dynamics of opposition in Morocco were similar to those in Egypt under Mubarak when the Islamists' capabilities were very different in these cases. It also does not explain why the dynamics differed in Egypt under Sadat and Mubarak when, as we shall see in Chapter 4, the Islamists were just as strong and threatening by the late 1970s as they were in the 1990s. Finally, one could expect that, given the relatively less conflictual experience with Islamists in Morocco and Jordan, the dynamics of opposition should be similar in these cases. Yet, they were not. The strength and historical experiences with Islamist political forces do not explain when the conflicts between moderate opponents and governments escalate and when they do not.

Secularist Forces

The strength of secularist forces also does not explain the divergent dynamics. Secularist forces in Egypt, Morocco, and Jordan had different historical bases. Morocco's secularist parties had the most legitimacy. The Istiqlal Party was a driving force in the independence movement, as discussed in Chapter 2, and although it was splintered, it was not significantly delegitimized.[11] In contrast, Egypt's Wafd Party had formed in 1919 as a major force against British intervention, but by 1952 it had become associated with conservative bourgeoisie interests, corruption, and weakness. Jordan's Nationalist Movement too had grown in response to British intervention, but it lost the showdown against King Husayn in the 1950s.[12] While the secularist leftist parties in Jordan were perhaps less discredited than the Wafd, they were certainly no stronger. Moreover, as in Egypt, they would be forced underground for nearly two decades. The legitimacy and historical strength of secularist parties in Jordan and Egypt remained more limited than in Morocco. Yet, opposition elites in Morocco chose not to mobilize the masses at the height of the economic crisis, contrary to what one may expect.

Venues of Activism

Finally, the venues through which these forces act do not appear to explain the different government–opposition relations. Opposition forces can use a variety of organizational structures to affect policy and demand access to power: political parties, trade unions, professional associations, student unions, and other civil society organizations. The loci of opposition have varied across the cases we examine. In Morocco, the opposition parties were tied to the labor movement, with the Istiqlal Party, closely linked to the UGTM, and the USFP closely linked to the CDT and to the student movement. These syndicates, as well other groups in civil society, were used to mobilize not only for better working conditions, but also for greater transparency, improved human rights conditions, and democracy.[13] These links also provided the opportunity for opposition elites tied to the parties to use general strikes to demand political changes.[14] In contrast, in Jordan the links between the labor unions and the secular opposition parties were weak by the mid-1970s, so the underground parties were most active through the professional associations, and particularly in the lawyers' and engineers' syndicates.[15] Parties were also particularly active in Egyptian professional syndicates. In addition, the National Progressive Unionist Party (NPUP), formed after 1978, had strong ties with the labor movement, and opposition parties used student movements and other nongovernmental organizations to mobilize opposition.

Opposition elites used these venues to put pressure on governments through demonstrations started by students, union workers, or other syndicate members – and even sometimes by those who were apparently anomic. It is important to keep in mind Tilly's observation that even the most apparently spontaneous demonstrations require a degree of organization and at least some access to resources.[16] Opposition elites used a variety of mechanisms to provide both.

Opponents in Egypt, Morocco, and Jordan have used different venues of opposition, but this does not appear to explain the dynamics of opposition. Indeed, as Table 3.1 shows, the characteristics of the government and opposition in Egypt, Jordan, and Morocco do not appear to be systematically related to the patterns of opposition during prolonged economic crises. The explanation for these dynamics is found in SoCs.

MODERATES AND RADICALS, INSIDERS AND OUTSIDERS

Before considering how inclusion in or exclusion from the system affects the characteristics of these parties, we need to differentiate between the ideological and legal bases of opposition groups. Ideological distinctions – between moderates and radicals – are defined by the amount of reform opponents seek: Those who prefer policies far from the status quo are more radical, while those who seek less reform are more moderate. This is distinct from the *type* of reform opponents seek (i.e., whether toward more secularist or Islamist social reform policies, toward more free market

TABLE 3.1. *Domestic Conditions in Egypt, Jordan, and Morocco*

	Egypt Under Nasir	Egypt Under Sadat	Egypt Under Mubarak	Morocco	Jordan
Socioeconomic Basis of Regime	Military officers	Business elites and military	Business elites and military	Urban notables (esp., from Fez, but also from Rabat and Marrakesh), large landowners, business elite	Transjordanian tribal elites, Palestinian–Jordanian economic elites
Historical Experience with Secular Political Organizations	Wafd Party of prerevolutionary period largely discredited	Wafd Party of prerevolutionary period largely discredited	Wafd Party of prerevolutionary period largely discredited	Istiqlal Party of independence movement not discredited	Leftist and Arab nationalists parties relatively weak
Historical Experience with Islamist Political Organizations	Strong: formation of Muslim Brotherhood under Hasan al-Banna in 1928	Strong: formation of Muslim Brotherhood under Hasan al-Banna in 1928	Strong: formation of Muslim Brotherhood under Hasan al-Banna in 1928	Weak	Moderate: Jordanian Musim Brotherhood established in 1946
Primary Loci of Opposition Activists in Civil Society	Professional associations	Professional associations, unions, student movements	Professional associations, unions, student movements	Trade unions, student movements	Professional associations

74

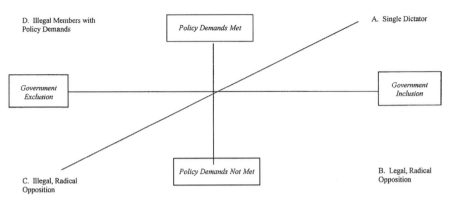

FIGURE 3.1. Distribution of Policy Goods and Political Access.

or socialist economic policies). There are moderate and radical Islamists as well as moderate and radical secularists.[17] Inclusion and exclusion simply designate whether or not groups are permitted to enter the formal political sphere.

To understand the relationship between ideological moderation and inclusion, we return to the question of how incumbent elites shape the political environment. Incumbent elites can distribute two types of goods. They can make concrete changes in economic or political policies that respond to the opponents' demands.[18] Because the extent to which a group is radical is simply the amount of change it demands in the present system, the more the government responds to the demands, the more moderate the opposition becomes. Incumbent elites can also grant access to the political process. They choose whether or not to grant elites the right to make their demands legally. As discussed in the previous chapter, through the decision to grant or withhold access to the political system, incumbents create exclusive, inclusive, or divided SoCs.[19]

These distinctions can be thought of as a continuum, pictured in Figure 3.1. To the right of the vertical axis are groups that have a legal right to participate in the political system. Moving to the right, actors have fewer restrictions placed upon their participation. In contrast, to the left of the vertical axis are groups that have no legal access to the political system. Moving to the extreme left are groups that incur greater and greater costs for their attempts to participate. Similarly, above the horizontal axis are groups that have at least some of their political demands met. Below the horizontal axis are groups whose demands are not met in the status quo. The closer a group's position is to the top of the graph, the more its demands are met. The farther the group's position lies below the horizontal axis, the more radical its demands.

Although actors are not located at the extreme positions, these ideal types are important reference points. At the extreme upper right (point A) are actors whose policy preferences are fully met in the status quo and who have unrestricted access to the political system. At the extreme lower left (point C) are the groups whose demands depart radically from the status quo and who have no legal access to the political system. At the extreme lower right (point B) lie the radical, legal opposition groups. These groups are given access to the political system, but their demands are not met in the status quo. Finally, at the extreme upper left (point D) are groups whose demands are fully met but who are excluded from the political system. These would be subjects of a benevolent dictator.

In reality, these extreme types rarely, if ever, exist. Empirically, we find more examples of types A and C than of types B and D, however. Authoritarian leaders illustrate positions close to the extreme upper right. King Hasan II, King Husayn, and Presidents Nasir, Sadat, and Mubarak, as well as members of their inner circle, were clearly included in the ruling coalition and given wide political powers. Even these leaders, however, experienced some restrictions upon their rule and often made some political concessions. As we saw in the previous chapter, neither King Husayn nor King Hasan II could afford to isolate themselves too much from the political spectrum, particularly not from its most important and powerful actors.

Illegal, repressed political opponents resemble points near ideal type C. Such opponents have no legitimate role in the political system and few, if any, of their policy demands are met. In Egypt and Morocco, these groups have included the Islamist parties as well as the extreme leftist parties, Ila al-Amam and the Movement of March 23 of Morocco, and the militant Islamist groups and Communists in Egypt. In Jordan, the Islamist Liberation Party has consistently remained outside the formal political system, since its demand for an Islamic state is incompatible with the monarchy. During the period of martial law from 1957 to 1989, the secularist opposition parties were also excluded from the formal system. Palestinian opposition groups, such as the Democratic Front Organization in Jordan (MAJD) and the Popular Front for the Liberation of Palestine (PFLP), were firmly repressed. Of the myriad parties participating in the formal political sphere prior to 1960, only the Muslim Brotherhood was allowed to operate openly, taking advantage of its role as a charitable association, its loyalty to the king, and its usefulness as a counterbalance against the more threatening secularist, pro-Nasirist opposition.

That examples of these extreme types are more apparent than others is no accident. Empirically, there is a strong link between the extent to which a group's demands differ from the status quo and the likelihood that this group is permitted legal participation in the political system. Where a divided political system exists – that is, incumbents allow some groups to participate in the legal political system while excluding others – the included opposition groups are more moderate than those that have been excluded. The reason for this lies in the nature of political coalitions.

Theorists recognize that adding members to a ruling coalition requires an increasing division of decision-making power and potential spoils. Consequently, elites prefer to rule with minimal winning coalitions or minimal connected winning coalitions.[20] That is, they prefer either the smallest number of members who can achieve and maintain power or the smallest number of members with similar policy demands. Only when elites come under fire do they expand the political regime, allowing opponents a legitimate voice in the system in the hope of reducing future political threats.

The inclusion of new members in the coalition is costly, however. Expanding participation in the system requires the additional division of selective incentives to political elites. It is not surprising that newly elected members of parliament in many developing countries drive new luxury cars or that government ministers live in upper-class houses. Incumbent elites must distribute these spoils to newly admitted elites regardless of the elites' policy preferences. In addition, incumbent elites need to grant policy concessions. The admittance of other elites is useful only if they can bring with them the popular support of their constituents. To maintain this support, the newly admitted elites need policy changes, real or promised, to take back to the streets. How much change is necessary is uncertain; thus expanding the ruling coalition is risky.

Consequently, political incumbents resist granting wider participation, and when they do so, they try to manage political expansion by admitting the more moderate groups first. Initial political reforms often are restricted to party or administrative reforms, which primarily benefit the incumbents' supporters. Even when constitutional reforms are finally undertaken, governments control the entry of new members into the political system. Incumbents prefer meeting moderate political demands to radical ones. Thus, ceteris peribus, opponents whose policy preferences are close to the status quo are less costly for the ruling coalition to absorb.

Consequently, governments often prefer to admit moderate groups into the system, excluding radicals.

Morocco's divided political system illustrates this well. On the one hand, Susan Waltz is correct when she notes that it is not strictly a question of ideology that determines whether or not a group is permitted into the formal political system. She writes:

> it is tempting to associate political marginality with ideological position. In fact, the experiences of both the left and the Islamists suggest that a finer analysis is required. Their histories reveal differential treatment of groups having a similar ideological position, suggesting that being part of the opposition is not only a function of ideological position but also a function of their group's relation to the monarchy, the size of the party or the group, and its position toward major national issues, such as the question of the Sahara.[21]

Yet, while a group's position on the ideological spectrum is not the determining factor in whether or not opposition is admitted to the political system, the party's positions on critical policies (i.e., the legitimacy of the monarchy, Morocco's right to the Sahara, the King's religious legitimacy) is. No party is allowed to participate openly if it is perceived to contradict the monarch on these issues. Thus, in Morocco, King Hasan II continued to outlaw Islamist political parties after he liberalized the political system in the mid-1970s. Furthermore, in regard to secularist parties, the palace was more likely to admit weak groups with ideologically radical demands, assuming they were willing to abide by the rules, than more popular radical groups. Thus, for instance, the palace legalized the PPS, a reconstituted version of the formerly outlawed Communist Party, but it continued to exclude the more radical and popular Movement of March 23.[22]

Authoritarian elites are also more likely to admit moderates and more pragmatic radicals because they are more likely to accept the conditions of participation. Formal inclusion and exclusion may not always appear to be the incumbent's choice, but fundamentally it is. In some cases, excluded opponents clearly want to be incorporated into the formal political system, and incumbent elites clearly are calling the shots. Such was the case of the Muslim Brotherhood in Egypt, which we will discuss in more detail shortly. Since the 1980s, the Brotherhood repeatedly stated that it would welcome admission as a political party.[23] At the same time, however, it refused admission as a social organization, which the regime offered. In other cases, parties appear to shun the system entirely, as the Liberation Party did in Jordan. Yet, in reality, the radical stance of the party simply meant that it demanded the downfall of the monarchy as the price of its inclusion. This was obviously too high a price for the palace, but it remained the palace's choice not to concede. That such demands are more likely to come from radical groups, however, is yet another reason that incumbents usually seek first to incorporate more moderate opponents.

Finally, we shall see shortly that opponents often moderate their policy demands (although not their true preferences) in return for inclusion in the system. When governments build walls that exclude an entire spectrum of opposition – as Morocco and Egypt have done in excluding the Islamist opposition – the excluded opposition is likely to contain radical elements. Opponents with radical preferences gain little from the government if they make more moderate demands. Thus, they continue to mobilize on their true policy preferences or on positions that they expect will gain popular support. In either case, these are likely to be more radical demands than they would propose publicly if they were included.

INCLUDED VERSUS EXCLUDED POLITICAL OPPONENTS

Even among groups preferring similar policy positions, however, the distinction between included and excluded opponents is significant. Included opponents have more cooperative relationships with the incumbent elites than do excluded opponents. This stems from the fact that they are invested in the maintenance of the regime, and thus they are restrained in the extent to which they press their demands. In contrast, excluded opponents try to threaten the government, either to demonstrate to incumbents that they need to accommodate them or to overthrow the existing order. At the same time, however, included opponents often have weaker relations with the masses than the excluded elites. They have the organizational capacity and freedom to mobilize openly, but the masses often view these elites as co-opted by the incumbents. When legal opposition groups are unsuccessful in obtaining their demands, as often happens during prolonged economic crises, they lose support to excluded opponents. The masses often view elites outside the system as more legitimate, but fear demonstrating their support for these groups, making it difficult for illegal opposition groups to mobilize this support.

Party–Incumbent Relations

Legal Opposition. Legal opposition elites are entitled to make demands within the formal political system, but they agree to boundaries within which they may do so.[24] Above all, the incumbents enlist opposition elites in the job of maintaining political order. For example, the first principle in the Jordanian National Charter was that the government is a "parliamentary monarchy," and the Charter went on to bind participants in the process of "maintaining social peace."[25] Similarly, the national pact in Tunisia stressed national unity and the legitimacy of the existing regime,[26] and the formation of the National Progressive Front (NPF) in Syria included only those who were willing to "toe the Ba'th Party line which, according to the NPF covenant, was binding for the entire front, and to accept Ba'th Party dominance within the system."[27] In Egypt, the presidency retained its "intrinsic integrity and independence"[28] even after the strengthening of the multiparty system. Similarly, in Morocco, opposition elites clearly understood that by participating in the legislative elections of 1977, they had reentered the pact with King Hasan II. They were bound to be his loyal opposition, what the King termed his "300 advisors" in parliament.[29] The parties were not to threaten the monarch's position.

Consequently, the opposition's ability to challenge the incumbent regime is strictly limited. For example, these elites may criticize corruption, but they often must refrain from naming specific persons or instances; they may argue the need for better social services, but they have no real budgetary control; and they may demand changes in the relative weight of parliamentary institutions and the head of state, but they may not challenge the leader directly. In both Morocco and Jordan, legal opponents were clearly prohibited from challenging the monarch's legitimacy.[30] They were also unable to criticize strongly the leaders' foreign policies, particularly King Hasan II's policies vis-à-vis the Western Sahara or King Husayn's policies toward Israel and the Palestinian Occupied Territories.

No one is under the illusion that the playing field is level. Indeed, in interviews with the author, members of the opposition in Morocco and Jordan invariably demonstrated the extent to which they were well aware that their participation in the system remained strictly at the discretion of their respective kings. This was particularly striking in Jordan, where both activists and observers pointed out the additional constraints that legalization had imposed upon the parties. Prohibitions on receiving foreign funding, subjection to government audits, limitations on the number of founding members required for parties, and restrictions on meeting places controlled parties in some ways more than when parties were banned.[31] Although Moroccan political activists had experienced these constraints for more than 20 years, they were also aware of their limitations and their role in supporting the state. A discussion at a youth meeting of a leftist party was telling in this regard. The discussion had turned to the problems of gaining legitimacy and support among the public (a problem we will discuss shortly), and many were arguing that the goals and platforms of the party were too intellectualized for the average Moroccan. The member noted, in reference to the limitations of the party: "Our problem is not that we are a community only for the intellectuals, but that we are a community for the intelligence (referring to the *mukhabarat*)."[32]

Furthermore, while party activists are legally allowed to mobilize, they are still subject to repression. Repression extends beyond the imprisonment of notable figures, such as former USFP Secretary General H' Hamad Boucetta and CDT leader Nubir Amaoui in Morocco or the Islamist opposition leader Layth Shubaylat in Jordan, to activists, journalists, and other apparent sympathizers in both countries. As Denoeux remarked with regard to Egypt:

even under the relatively liberal climate of the Mubarak regime, election fraud, intimidation, and harassment of opposition parties and their members remain common practice. When all is said and done, opposition parties operate only by the goodwill and sufferance of the Mubarak government, and they remain very vulnerable to an always-possible state crackdown.[33]

Elections are also accompanied by alleged electoral fraud and intimidation, and incumbents unilaterally change the rules of the game to suit their purposes. In Egypt, the continued state of emergency allowed the regime, at will, to prohibit opposition parties from organizing meetings. In addition, electoral engineering favoring the ruling party, combined with ballot stuffing, helped the NDP dominate the People's Assembly throughout Mubarak's rule.[34] In Morocco, King Hasan II instituted a rule requiring that all candidates be members of political parties, implicating the parties in the role of governance at the height of the economic crisis. In contrast, in 1993 King Husayn sought to limit the role of political parties, establishing a new one-person, one-vote law that favored tribal elites. Through a combination of formal and informal mechanisms, the kings attempted to keep the legal opposition strong enough to be useful, satisfied enough to be loyal, and weak enough not to challenge the system. As one Moroccan put it, it was the politics of bread: Everyone is allowed a slice, but no one is allowed to take the whole loaf.[35]

Nevertheless, legal opponents do challenge established boundaries (indeed, this is to the benefit of both the palace and the opposition),[36] but when they push too hard, they are punished.[37] In some cases, the punishments are relatively minor. For example, when the international community forced King Hasan II to accept a referendum on the Western Sahara in

September 1981, the Secretary General of the USFP denounced the King's abandonment of the territory. The announcement crossed a boundary, namely, that the opposition should not challenge the King's foreign policy. The Secretary General was subsequently arrested and given one year in prison. Yet, the message sent, the King pardoned him in February 1982.[38] Similar responses have been seen in Jordan. Most notably, the Islamist MP Layth Shubaylat challenged the boundary of acceptable politics; his public challenges to the King and the government led to his incarceration in 1992 and 1995.

Legalized opposition parties also have some impact on policy, although it is limited. In Egypt, party newspapers and some parliamentary debates were particularly important in raising political awareness on critical issues.[39] This was also the case in Morocco, and many USFP demands were met, at least partially. For instance, in 1980 the King responded to USFP calls for a rent freeze by decreasing the rents for low-income Moroccans by one-third. In Jordan, as Rex Brynen has noted, King Husayn responded to mounting opposition complaints by overturning the government and appointing a new prime minister, although he also "studiously avoided any indication that he [was] bound by parliamentary election results in choosing either prime minister or cabinet."[40] Kings often failed to acknowledge the opposition's impact on policies, but many opposition elites pointed to such examples and argued that they did indeed achieve limited policy demands by working within the system.

They also earn selective incentives by acquiescing to the rules. For instance, opposition members in parliament find that the opportunity to make speeches and ask questions of government ministers brings them media attention and raises their status.[41] As Hinnebusch notes with regard to Egypt:

> For opposition activists, the rewards are either personal advancement – the chance of co-optation – or ideological – the chance to espouse ideas, reshape public opinion, and occasionally even influence policy. Even if the regime is the big winner, participation is thus meaningful for them, affects outcomes, and in the long run may lead to the institutionalization of greater power sharing.[42]

Opposition elites do not want to lose these privileges.

Because they rely upon incumbents for the opportunity to participate in the system, these elites have different relationships with state elites than do illegal opposition forces. They often develop close relationships with them. They work within the formal structures of government, making their demands in parliamentary sessions, party meetings, and proclamations in daily newspapers. In addition, these elites have often gained close access to the centers of power, attending private sessions with upper elites and sometimes even maintaining close personal friendships with them. Even where personal ties are not strong, however, they have accepted a role in maintaining internal stability, and this role draws them into a closer relationship to the central power than that of illegal opposition elites.

The result is that legal opposition elites want to challenge the government, but they are unlikely to challenge too strongly. 'Abdallah al-Akaylah, a major spokesman of the Islamic Action Front (IAF), explained the logic of the relationship at the international conference in London in 1992 so clearly that it is worth quoting at length. In the statement, he explained:

1. The Islamic Movement of Jordan understands the position of the Jordanian State and knows that its resources are very limited. The State's economy largely depends on foreign aid, and therefore there is a limit to what any Jordanian regime can do....
2. The Movement realizes that Jordan lacks the essential requirements for the establishment of an Islamic state, and the regime is assured that the Islamic Movement does not seek to topple it or replace it with an Islamic regime.
3. The Movement, thanks to its social power and the services it renders to the public throughout Jordanian society, constitutes an element of security for the regime against any coup attempt....
7. The regime and the Islamic Movement show a certain degree of flexibility in dealing with each other during crises whether the tension was initiated by the regime or by the Movement itself....
9. The demands of the Islamic Movement at most are reformatory in nature and encompass all aspects of life. However, they do not in any way threaten the regime or propose an alternative to it....[43]

In short, legal opposition elites see themselves as an integral part of the regime. They become committed to maintaining it, and they focus on gaining the most they can while playing within the rules. Noha El-Mikawy noted this attitude in the Egyptian parliament after Mubarak incorporated the opposition. In contrast to the earlier period, "there was a difference reflected in the battle of maneuvers between opposition parties and the [ruling] NDP inside Parliament. The opposition was not caught in a battle of principle. The opposition thought in terms of what was politically expedient."[44]

This commitment can be broken, but included elites believe that the costs of doing so are extremely high. They fear not only repression, but also exclusion from the very system they have fought so hard to enter and from which they benefit. While they seek the implementation of their policies and greater political power, they fear losing the privileges of participating.

As Krane summarized:

Operating within the ever-shifting zone of "semifreedom," these individuals and groups strive for basic institutional and/or policy changes while attempting to avoid the extremes of co-opted loyalty to or violent rejection of the mixed regime. [Their decision to do so] may flow from one or more motives: (1) ideological or philosophical agreement with the regime, (2) receipt of tangible rewards conditioned on loyalty, (3) rational calculus over the benefits and costs of any political action vis-à-vis other personal priorities . . . and (4) inability or willingness to exit or voice.[45]

In short, these opponents challenge the regime, but they do so within limits.

EXCLUDED OPPOSITION GROUPS. In contrast to the legal opposition, illegal opposition groups have less extensive ties to the government. Incumbent elites may have some contact with excluded opposition elites and allow them to make some demands, acting as a safety valve. Major opposition figures such as the Communist Party leader 'Isa Madanat in Jordan or Islamist Ahmad Yasin in Morocco met with the palace elite, even from their jail cells or while under house arrest.[46] Similarly, the palace summoned the former Ba'thist, Jamal Sha'ir, to a meeting after he published an editorial in 1975 calling for an advisory body to substitute for the closed parliament and encouraged him to form a political group.[47] Many opposition leaders associated with the banned leftist parties were subsequently included in the National Consultative Council (NCC). Even more clearly, Mubarak allowed the Muslim Brotherhood to participate in elections, although it refused to legalize it as a political party.[48] However, these roles are not guaranteed, and as long as parties are not formally entered into the system, individual elites who enter independently (e.g., joining the NCC, meeting with the palace) are often perceived as having been co-opted.

Exclusion alters the incentives of opposition elites. Included opposition groups have pledged to help maintain the system, and thus their value to the incumbents is based, in part, on demonstrating their ability to help maintain the status quo.[49] Excluded opponents have made no such pledges. As Carrie Wickham has noted, even the Muslim Brotherhood in Egypt, which ran in parliamentary elections, served on boards of professional associations, and operated openly, did so without agreeing to "safeguard the interests of those existing [in] power."[50]

This has important implications. Excluded opponents benefit from challenging the regime. They want to prove their ability to disrupt the status quo, challenging the system enough that incumbent elites are forced to meet their demands. Indeed, it is precisely because those individuals from excluded groups that choose to work with the regime are seen as helping to stabilize an unacceptable status quo that they are ostracized from their parties. The relations of excluded opposition elites with incumbents are strikingly different from those of included elites.

Mass–Party Linkages

Legal Opponents. Although legal opposition elites have closer ties to the regime than excluded elites do, they do not necessarily have stronger ties to the masses. Legal opposition elites attempt to mobilize popular support through political parties, trade unions, or professional associations for two reasons. First, to help maintain political stability, it is important for them to allow and promote the popular frustration within defined limits, thereby helping provide stability. At the same time, their ability to mobilize the populace is critical if they are to gain political concessions from incumbent elites. Gellner noted this dynamic in patron–client relationships:

[P]atrons may incite their followings into rioting simply to demonstrate their power to their rivals or to the central authorities. After all, politicians seek clients largely because a dedicated following provides them with a certain leverage towards competitors and the government. Therefore, a patron should be expected to rouse his clients, from time to time, into destabilizing political activities, either to show his opponents what good weapons he controls or to protect himself against attempts to undercut him on his turf.[51]

Although these opposition leaders promote political unrest in order to maintain their legitimacy among the people and to provide an important pressure valve for the regime, their relationship with the status quo is well recognized. Because the Jordanian and Moroccan opposition party elites failed to overturn the regime in the 1950s and 1960s, many perceived them as being at the mercy of the kings. Incumbent elites allowed their participation only as long as they helped to maintain the regime. Thus, a wide segment of the masses lost faith in the parties.[52] Polls found that, even after liberalization, Jordanians did not believe their political parties could significantly impact policies.[53] Similarly, a 1980 survey of Moroccan students found that although Moroccans were generally well informed about politics, they refused to participate because they felt that the "quasi-democracy" was "neither representative nor responsive to their needs."[54] Indeed, in a country of approximately 24 million persons, the four largest parties (the Istiqlal, USFP, MP and RNI) were estimated to have fewer than 550,000 members combined.[55] Similarly, Khalil al-Shubaki argues that in Jordan there were 23 parties with about 13,000 members. This corresponded to approximately 3 members for every 1,000 Jordanians spread across an astonishing number of weak parties.[56] Finally, daily conversations in both countries suggested that the masses often saw legal opposition parties, at best, as limited forces for change and, at worst, as sycophantic stooges co-opted into supporting a corrupt regime.

Despite its very different history, similar skepticism was pervasive in Egypt. A public opinion poll conducted by *al-Ahram* in 1994 found that while 73 percent of Egyptians believed that a multiparty system was beneficial in general, only 36 percent of respondents felt that the current multiparty system was useful.[57] Similarly, only 36 percent of respondents felt that any of the parties represented them, with 40 percent stating that no parties reflected their positions and 22 percent having no opinion. Perhaps even more significantly for opposition parties, the majority of these respondents (21.3 percent) believed the ruling NDP represented them, in contrast to 7.7 percent who supported the Wafd, 5.9 percent who supported Islamist groups, and 2.5 percent who supported the NPUP and the SLP.[58] A study by the al-Ahram Center for Strategic and Political Studies had similar findings. Thirty-three percent of respondents could not recognize any political parties, and 9 of Egypt's 15 parties were recognized by less than 7.5 percent of the public. Only 4.7 percent of those surveyed were members of political parties.[59] It was not surprising that some have estimated the turnout in Egypt's parliamentary elections to be only 20 to 30 percent in the urban areas and even lower in the countryside.[60]

The chasm between the masses and opposition elites widens when party elites benefit from their relations with the state. Participation in government is particularly problematic, as both the Istiqlal and the USFP learned in Morocco. By accepting ministerial portfolios, parties jeopardize their role as the opposition, and they are implicated in the government's policies.[61] In other cases, the continued willingness to play a role that is intended, at least in part, to shore up the regime receives criticism. In Egypt, even the left-wing NPUP, which claimed to speak for the workers and peasants, was "marred by too many prominent intellectuals and armchair leftists" to represent the masses.[62] The very act of cooperation with the regime tarnished the opposition's legitimacy and provided these leaders with incentives and opportunities that differed dramatically from those of their constituents. The problem is exacerbated when party activists sometimes adopt an elitist attitude, nearly dismissive of the very constituencies they claim to represent.

Legal opposition groups also face institutional barriers to developing ties with the masses. Parties have limited access to state-controlled media and meager financial resources. In Egypt, legal political parties were given material resources as well as the right to publish newspapers, which was denied to illegal entities.[63] However, they were dwarfed by the regime, which maintained control over the media, the distribution of jobs, and other material resources.[64] In Morocco, the regime subsidized party newspapers, allowing each party a limited voice. However, access to television and radio was strictly controlled. In a country with nearly a 50 percent illiteracy rate,[65] this severely handicapped the Moroccan parties' ability to reach the public. In Jordan, parties received no such formal government support. Furthermore, foreign support was strictly prohibited. This restriction, put in place and enforced only after the parties' legalization, actually weakened the opposition. Most of the parties that emerged after liberalization were mere skeletons, with an organizational structure but little mass support.[66] Parties with a longer history of activism found their budgets restricted after legalization and the end of the cold war.[67]

The result is that the ties between the masses and the political parties are extremely weak. Party elites, recognizing that they are dependent on the regime rather than the people, do little to adjust their platforms to make them relevant to the people's concerns.[68] Nor do they focus as much on providing important social services to address their constituents' concerns. Such activities are more likely to be found outside the formal political parties.[69] The Egyptian system was thus described as a "system of party formation from the top [which] has resulted in a party framework that is more indicative of authoritarian bureaucracy than the diverse political desires of the Egyptian people."[70] The same could easily have been said of Morocco, Jordan, and much of the Third World.

EXCLUDED OPPOSITION. Illegal opposition groups differ from the legal opposition in several ways. While more moderate excluded groups are sometimes permitted to operate openly, illegal groups communicate more frequently through secret meetings or underground fliers, cassettes, and magazines. Illegal opposition groups often also use a strict hierarchical organization to avoid government repression. These organizations rely upon military discipline, elaborate rituals, and a series of small, linked cells in order to decrease the likelihood of exposure and subsequent repression.[71]

These groups clearly experience even more stringent restrictions on mass communication than the legal political opponents. However, not having accepted the restrictions of the formal political system, they circumvent government control.

More importantly, although these groups can more easily obtain financial support from foreign actors, they act primarily for and with the support of the masses dissatisfied with the formal political system. In divided SoCs, legal opposition groups focus on maintaining the incumbents' support, while illegal groups seek support from the people. Consequently, these groups provide important social welfare services, which increase their support from the poor, the unemployed, and the underemployed. Indeed, Ahmed Abdalla concluded, "The Islamist extremists may not all themselves be unemployed, but unemployment feeds a general atmosphere of disappointment upon which fanaticism feeds."[72] The same holds true for radical secularists.[73] Different illegal groups draw their support from different constituencies – urban and rural, north and south, educated and unschooled.[74] At the end of the day, however, all receive their support from those who are increasingly dissatisfied with their daily lives and the legal political parties that fail to represent them.

Gauging these organizations' popular support is nevertheless difficult. Although elites in illegal opposition groups are sometimes able to capitalize on openly expressing their opposition to the regime, their followers seldom can. In both Jordan and Morocco, even graffiti linking individuals to covert political parties was enough evidence to put a suspected party sympathizer in jail.[75] In addition to the fear of immediate repression, people know that actions that reveal their political allegiance can some day be used against them. Thus, the same individual who would be willing to express opposition to the regime in a legally sanctioned gathering may refuse to join an illegal one, fearing greater repression.

Consequently, while illegal opposition groups often have strong ties to the masses, they may find it difficult to estimate the exact strength of their appeal or to mobilize open demonstrations of their support.[76] The need for clandestine organization makes it difficult to create large, centralized organizations. Movements tend to appear fragmented, weak, and relatively disorganized, as the case of Islamists in Morocco.[77]

Despite this, the excluded, anti-regime opposition may expect popular participation if or when it is able to mobilize successfully against the regime. As Tessler noted with regard to Moroccan youth, the low popular participation in formal political parties was a "condemnation of the system and an indication of their alienation." They stood poised at the edge of the system, willing to participate with the excluded radical leftists or Islamists to challenge the regime.[78] A description of the Iranian Hizballah also illustrates the potential organizational power of underground opposition movements. As Denoeux explains:

> The informal organization of Hezbollah did not diminish its effectiveness. In fact, it may well have lain at the heart of the Hezbollahis' ability to act swiftly. Hadi Ghoffari, head of Hezbollah in the early 1980s, said "the party of Allah is an ethereal organization. It is everywhere and yet nowhere. It is everywhere because it is nowhere."[79]

PREFERENCES OVER MOBILIZATION

As a result of these very different linkages with incumbent elites and the masses, opposition elites have divergent preferences concerning mobilization. Legal opponents want to mobilize in order to gain their demands, but they do not want their mobilization to become out of control. The reasons for this should be quite clear. They have made an implicit agreement with the government to maintain control; in return, they receive access to the formal political sphere, some policy concessions, and selective incentives. In contrast, excluded opposition elites prefer to use more radical methods of challenging the status quo. They have not made agreements with the government and thus have no particular need to curb their attacks. Indeed, excluded opposition elites can benefit from creating crises.

Thus, sympathizers and members of illegal opposition groups prefer to join in already existing strikes and demonstrations. This grants them a higher level of assurance. First, they gain some "safety in numbers," since the members of the unions, parties, or other legal groups, facing lower costs, are likely to be out in the streets as well. In addition, they expect the authorities to use less repression when putting down a legal demonstration. The authorities find it more difficult to justify the harsh repression of legal opponents, and – unable to separate legal and illegal opponents fully – they are forced to take a somewhat more lenient line toward both legal and illegal demonstrators.[80] Finally, the presence of both legal and illegal opposition groups in the same demonstration makes it more difficult to identify sympathizers of the excluded opposition groups. After the riots are over and people have returned to their homes, participation in a legal movement does not necessarily identify the participant as sympathizing with the illegal movement. In short, for illegal opponents, exploiting an ongoing protest is less costly than mobilizing independently.

TOWARD A REVISED MODEL OF OPPOSITION–GOVERNMENT INTERACTIONS

There are two important lessons in the empirical literature. First, incumbent elites take an extremely active role in manipulating their political environments. By admitting various opponents into the formal political sphere, they can create divided or unified SoCs. SoCs are distinct from the form of political regime. Second, the SoCs affect the nature of political opposition groups that exist and the dynamics of government–opposition relations within the regime. A simple model of government–opposition relations will make it possible to analyze the influence of SoCs on these relations.

Rules of the Game

The model, depicted in Figure 3.2, is one of complete information. There are three players: two opposition groups and the incumbent elites. The opposition groups are ordered ideologically, so the first is more moderate and the second more radical. They decide whether or not to make political demands on the incumbents. They can do so jointly or independently. The incumbents decide whether to negotiate with the opposition group(s) or to repress their demands.

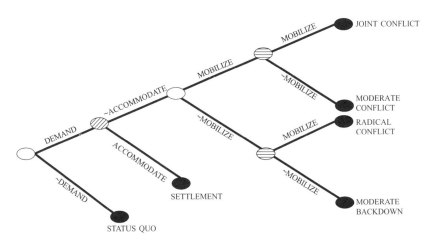

FIGURE 3.2. Model of Government–Opposition Interaction.

The model begins from the perspective of the most moderate opposition party, which decides whether or not to make demands on the incumbents. If the moderates challenge the government, incumbent elites decide either to negotiate or to refuse the opposition's request. In the case of negotiation, a settlement is reached that is between the incumbent's and the challenger's preferred positions. If the government refuses negotiations that satisfy the moderate's demands, the challenger can choose to exploit the masses' discontent, mobilizing a protest to put additional pressure on the regime. If the opposition group mobilizes unrest, there is conflict; otherwise, the outcome is that the moderates back down.

Two types of conflict between the moderate opposition and the government are possible. As shown in Figure 3.2, the more radical opposition group may choose to join in the protest movement, pressing its own demands.[81] If this occurs, a Joint Conflict exists; otherwise, the government and the moderates enter into a Moderate Conflict. If the moderates choose to back down, the radicals may still mobilize, creating a Radical Conflict; otherwise, the moderates back down. In any case, when the conflict exists, there is some probability that the opponents will obtain their demands, some probability that they will be repressed, and a cost to be paid for mobilizing the masses. As crises continue, the probability that demands will be obtained increases. Thus, as crises continue, the expected utilities of both independent and joint conflicts increase. If the opposition group chooses not to make demands, the Status Quo remains.

The expected values of the outcomes for each actor consist of changes in the policy position and the costs incurred in gaining such changes. For each actor, the expected values of policy changes are considered to be a function of the policy implemented and the actor's preferred policy. To simplify, the policies are considered to be unidimensional, as shown in Figure 3.3. The moderates' preferred policy is held at 1; the incumbents' preferred position is the Status Quo (SQ), which is set at 0; and the radicals' preferred policy

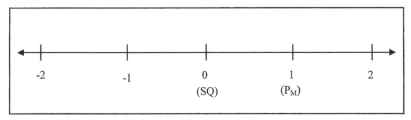

FIGURE 3.3. Ideological Spectrum.

is P_R, which, to satisfy conditions, may be less than -1 or greater than 1.[82] Thus, the SQ is valued -1, 0 and $-|P_R|$ for the moderates, incumbents, and radicals, respectively.

The model measures the government's and the oppositions' expected values of policy concessions by the distance between their preferred policy and the current policy. It assumes that there are constant returns to policy change; actors are neither ideological nor pragmatic.[83] The incumbents' and opponents' expected values of any given policy can thus be generalized as $-|P_I - \pi_J P_J|$ where P_I is the preferred policy position of actor i, π_J is the probability of obtaining actor j's preferred policy in a conflict between incumbents and actor j, and P_J is the policy preferred by actor j.[84] Thus, the government's expected losses if it fully concedes to the policy demands of moderate or radical groups are $-P_M$ and $-|P_R|$, respectively. That is, the incumbents' expected value is -1 if it fully concedes to the moderates and $-|P_R|$ if it concedes to radicals. The expected value of full concessions to their own policy demands for both moderates and radicals is 0 (i.e., $-|P_M - P_M|$ and $-|P_R - P_R|$, respectively). The function is neutral in regard to the actors' ideological preferences; a one-unit change in policy results in a one-unit movement in the actors' utilities, regardless of how near or far the policy movement is from the actors' own preferred policies.[85]

Given this function, the expected payoffs for the model's outcomes are presented in Table 3.2. The model's expected payoffs include both the expected value of the resulting policy position and the costs of conflict. For instance, moderates' expected value of a policy gain in an isolated conflict with incumbents is $-|1 - \pi_M|$. Importantly, in this model, opponents are affected by the policy concessions that other opposition groups receive as well as those that they receive themselves. If the moderates obtain policy concessions, radical opponents' expected utility for the current policy changes from $-|P_R - 0|$ to $-|P_R - \pi_M|$. It should be clear from this that radical opponents for whom $1 < P_R$ benefit and those for whom $-1 > P_R$ lose when the moderates obtain concessions. Similarly, moderates gain when radicals obtain policy concessions such that $\pi_R < 2$, and they lose when radicals obtain concessions $\pi_R > 2$.

In the event of a joint conflict, when both moderates and radicals mobilize, the expected utility for each group is a function of the likelihood that they succeed in obtaining demands (π_J) and, within this, that each group obtains its preferred policy. The likelihood that moderates obtain their preferred policy position is designated α, and the likelihood that the radicals obtain their preferred policy is $(1 - \alpha)$. For example, the expected

TABLE 3.2. *Expected Payoffs for Outcomes in the Model*

Outcome	Moderates	Radicals	Incumbents
Moderate Conflict	$-\lvert 1 - \pi_M \rvert - C_M$	$\pi_M(-\lvert P_R - 1\rvert)$ $+ (1 - \pi_M)$ $(-\lvert P_R\rvert)$	$-\pi_M - C_G$
Radical Conflict	$-\pi_R(\lvert P_R - 1\rvert)$ $-(1 - \pi_R)$	$-(1 - \pi_R)\lvert P_R\rvert$ $- \theta C_R$	$-\pi_R(\lvert P_R\rvert) - C_G$
Joint Conflict	$\pi_J[(1 - \alpha)$ $(-\lvert 1 - P_R\rvert)]$ $-(1 - \pi_J) - \beta C_M$	$\pi_J[-\alpha(\lvert P_R - 1\rvert)]$ $- (1 - \pi_J)\lvert P_R\rvert$ $- C_R$	$\pi_J[-\alpha$ $-(1 - \alpha)\lvert P_R\rvert]$ $-C_G$
Status Quo	-1	$-\lvert P_R\rvert$	0
Moderate settlement	$-\lvert 1 - S_M\rvert$	$-\lvert P_R - S_M\rvert$	$-S_M$
Moderate BackDown	$-R_M$	$-\lvert P_R\rvert + R_R$	R_G

value of the policy gains from a joint conflict for the moderates is thus $\alpha + (1 - \alpha)P_R$.

In addition, the model allows for the costs of mobilization to vary according to whether the opposition groups enter into the conflict independently or jointly. The cost of mobilization is designated C_M when moderates mobilize independently and βC_M if the radicals join in as well. The costs are θC_R for radicals if they enter independently and C_R if they join the moderates. The change in the cost of mobilization between independent and joint conflict is thus represented by the multiplicand β for the moderates and θ for the radicals. When β or θ is greater than 1, the costs of mobilization are increased, and when they are less than 1, the costs of mobilization are decreased. For reasons discussed in Chapter 2, in the unified SoC the costs of isolated conflict are greater than or equal to those of joint conflict (i.e., $\beta \leq 1$ and $\theta \leq 1$). In the divided SoCs, the costs of joint conflict are greater than the costs of isolated conflict, (i.e., $\beta > 1$ and $\theta > 1$).

If neither moderates nor radicals challenge the incumbents, all actors obtain their expected utility for the Status Quo. If the government and the opposition reach a settlement, the costs to both parties are minimal (here, assumed to be 0), and they receive the values for the policy obtained. If the opposition chooses to back down, there remains some probability that the radical opponents are accommodated or continue to mobilize an independent protest. In addition, the moderates have shown themselves to be weak and have lost some of their support. The government and the radicals may each gain a portion of this support.[86]

The expected utility of conflict depends upon the decisions of the second opposition force. If the conflict remains limited to the government and the moderate opposition, this group obtains the expected value of conflict and pays the costs of repression and mobilization. The government loses the expected value of conflict and pays the costs of repression. Thus, the moderate opposition's and government's expected utilities of Isolated Conflict are $-|1 - \pi_M| - C_M$ and $-\pi_M - C_G$, respectively. If a radical opposition group takes advantage of the conflict to press its own demands, the actors then gain the expected value of Joint Conflict.

Several simplifying, but reasonable, assumptions about the government's and the oppositions' preferences are used in analyzing the model. First, the model assumes that the policy outcome reached through negotiation, S_M, is between the status quo position and the moderate's optimal policy. Thus, the government will always prefer the Status Quo to Settlement, and the opposition will always value Settlement over the Status Quo. Second, the opposition will prefer the Status Quo to BackDown, while the incumbents, in contrast, will always prefer BackDown to the Status Quo. Thus, for the government, BackDown > Status Quo > Settlement. For the moderate opposition, Settlement > Status Quo > BackDown. Third, the government always prefers an Isolated Conflict (by either the Moderates or the Radicals) to a Joint Conflict, since the probability that the government makes concessions in a Joint Conflict is greater than that in an Isolated Conflict, and the concessions made in a Joint Conflict will be no less costly than those made in an Isolated Conflict. Because minor confrontations are less costly for incumbents to control than major ones, incumbent elites prefer Isolated to Joint Conflicts. The assumptions can be summarized:

The Government's Preference Orderings:

BackDown > Status Quo > Settlement
Independent (Moderate or Radical) Conflict > Joint Conflict

The Opposition's Preference Orderings:

Settlement > Status Quo > BackDown

Initial Analyses

Examining how incumbents can shape the political environment and influence the strategic actions of moderate and radical opponents will be the focus of subsequent chapters. Using simple backward induction, however, a few factors are clear in the case of perfect information:

Remark 1. Moderates should make demands only when they prefer Moderate Conflict to the Status Quo. If this is not the case, incumbents prefer the Moderates' BackDown to the Settlement and therefore refuse to make concessions. The Moderates, preferring the Status Quo to BackDown, should have preferred not to make demands.

Remark 2. When Moderates make demands, a Settlement will result if incumbent elites prefer Settlement to Mobilization.

Remark 3. When Moderates prefer Conflict to the Status Quo, Conflict results if the incumbent elites prefer Mobilization to Settlement. The Status Quo remains unchallenged otherwise.

From these observations, it should be clear that the incumbents can influence the level of demands made upon them by altering their opponents' expected utilities of conflict. In part, this is common knowledge: It drives the expectation that the lower the costs of conflict and the higher the probability of success, the more likely that opponents will challenge incumbent elites. The next two chapters, however, focus on how incumbents manipulate SoCs to alter the opponents' willingness to make demands even as their chances of success increase.

4

Dynamics of Opposition in Unified SoCs

This chapter explores how cost structures in the unified SoC affects the level of contestation between opponents and the ruling elites. Government–opposition relations in the unified SoC are consistent with the conventional wisdom: As governments become weaker vis-à-vis their opponents, the opposition is more likely to demand reforms. In prolonged economic crises, then, the opposition is increasingly willing to challenge the government as the crises continue. Furthermore, once moderates demand reforms, they remain willing to do so (ceteris paribus) until their demands have been met. Groups with diverse interests thus join together to put pressure on the government.

The underlying logic is simple. Opponents in the unified SoC do not expect to be repressed more severely when they join with more radical groups to demand reforms than they are if they mobilize alone. Where all opposition groups have been excluded from the system, they have little to lose; and where all have been included, mobilizing in concert with other included opposition groups does not cross agreed-upon boundaries. Rather, moderate opponents should prefer joint conflicts to independent ones. The probability that they succeed in obtaining reforms should be higher in this case, and the costs of mobilizing may be lower. Because moderates can expect their demands to be met before more radical demands (recall our discussion in Chapter 1), they should continue to escalate the conflict until their demands are met.

To see why this is so, we first use the model presented in the previous chapter to develop hypotheses about the dynamics of government–opposition relations in the unified SoC. We then apply these hypotheses to the cases of Jordan and Egypt under Nasir and Sadat. In both cases, the conflict between the government and the opposition intensified during the economic crisis, coming to include a broad range of opponents.

THE ESCALATION OF OPPOSITION: DYNAMICS IN THE UNDIVIDED ENVIRONMENT

An illustrative case of the model presented in Chapter 3 demonstrates why opposition groups are likely to increase their opposition to the regime as economic crises continue. The general equilibrium conditions for the mobilization subgame (shown in Figure 4.1) are summarized in Table 4.1. In order to clarify how the government's ability to use SoCs to manipulate the costs of mobilization affects the dynamics of opposition, these conditions are presented in simplified form in Table 4.2.

Three assumptions make this simplification possible. The first assumption is that the likelihood that joint opposition succeeds in obtaining demands is simply the sum of the probability that each individual group succeeds.[1] (The probability of success is set at 1 in the case where the sum of the individual probabilities is more than 1.) The second assumption is that the radicals and the moderates do not differ significantly with respect to their preferred policies.[2] We continue to assume that the radicals' preferred policy is slightly farther from the status quo than that of the moderates, and consequently that the government will meet moderate demands before they satisfy the radicals. Yet, to isolate the influence

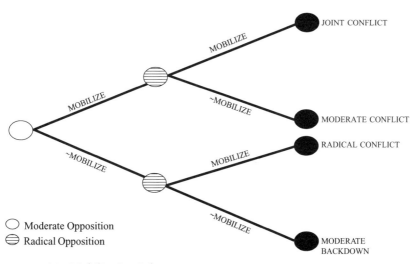

FIGURE 4.1. Mobilization Subgame.

TABLE 4.1. *Equilibrium Conditions in the Mobilization Subgame*

Outcome	Conditions for Moderates	Conditions for Radicals
Joint Conflict	$\pi_J[(1-\alpha)(-\lvert P_R-1\rvert)]$ $+\pi_J-\beta C_M>0$	$(\pi_M-\alpha\,\pi_J)(-\lvert P_R-1\rvert)+$ $(\pi_J-\pi_{M)}\lvert P_R\rvert-C_R>0$
Joint Conflict	$\pi_J[(1-\alpha)-\pi_R][(-\lvert P_R-1\rvert)]$ $+(\pi_J-\pi_R)-\beta C_M>0$	$(\pi_R)\lvert P_R\rvert-\theta C_R>0$
Moderate Conflict	$\pi_M-C_M>0$	$(\pi_M-\alpha\,\pi_J)(-\lvert P_R-1\rvert)+$ $(\pi_J-\pi_{M)}\lvert P_R\rvert-C_R<0$
Radical Conflict	$\pi_J[(1-\alpha)-\pi_R][(-\lvert P_r-1\rvert)]$ $+(\pi_J-\pi_R)-\beta C_m<0$	$(\pi_R)\lvert P_R\rvert-\theta C_R>0$
Moderate BackDown	$\pi_M-C_M<-R_M$	$-\lvert P_R\rvert+R_R>(\pi_R)\lvert P_R\rvert-$ θC_R

TABLE 4.2. *Dynamics of Protest in Unified SoCs*

$\longrightarrow$

Conditions for Radicals/Moderates	$\pi_M<C_M$ and $\pi_J<\beta C_M$ (Moderates will not mobilize)	$\pi_J-\beta C_M$ but $\pi_M<C_M$ (Moderates will mobilize jointly or alone)	$\pi_M-\beta C_M$ (Moderates will mobilize jointly or alone)
$\pi_J\lvert P_R\rvert<C_R$ (Radicals will not mobilize)	Status Quo	Moderate Conflict	Moderate Conflict
$\pi_J\lvert P_R\rvert-C_R$ but $\pi_R\lvert P_R\rvert<\theta C_R$ (Radicals will mobilize jointly, but not alone)	Status Quo	Joint Conflict	Joint Conflict
$\pi_R\lvert P_R\rvert-\theta C_R$ (Radicals will mobilize jointly or alone)	Radical Conflict	Joint Conflict	Joint Conflict

Note: Arrows show the direction of changing preferences as the probability of success increases.

of the different cost structures on the dynamics of mobilization, I assume that the oppositions' preferences are not significantly different. (The importance of different preferences will be explored in Chapter 6.) Finally, to consider the influence of different SoCs during economic crises, we assume that as economic crises continue, the opposition expects that its gains from mobilization will be greater than they were previously.[3] These assumptions allow us to isolate the effect of the changing costs of mobilization, specifically β and θ, on the dynamics of conflict.

The outcomes shown in Table 4.2 demonstrate why conflict should escalate only in prolonged economic crises. In this table, the oppositions' preferences move from left to right and from top to bottom as their probability of success increases. Both groups may initially prefer the Status Quo to any Conflict. As the probability of successfully opposing the government increases, the expected utility of conflict increases. When there is only one opposition group, it should be obvious that once the opposition prefers Conflict to the Status Quo, it will continue to do so. During economic crises, the expected utility for Conflict is increasing and that of the Status Quo remains constant.

Opponents who have become willing to challenge the regime will continue to do so as economic crises continue. To understand this, recall that in the undivided political system, the costs of Joint Conflict are less than or equal to those of Isolated Conflict. Consequently, as the crises continue, groups that previously preferred the Status Quo to Conflict may come to prefer Joint Conflict to the Status Quo, and later possibly Isolated Conflict to the Status Quo.

Is it possible, then, that the entrance of more radical opponents into a conflict will make the moderates unwilling to mobilize against the government? The answer is "no" in the undivided SoC. Knowing that another opposition group will challenge does not decrease the willingness of the first to challenge the regime. Thus:

> As the probability of success increases in a unified SoC, a moderate group that has previously challenged the government will continue to do so, regardless of the radicals' strategy, until its demands have been fully met.

PALACE INTERACTIONS WITH EXCLUDED OPPONENTS: THE CASE OF JORDAN

Government–opposition dynamics in the undivided SoC are well demonstrated in Jordan. As the economic crisis continued throughout the 1980s, opposition groups of very different ideological tendencies increasingly demanded political change. Jordan's exclusive, unified SoC had stifled the opposition at the beginning of the economic crisis, but it had not divided it.

Although opposition groups were illegal in the early 1980s, they were not entirely inactive. Political opponents tried to rally social forces, using the professional associations, informal organizations, and underground parties and publications as catalysts for unrest. The most moderate opponents could sometimes express their demands more openly. In March 1982, the government permitted a notable family with ties to the palace to edit a magazine, *al-Ufuq al-Iqtisadi* (*The Economic Horizons*), openly campaigning for greater democratic freedoms,[4] until it stopped the publication five months later. Similarly, the Minister of Interior allowed a former Ba'thist-turned-government minister, Jamal al-Sha'ir, to form the Democratic Unionist Association in 1983, with apparent encouragement of the palace.[5] Even more clearly, the palace permitted the Muslim Brotherhood to participate in politics, even though it was legally operating as a charitable society. Such concessions were limited and fleeting, however; they provided a pressure valve for the system, but they did not commit the opposition to maintaining the system.

The King also undertook a series of minor institutional reforms in the early 1980s, but he did not incorporate the opposition into the system. In 1982, he enlarged the National Consultative Council (NCC),[6] including more urban, educated elites. Two years later, he reopened parliament, holding by-elections for empty seats in 1985.[7] For the first time in 10 years, deputies returned to their seats. However, political parties were still illegal; parliament remained impotent; civil and political liberties were severely restricted; and the opposition demands remained unmet.

Moreover, the increasing economic discontent after 1983 strengthened the opposition. Islamists gained the most. They provided welfare services that the masses increasingly needed. Through their close relationship to the palace, prominent leaders in the Muslim Brotherhood had also been given access to government portfolios, particularly to the Ministries of Education and Religious Affairs and Endowments. These ministries allowed the Brotherhood to have an important influence on school curricula and the mosques. In the legislative by-elections, Islamists won three of the eight seats available, and 'Abdallah Akaylah, a Muslim Brotherhood member of parliament, estimated that the Brotherhood had the support of 10 percent of the population.[8] Although not an overwhelming majority, in the regional context of rising political Islam, the Brotherhood was emerging as the single strongest organized political force in the country.

The Brotherhood increasingly demanded political reform. This was perhaps surprising, since it had long enjoyed good relations with the palace. After 1979, when King Husayn responded to pressure from Syria by temporarily curtailing the Brotherhood's activities,[9] the Muslim Brotherhood leader Muhammad 'Abd al-Rahman al-Khalifah declared,

"We understand our government.... We have accepted these constraints without reserve in order not to create internal dissension."[10] In the early 1980s, however, the arguments surfaced that the Jordanian monarchy was not "wholly Islamic" and that legislation needed to be based upon the *shari'a*, particularly in the secondary schools and universities. The King refused to entertain such demands, and in the early 1980s, the government prohibited some of the Brotherhood's publications and restricted their meetings with groups in other countries.

The rift between the palace and the Brotherhood widened. By 1985, in part as an attempt to reconcile his relationship with Syria, Husayn publicly attacked the Brotherhood. In a vehement statement, he said he had been "deceived" by "those who cloak themselves in our Moslem faith." He warned against the "evil designs of this rotten group [the Brotherhood]" and vowed to expose the "evildoers, deceivers and conjurors and [prevent] them from achieving their goals."[11] Then, with the palace's blessing, the *mukhabarat* moved against some of their most prominent figures, including Akaylah, who was forced to resign from his position in the Ministry of Education and was then barred from returning to his teaching post at the University of Jordan.[12] Finally, the Law on Sermons and Guidance in Mosques was passed, giving the government the right to censor sermons and ban preachers.

In part, the confrontation was the result of the King's foreign policy choices. His engagement with Yasir Arafat in the Arab–Israeli peace process had raised considerable ire. Furthermore, as the economic situation worsened, he turned from his alliance with Iraq toward restoring relations with Syria.[13] Distancing himself from the Muslim Brotherhood could help in that regard, since Syrian–Jordanian relations had been severed as a result of Syria's claim that Jordan supported its Muslim Brotherhood opposition. Distancing the palace from the Brotherhood could also facilitate the Arab–Israeli peace process. As a high-level official explained the King's statement:

It wasn't that the King wanted to appease the Syrians on the eve of [Prime Minister] Rifa'i's visit to Damascus [to reconcile Jordanian–Syrian relations] as much as it was an earlier apprehension of the dangers of fundamentalism. We came to realize what rejection they [the fundamentalists] would form to the continuation of the peace process.[14]

Yet, to understand the increased tension between the King and the opposition as solely the outcome of foreign policy changes misses an important point: The Islamists in the unpartitioned environment were undeterred from confronting the King. Although the Muslim Brothers were willing to compromise with the King when they were relatively weak, they were not willing to remain silent as they gained strength and their demands increased. They did not fear the threat of other groups joining in the fray. Rather, they used popular discontent to demand greater political change, and the King fought back.

The first major popular unrest occurred in 1986 on the campus of Yarmouk University. There, on May 11, students gathered in a warning strike to demonstrate against newly imposed school fees and to demand the Arabization of the university's curriculum. They also demanded an end to the rigid control over students' political and social lives, representation on the university committees, and the release of detained colleagues. The authorities responded to the initial demonstrations with several arrests, and the protests grew to include nearly 1,500 students. The students continued not only to express their economic concerns, but to demand political change as well. The regime answered swiftly. After an unsuccessful attempt at mediation, riot police stormed the campus, leaving at least 3 dead, many injured, and nearly 800 students arrested. The King blamed the Communist Party and the Muslim Brotherhood for instigating the unrest.[15] The opposition clearly spanned the ideological spectrum and had the potential to coalesce, using economic grievances to make political demands.

Through the end of the 1980s, dissatisfaction with the government increased among both secularist and Islamist opponents, centering on charges of corruption, limited freedom of speech, the underrepresentation of the urban majority in the NCC, and the failure of national legislation to conform to Islam. Much like, and perhaps inspired by, the Palestinians in the *intifadah*, they increased their attempts to mobilize discontent, using the limited means available to them. The government allowed demonstrations in support of the *intifadah* and, in May 1988, the King relinquished control over the West Bank, but tensions mounted. The government reportedly detained dozens of left-wing opponents who, in conjunction with the PLO, called for the overthrow of the Hashemite regime.[16] In a move to control the press, the regime dissolved the editorial boards of Jordan's major newspapers and replaced them with handpicked members. Subsequently, the editor of the newspaper *al-Ra'i* wrote, on behalf of the regime, that the professional associations had exceeded their role. The associations boycotted the paper, and the government threatened to shut the associations down. Indeed, most opposition elites believed that such an action was inevitable.[17]

However, the economic crisis had become unmanageable, forcing Jordan to accept IMF-directed adjustment plans. On April 17, 1989, Jordanians awoke to dramatic price increases on basic goods. Subsidies were cut, and prices increased 10 to 50 percent on diesel fuels and cigarettes. For a population that had seen its average annual per capita income decline by 50 percent in six years, this was unacceptable.[18] Almost immediately, rioting began in the south and spread to Amman. Although the Palestinian refugee camps and the city of Irbid did not join in the unrest, the violence escalated into what some opponents active in the then-underground parties and the professional associations have called the "Jordanian intifada."[19] Clashes continued for three days, leaving at least 7 killed and 34 injured.[20]

Theories of how the violence began abound. Some say that a few of former Prime Minister Mudar Badran's men, connected with the Muslim Brotherhood, began it in an effort to discredit the incumbent government.[21] Others state that it began when truck drivers, unlinked to any political group but most affected by the dramatic rise in fuel prices, took to the streets. Most political analysts and party members agree that the organized opposition did not start the rioting.[22]

Yet, opposition in almost all sectors of society used the incident to make political demands. Underground parties with links to the outlying areas used pamphlets and phones to promote the unrest and press their agendas.[23] As a result of these activities and in an attempt to thwart further unrest, the authorities detained approximately 150 members of the Communist Party.[24] The professional associations, unions, women's organizations, student unions, outlawed parties, tribal federations, tribal youth organizations, and individual clans issued pamphlets and communiqués expressing their demands. Although they had different emphases and varying demands, all of them called for political reforms: greater personal freedom, the lifting of martial law, relegalization of political parties, and the resumption of parliamentary life. All charged the government with nepotism, corruption, and fiscal mismanagement, calling for the resignation of Prime Minister Zayd al-Rifaʿi.[25]

King Husayn, who had been in the United States when the riots began, returned immediately, calming the political scene and announcing measures toward political liberalization. Although the regime claimed that the riots were not personally against the King, he apparently understood their message. Notably, the Palestinians, often considered the King's greatest political threat, chose to stay out of the rioting immediately following the price increases. The violence occurred in the heart of the King's traditional stronghold, among the Transjordanians in the south. It demonstrated not only the strength of the discontent, but also the limitations of a system based upon the co-optation of tribal elites. These elites had become either unable or unwilling to restrain their local populations. In addition, however, in the proliferation of demands that a wide range of organizations and associations made in the aftermath of the riots, Jordanians of both East Bank and Palestinian origins voiced similar demands. As a senior government official explained, "The real issue was a popular rejection of a whole government system that does not allow for the minimum required level for political expression of participation."[26]

Although the rioters had not directly challenged the King's legitimacy, the breadth of the opposition demonstrated a grave threat: There was increasing potential for opposition that spanned both ideological positions and national origins. Moreover, it represented the first direct clash between the King and the Transjordanian population, neither instigated nor abetted by outside forces. As a result, "the barrier of fear [had] collapsed. People [were] much more aware of their power to make change. They [were] saying, 'enough is enough.'"[27]

Prime Minister Zayd al-Rifa'i resigned on April 24th, and the King put his cousin, Field Marshal Zayd Bin Shakir,[28] in his place. The King also announced important political reforms.[29] He called the first general elections to be held since 1966.[30] Political prisoners were granted amnesty; reasonable criticism in the press was allowed; and although martial law remained in effect, parties were allowed to reorganize publicly.[31]

Immediately, the palace and the opposition set about negotiating the rules by which the opposition could formally enter the political arena.[32] In April 1990, the King appointed a 60-member committee, including representatives from the groups that had called for political reform, to draft initial guidelines. By June 1991, the National Charter (*al-Mithaq al-Watani*) was ratified at a conference of 2,000 leading Jordanians. Although opposition activists and observers are quick to point out that their role in the negotiations was, in reality, to raise their hands in agreement to the palace-sponsored proposal, it was nevertheless significant that the opposition parties gave their agreement.

One of the document's purposes was to set the framework within which political parties could operate. Much like the parties in Morocco, legal political parties in Jordan had to accept the legitimacy of the Hashemite monarchy and operate without foreign funding or influence. During this time, political opponents once again resurfaced, acting openly in the formal political sphere. On July 5, 1992, using these guidelines, parliament passed the Political Parties Law, making way for the relegalization of parties that had been banned since 1957.

This political liberalization was clearly the result of the economic decline suffered from the beginning of the 1980s. As we would expect, the increased popular discontent accompanying economic decline fueled the movement. While most of the masses were unconcerned with political liberalization, they were willing to support the movement toward reforms in the hope that these would usher in greater economic growth.[33] In response to economic difficulties, more Transjordanians became actively critical of the regime. The common grievances, along with the King's attempt to integrate the Palestinian population, allowed Palestinians and Transjordanians to work together in pressing their demands. Most importantly, in a unified SoC, there were no strong disincentives toward a joint conflict. Indeed, because all groups had been left out of the system, all expected to gain from an escalated conflict.

TOWARD A UNIFIED, INCLUSIVE SoC

Before we examine how the liberalization affected the dynamics of opposition in Jordan, it is important to distinguish carefully between liberalization, as seen in Jordan, and democratization. Liberalization represented a very deliberate change in King Husayn's strategy toward his opposition. The demonstrations that erupted at the end of 1989 had surprised the King, but they had not threatened to topple him, at least not in the short run. It was therefore not immediately clear what his political response would be. While opposition groups demanded reform, the King consulted with palace supporters. Views were mixed,[34] but the King eventually decided to call for new elections and the first lifting of martial law since 1957. The change was dramatic, but it did not represent a loss of the King's control. As one observer noted:

What's happening here [in Jordan], then, is new and different – a fundamental, perhaps generational, transition that is both less threatening and more promising than the crisis-mongers would have you believe. Husayn is not so much losing his grip as he is loosening it in a calculated effort to tighten the hold of his Hashemite dynasty.[35]

The reforms were not intended to alter the King's hold on power. For instance, the press was allowed greater freedom than it had enjoyed in the previous decades, but the newspapers remained subject to close censorship as well as self-censorship. The three leading newspapers were still under majority ownership of the government, with their editors firmly beholden to the palace. As George Hawatmeh, former editor-in-chief of the *Jordan Times*, summarized:

Democratization in Jordan was not a revolution; and those who manned the transformation of the process, including the top editors of the mostly government-owned papers, were men who had served and known the regime well. The hierarchy now moved at the same pace as the regime did. It was all going to be a peaceful, slow process of change.[36]

Similarly, as the former Prime Minister and attorney Ahmad Obeidat concluded, the palace controlled the courts, giving them little incentive to challenge the regime.[37] Indeed, to the applause of conservatives, King Husayn was changing the rules of the game without changing the real distribution of power. Fahad al-Fanek, a prominent Transjordanian columnist, concluded:

We have a king of our own and he is supposed to be the guardian and arbitrator. And he is doing just that, because he has the right to overrule a court by giving a pardon, to override parliament by not approving a new law and to fire the government if he thinks it is doing something wrong.[38]

Yet, within the political sphere, nearly all actors were permitted to participate.[39] Although the Algerian situation raised concern about allowing Islamist political parties, the Kingdom opened participation to parties of all political ideologies. In part, this was because the long history of the Muslim Brotherhood meant that their participation appeared less threatening in Jordan than it did in other Arab states. In addition, moderates such as Ibrahim 'Izz al-Din argued: "You cannot deny people the right to organize as they wish. The best thing is to give every group the chance to operate publicly. If you try to suppress any opinion or trend, you will have problems such as we have witnessed in many parts of the world."[40]

PALACE INTERACTIONS WITH THE LEGAL OPPOSITION

While the efforts toward liberalization and the hope of greater reforms initially reduced opponents' willingness to challenge the incumbent regime, they did not do so for long. In the early period of liberalization, Jordan's political situation resembled that of Morocco in 1984, when Moroccan party elites chose to remain apart from the popular unrest in the hope that the elections would bring them increased political influence. In Jordan, as well, opposition elites and the masses expected that the government would become more accountable, corruption and nepotism would decline, and the people would soon have true influence. These expectations seemed reasonable, given the King's unusual foreign policy position during the Gulf War. Instead of siding with his Saudi and U.S. sponsors, King Husayn had remained apart from the allies, sacrificing foreign aid in the process. In addition, he allowed groups to mobilize popular rallies in support of Iraq, to set up 24-hour news stations through which interested parties could see the war's progress, and to send volunteers and material aid to the Iraqis. Before the Gulf War, the Muslim Brotherhood formally joined the cabinet for the first time.[41] Finally, the press and public discourse featured elites proclaiming how democracy would help make the necessary economic reforms feasible. Liberalization seemed a necessary solution at a difficult time.[42] In 1992, with expectations running high, an estimated 1 million Jordanians turned out to see the King return from his hospitalization abroad.[43]

The oppositions' expectations went unfulfilled, however. In addition to his domestic concerns, King Husayn continued to work toward peace with the Israelis, in part as a way to rejoin the international community and ease his economic problems. An active, influential opposition could be a stumbling block to accepting a peace agreement, however. Thus, the regime quickly set limits on Jordan's political liberalization.

By the following year, some Islamists were becoming disappointed. The Muslim Brotherhood–dominated IAF had been particularly successful in the 1989 elections, winning seats for 22 of its 26 candidates and controlling more than one-quarter of the 80-member lower house. In addition, independent Islamists gained 12 seats, giving the Islamist bloc 34 seats. The Islamists' dominance made both the palace and secular leftists uneasy.

Consequently, some argue that the palace took early measures to check the Islamist forces. That same year, the King appointed only one Islamist member, Ishaq Farhan, to the 40-member Senate, leaving it dominated by Transjordanian loyalists.[44] Furthermore, much to its disappointment, the Muslim Brotherhood was offered only one seat in Mudar Badran's first cabinet, which it chose to reject.[45] Although the palace would subsequently allow the Brotherhood to enter the government as tensions mounted before the Gulf War,[46] it dismissed the government soon after the Gulf War, in June 1991.[47] Throughout 1991 and 1992, the Ministry of Interior banned large public meetings held by the Islamists, and in passing the Political Parties Law of 1992, the government officially barred political parties (broadly interpreted to include the Muslim Brotherhood) from using mosques, schools, and other religious institutions for political activities.[48] Although it chose to accept the election results, the palace played down the strength of the Muslim Brotherhood, saying that only 10 percent of the 1.6 million eligible voters cast their ballots for the fundamentalists and that only 25 percent of voters supported the Muslim Brotherhood and its sympathizers.[49]

A more significant reversal of the liberalization efforts took place after the Palestinians and Israelis accepted the Oslo Agreement in 1993. While reportedly furious at having been excluded from the Palestinian–Israeli negotiations, King Husayn also recognized the opportunity that the Oslo Agreement presented him. The major obstacle to forging a separate Jordanian–Israeli peace agreement had dissolved.

Consequently, the King tightened his control over policy making. Revisions in the electoral law issued on August 13, 1993, just months before the November 1993 elections, clearly disadvantaged leftist and Islamic opponents. Procedurally, objections centered on the extent to which the one-person, one-vote electoral scheme favored tribal candidates at the expense of the political party candidates, as well as the gerrymandering that favored the conservative East Bank communities over the urban areas and Palestinian camps.[50] The opposition also argued that selective repression of leftist and Islamist candidates and their supporters increased before and during the elections.[51] Grievances led to formal statements, by the IAF and others, denouncing the electoral procedures.[52]

In addition, both parliament and the cabinet were barred from any real policy-making role. Neither was even informed of the details of the Washington agreement signed in July 1994 or the peace treaty of October 1994 until after they were signed.[53] The peace treaty did, in part, ease Jordan's economic problems. The United States, Britain, France, and Germany wrote off $830 million of Jordan's foreign debt at the end of 1994, and Jordan was allowed to reschedule $2.2 billion of foreign debt that would have come due before mid-1997.[54] Yet, if the restrictions on political reform and the economic benefits of the peace treaty were made in an attempt to maintain stability, they had the opposite effect.

The opposition continued to challenge fundamental policies of the government. Backed by increased popular discontent, widespread disapproval of the peace accord, failure to see an end to the economic crisis, and a common demand for political power, a broad political coalition formed to oppose Husayn's policies. By early 1995, Islamists and leftists had formed an Anti-Normalization Committee.[55] They directed their attacks at the King's most fundamental policies, and they threatened the King's legitimacy. Furthermore, these attacks made the continuation of the peace process,[56] which relieved Jordan of some of its debts and regained support from its international allies, more difficult. They were thus problematic, because returning to the international fold and regaining economic support was critical for the King if he was to defuse popular discontent and maintain his rule. Furthermore, the continued pressures for political liberalization attacked the King's power. The feasible political changes had already taken place; to ask for greater freedoms and a more essential policy-making role in the Kingdom was to ask for significant concessions from the palace. The opposition planned to hold a National Conference at the end of May 1995.[57] Modeled after the National Charter Conference held four years earlier, the conference was intended to draw up a "Charter of Honor," demonstrating the opposition's frustration with the "liberalization" (or deliberalization) that it had witnessed so far.[58]

As the conflict between the King and his opponents intensified, King Husayn signaled that he would respond with increased repression. Continued criticism of the peace treaty was disruptive and unacceptable, and those willing to step across the line would be punished. In November 1995, Prime Minister Zayd Bin Shakir warned, "Any denial of [Jordan's] achievements is tantamount to treason,"[59] and took steps to tighten the Press Law in order to "safeguard a 'responsible' press."[60] One month later, King Husayn reiterated that he was ready for "a show-down with the opponents of his policies towards Israel and in the region generally."[61] In part, this angry response was in reaction to Jordanian opposition to the peace treaty, which had only intensified after Jordanians watched King Husayn and Queen Nur grieve at the assassination of Israeli Prime Minister Yitzhak Rabin.[62] Yet, even as the peace treaty became a fait accompli, the cycle of escalation and repression continued.

In a unified SoC during a prolonged economic crisis, the opposition front remained united. In 1996, the economic situation had deteriorated, leading to announcements that the government would once again raise bread prices (i.e., lower subsidies) by 300 percent. Despite an attempt to prepare the public, and despite King Husayn's personal appeal on July 12th to the Jordanians to support the government's decision, opposition escalated. On July 21st, activists broke into parliament on the first day of the extraordinary session. Parliamentary opposition members ranging from the leftists to the Islamists spoke out strongly against the rising prices, and a petition with 30,000 signatures, including those of 41 members of parliament, was presented to parliament. It asked the government not to implement the price increase; otherwise, the parliamentary opposition warned, the government could face a no-confidence vote.[63] Yet, on August 16th, the government raised the price of bread while King Husayn closed the parliamentary session. Widespread public rioting shook Jordan for a second time in less than a decade, and the palace responded by calling in army units and imposing a curfew.[64]

The palace clamped down. Ignoring the opposition, it sponsored the 1997 Press and Publication Law, providing more restrictions on publications and more severe penalties for infractions.[65] It also refused to engage in serious dialogue with the opposition about revising the 1993 Electoral Law. As a result, 10 opposition parties boycotted the upcoming elections by August 1997. The national turnout rate was a low 54.5 percent, and in urban areas where political parties were strong, it plummeted to as low as 20 percent.[66] Once again, the opposition coalition spanned the ideological spectrum and the Palestinian–Transjordanian divide,[67] and it was willing to put pressure on the King.

As popular support for Husayn reached its nadir, the opposition called for public demonstrations. The demonstrations were called in support of Iraq, whose relations with the United States were becoming increasingly tense. They were particularly important because the government had banned the demonstrations, in marked contrast to its response during the 1991 Gulf War. Furthermore, the included opposition was willing to risk crossing the line, choosing to mobilize the demonstrations despite the prohibition. On February 13, opponents organized a protest after Friday prayers at a mosque in Amman, and over 2,000 persons demonstrated. The following week, demonstrators marched in the typically loyalist southern town of Ma'an. The confrontation between the police and demonstrators lasted for three days, leaving one killed and the town under curfew for one week.[68] The opposition, objecting to the repression, called for the government's resignation.

Although the opposition failed to confront the government three months later, when it prohibited a rally commemorating *al-Nakbah* (The Catastrophe),[69] the opposition front remained united. On June 13, 1998, these members, now including the nine political parties, the Muslim Brotherhood, the Lawyers' syndicate, and 11 prominent individuals,[70] came together formally to form the Conference for National Reform, holding their first National Congress on July 25, 1998.[71]

The palace threatened to redefine the role of the professional associations[72] and to separate religion from politics.[73] It restricted freedom of the press once again. Despite these threats, however, the Jordanian opposition continued to challenge King Husayn. Pressures from a wide range of opposition groups increased, making economic reforms dangerous, as the riots of August 1996 demonstrated.

The significance of this broad coalition should not be understated. There was little love lost between the two sets of opposition groups. In 1989 some Islamists had accused a prominent female secularist candidate, Toujan Faysal, of "apostasy," declaring her incompetent, dissolving her marriage, and promising immunity to anyone who would "shed her blood."[74] Similarly, secularist party members often made derogatory comments about their Islamist partners.[75] In addition to ideological differences, there were power struggles among the coalition partners that constantly threatened to tear them apart.[76] Similarly, the Palestinian–Transjordanian divide was not easy to overcome. In the past, divisions over the relative importance of the Palestinian issue had led to splits among the parties. Although King Husayn's relinquishment of the West Bank alleviated tensions, important differences remained between the Transjordanian and Palestinian views on this and other matters.[77] Yet, despite all the divisions and tensions, the coalitions continued to challenge the palace.

The unified SoC was marked by a spiraling conflict between the King and his political opponents. As the situation worsened, the probability that the opposition would succeed in mobilizing unrest increased. Because no political opponents would be disadvantaged in an exploited conflict, they were willing to coalesce to press their demands. The King's only hope of controlling the situation was to co-opt greater portions of the political field while increasing the costs of mobilization through greater repression. Not surprisingly, by 1998 most activists and observers agreed that the system had returned nearly full circle to the dark years of 1988.[78]

Yet, while opposition groups feared the King's retribution, they did not fear each other. Indeed, repression only united them further. No segment of the opposition expected to pay higher costs to mobilize a joint conflict than an isolated one. Instead, they believed that political pluralism, and a jointly fought struggle to obtain it could benefit all. As the Muslim Brotherhood leader Khalil al-Shubaki explained with regard to the Brotherhood's cooperation with leftist parties:

It is coordination over a common cause. It does not mean that we recognize the legitimacy of their thoughts. We believe in political pluralism as long as it is within the general Islamic framework. What we want for ourselves, we want it for others too.[79]

GOVERNMENT–OPPOSITION DYNAMICS IN A UNIFIED SoC:
NASIR AND SADAT

In Egypt, Nasir and Sadat also experienced the increased united opposition characteristic of a unified SoC. As the economic situation worsened
and the Israeli–Egyptian Peace Treaty, intended in part to alleviate these
problems, heightened public criticism, they came under intense pressure
from both leftists and Islamists. Both presidents initially responded to
the increased discontent with announcements of liberalization, but they
reimposed restrictions on political activity when pressures mounted.

Opposition in Nasir's Unified, Exclusive SoC

Like Jordan, Egypt had a unified SoC when its economy took a downturn
after 1966. Discontent increased further following the 1967 war, as described in the Introduction. The revolutionary regime had clearly failed to
deliver on its promises. For the first time since 1956, Egyptians questioned
the legitimacy of the one-party system. Demands for multipartyism and
liberalization – virtually unthinkable before the war – now appeared.[80]

   In the unified SoC, opposition movements took advantage of the increased popular discontent surrounding the economic crisis to demand
political reforms. The first significant demands on the government had
appeared as early as August 1965, when it rounded up as many as 27,000
adherents of the Muslim Brotherhood in a single day. This "Last Muslim
Brotherhood Conspiracy" foreshadowed the interplay between economic
decline and political opposition, as many of the leading conspirators were
young members of the "new middle class" – engineers, scientists, and
students – who were finding their expectations shattered.[81]

   Tensions escalated after the 1967 war as the masses exhibited a willingness to mobilize for political demands that was unprecedented under
Nasir's regime. In June 1967, this took the form of support for Nasir. Secretary General 'Ali Sabri had apparently arranged for small-scale demonstrations to demand that Nasir withdraw his resignation, but millions
poured into the streets. The semiautonomous movement was surprising,
and it foreshadowed events to come.[82]

   Opposition escalated. In February 1968, the first real riots since 1954
erupted in Cairo and Alexandria when thousands of students and workers took to the streets in outrage over "lenient" sentences for military
officers tried for Egypt's defeat in the 1967 war. Demonstrators marched,
shouting not only "Death to the traitors!" but also "No socialism without

freedom!"[83] The riots ended after five days, with 10 individuals killed, 50 injured, and 500 arrested.[84] The Minister of Education, Labib Shukayr, blamed the Muslim Brotherhood for instigating the riots, and it is clear that some Muslim Brotherhood cells participated, but they were not the sole organizers.[85] Individuals representing a wide ideological spectrum joined together to demonstrate their dissatisfaction.

The cause of the riots was not only the immediate sentencing of the military officials, but also the growing discontent with Nasir's seemingly corrupt and impotent regime. That the military officers allegedly responsible for Egypt's humiliating defeat in the 1967 war were let off so easily seemed to confirm that the regime was built upon cronyism and self-interest, with little concern for average Egyptians. It was anger at the closed policies and economic failure of Nasir's regime that drove demonstrators into the streets. As Carrie Wickham put it, not only the officers but "the regime itself was on trial."[86]

The violence was put down, but discontent remained. The following month, workers, engineers, journalists, doctors, and lawyers echoed the earlier demands. Most notably, the general assembly of the Judges' Association piggybacked on the unrest, demanding independence from the ASU;[87] strengthening of the rule of law, with the end of the use of special courts; and further political liberalization. These demands were clearly intended to put pressure on the government. Announced in the aftermath of the February riots and only two days before Nasir planned to address the public, the announcements attacked the regime at its weak point. Furthermore, in timing the announcements as they did, the Judges' Association entered into a direct confrontation with the government, which had asked them to wait until after Nasir's March address to publicize their demands. The government saw the statement as an attack on the regime, made partly in support of the demonstrators.[88]

Nasir responded on March 31, 1968, with a declaration of reforms intended to reinforce and broaden the regime's base.[89] In the March Declaration, the president announced plans to prepare a new constitution granting greater freedom of "thought, expression, publication, opinion, scientific research and the press." Reaching out to the middle class, he also promised that the constitution would protect property rights, strengthen government institutions, provide for judiciary independence, and reinforce the rule of law. Statements subsequently published in *al-Ahram*, particularly those by Nasir's close adviser, Mohammad Haykal, reiterated the message. A cabinet reshuffle, disbandment of a "particularly notorious" branch of the security forces, and reforms within the ASU, most notably the ouster of ʿAli Sabri in May, and new elections for parliament, which returned only 27 percent of the incumbents, were intended to broaden the government's support base and weaken opponents of liberalization.[90] In addition, Nasir released approximately 1,000 of the least threatening imprisoned Muslim Brothers and granted greater concessions to students – allowing a new student newspaper and reducing the University Guard's authority.

Despite these initial concessions, demands for continued reforms came from all quarters. Opposition exploded a second time in November 1968, when students took to the streets in response to reforms that would have stipulated a reduction in enrollments.[91] Workers in the ETUF also continued to demand more latitude, although the only apparent concession to the workers was to allow them to publish *al-ʿUmmal* weekly instead of monthly.[92] As Mark Cooper notes, "Mass anti-regime violence became a permanent feature of the polity after the June defeat."[93]

The initial moves toward reforms were soon reversed. In part, this was due to Nasir's deteriorating health. Following a heart attack, Nasir traveled to the USSR for treatment, returning to focus primarily on foreign affairs while delegating domestic affairs to senior advisers – Sami Sharaf, Sharaʿwi Gomaʿa, and Amin Howaydi – who were closely tied to internal security.[94] In addition, Egypt came under pressure from the USSR to reinstate ʿAli Sabri, who returned to his post at the ASU, thus reestablishing the power of the ASU over parliament and undertaking further land reforms. In August 1969, the government also dismissed more than 200 judges in the "massacre of the judges"[95] and created a new Supreme Court and Supreme Council of Judicial Organizations, bringing the judiciary under the President's direct control.[96]

The reinstatement of repressive measures was not due to Nasir's weakness and external pressures alone. The same dynamics would be repeated as Egypt's economic crisis continued under Sadat. As in Jordan, the fundamental difficulty of attempting liberalization in a unified SoC was clear: With no significant divisions among the opposition, opponents met limited concessions with demands for further reform.

Government–Opposition Relations Under Sadat

Sadat changed the relationship between the government and its opponents after he assumed power in November 1970, but he did not alter the SoC. Islamists, in particular, were granted greater freedom.[97] However, despite limited liberalization, Sadat did not formally include opponents in the regime. Consequently, he soon faced the same challenges that Nasir had before him: The more reforms Sadat instituted, the more opponents took advantage of them to demand further liberalization.

Early in his presidency, Sadat implemented liberal reforms in an attempt to shore up his power and weaken his opponents. He immediately promised to strengthen the rule of law, and reforms instituted the following year granted greater political freedoms. He released political prisoners, reinstated previously dismissed judges, and even personally burned 22,000 transcripts of phone conversations recorded during Nasir's rule. He lifted most censorship to foster "intelligent criticism," and he encouraged popular participation, holding elections at every level of government (five elections) in 1972.[98]

The reforms helped to consolidate Sadat's position vis-à-vis his internal rivals, but they also contributed to pressure on the government. In part, this was because Sadat had apparently thrown in his lot with the liberalizers, and as Bruce Rutherford argued, "The process became self-reinforcing: the more liberalizing steps that he took, the more Sadat became dependent on the advocates of liberalization for support and, thus, the more pressure he faced to continue liberalizing."[99] In addition, continued economic decline, with rising unemployment and declining real wages, spurred general discontent.[100] This malaise was coupled with clear political problems – Egypt's humiliating conflict with Israel, its apparent dominance by the USSR, and stifled domestic freedoms. Opposition elites ranging from Marxists to Islamists thus took advantage of the heightened discontent and any political openings to mobilize popular support, demanding reforms.[101]

The early 1970s saw increasing unrest. Riots erupted in January 1972. The catalysts were the appointments of a conservative Prime Minister and First Secretary of the ASU[102] and rumors of austerity plans. Student demonstrators spilled out of the university and into the streets of downtown Cairo, sparking riots from January 24th to the 27th. Led by leftist forces, the demonstrations obtained the support of a wide range of opponents' with varied demands. Kepel explains:

But since [Islamists] were still too weak to put forward slogans of their own, they preferred to give the leftist slogans a slight twist, a Muslim cast. War against Israel, for example, which the leftist students called "the national liberation struggle of the Arab peoples against imperialism's policeman in the Middle East," was described by [the Brotherhood founder Hasan] al-Banna's disciples as the *jihad* that would put an end to the usurpation by infidels of one of the lands of *Dar al-Islam*. On this kind of basis, there were no obstacles to action.[103]

The Egyptian opposition challenged the government throughout the early 1970s. Students continued to demonstrate in April and December of 1972 and in January and February of the following year. Workers took to the streets in February, March, and April 1972 as well, and religious conflicts erupted from August to November. Even the military harbored dissent – with reported disturbances in February, July, October, and November 1972 and February 1973. As Mark Cooper concluded:

> Simply put, the government's policy was going nowhere. Economic reform and moderate liberalization produced no tangible improvements, and the people were becoming restless. War costs continued without war. The private sector fell into a recession. Reform of the public sector did not even appear to be implemented. The students were back out on the streets. The government was lambasted in the press and the Assembly.[104]

Under attack from all quarters, Sadat sought to weaken the opposition without making significant changes in the regime. He expelled the Soviets and moved toward war with Israel in an effort to counter his critics. In May 1974, he released a number of political prisoners. The People's Assembly passed a law reinstating, where possible, public sector employees who had been dismissed between 1963 and 1972 for political reasons. In the spring of 1974, Sadat also circulated the "October Working Paper," which promised political liberalization and proposed that the private sector play a greater role in economic development.[105] In July, the Assembly passed a law desequestering the land and property; by October, the government had returned about 10,000 *feddans* of land to nearly 500 people. The *infitah* was intended to alleviate the economic hardship and accompanying political tensions that plagued Sadat's presidency. Yet, as an editorial in *al-Iqtisadi* explained in March 1974, "Economic change [was not to] mean a change in the political system."[106]

Unfortunately for Sadat, it also did not mean a change in his opposition. Even Islamists whom he had released from prison took advantage of the increasing discontent to demand reforms. In 1974, Salih 'Abdallah Sariya led militant Islamists in an attack on the Military Technical College in an apparent attempt to overthrow Sadat. He and 96 others were arrested in connection with the incident.[107] The more moderate Muslim Brotherhood also attacked the government, calling its claims of liberalization – and later of democracy – a "thin veneer." Not only had Sadat failed to appease Islamists by claiming to be the "Believer President" and granting concessions unheard of under Nasir; he had actually made it more difficult to repress Islamist opposition. He could denounce leftists and Marxists as atheists, but the denunciation of Islamist opposition – indeed, even explaining the existence of such opposition – risked calling into question Sadat's legitimacy.[108]

Although he would often portray unrest as instigated by Communists and foreign influence, Sadat experienced increasing opposition on all fronts. In January 1975 over 1,000 workers, students, and others participated in violent demonstrations, stopping trains and trams and attacking offices, buses, and cars. They finally marched to the Ministry of the Interior, shouting slogans such as "Where is our breakfast, hero of the crossing?" "Nasir, where are you?" and "Out with Hijazi," (the current Prime Minister).[109] Again the security forces made widespread arrests, and this time the government blamed the Marxists. That same year, the government announced it had uncovered several alleged plots, by both Islamists and Communists, to overthrow Sadat.

The next year, yet another round of popular strikes and demonstrations shook the country. In January, Islamist students at al-Azhar University demonstrated, demanding that the state adopt the *shariʿa* as its fundamental law. Leftists also put pressure on Sadat's regime. In February, students demonstrated outside the offices of the newspaper *al-Akhbar* against the anti-Nasirist approach of its editor, which reflected Sadat's campaign. A long series of alleged demonstrations, strikes, and coup attempts by the leftists, Islamists, the military, and the masses appeared during the year. Popular discontent continued to rise across the political spectrum and even within the ASU.

Sadat's earlier reforms had not only failed to ease tensions; they had exacerbated the crisis. The economic situation had become worse, not better. Inflation was rampant, with an estimated price increase of 20–35 percent on all goods and an escalation of food prices of nearly 40 percent between 1973 and 1974.[110] By the spring of 1976, the leftist-oriented *al-Taliʿah* estimated that purchasing power had declined for 80 percent of the population since the October 1973 war. In a speech before parliament that year, Prime Minister Mamduh Salim warned that Egypt faced severe and continuing hardships.[111] At the same time, some Egyptians who had capitalized on Egypt's open-door policy were becoming extraordinarily wealthy, and their imported luxury items stood in stark contrast to the conditions of ordinary Egyptians. Critics complained of "vulgar consumption" and "economic apartheid." By 1976, even *al-Iqtisadi* warned:

> The consumption liberalization, and what it entails in the way of an explosive inflation, has changed the structure of Egyptian society dangerously. After being divided into a poor class, a large middle class and a rich class, it has now become composed of a destitute class and a rich class, while the middle class has been transformed into a treadmill, straining on the path to maintain a minimum standard of living.[112]

Furthermore, it had become the prevailing opinion that "the economic opening, which general policy has called for since the victory of October and which requires for its execution scientific administration at the highest level of ability, needs as well a political opening."[113]

Sadat thus instituted ever more significant political changes to reduce the opposition. In 1975, the government announced that membership in the ASU was no longer required for membership in professional syndicates.[114] In union elections the following year, the government repressed rank-and-file union militants, but it also allowed union leaders outside the ASU to gain positions in the June 1976 elections.[115] More importantly, Sadat announced that he would accept the establishment of competing platforms within the ruling ASU. On October 22, 1975, Muhammad Abu Wafia announced the social democratic platform, which would become the "center" platform. In the next two weeks, nearly 10 platforms were established, generally led by elites who enjoyed solid relations with the regime.[116] The exercise soon spiraled out of control, however, and platforms emerged that were more threatening. Seven of the last 19 platforms to be announced contained religious references, as opposed to only 1 of the first 10; they also contained references to Nasir and appeals to specific groups (e.g., workers, youth). Most importantly, the diversity of the platforms announced, and the lower levels of elites establishing these platforms showed, the desire and willingness of a wide variety of opponents to join in the political game.[117] In short, Egypt saw a "new form of political activity."[118]

The activity went far beyond the ASU and the regime's expectations, and it appeared threatening. The large number of platforms could make for tumultuous debates. More importantly, the platforms – which began to act suspiciously like parties – could spark other political activity that might be more difficult to monitor. This was particularly problematic because many of those announcing platforms, apparently anxious to enter the political realm, were relative outsiders, and their criticism could have shaken the established order. In short, their activity was unprecedented and potentially divisive. It was not what the government had intended.[119]

It is important for our analysis to recognize how limited the sphere of activity was to remain. The First Secretary of ASU responded to the activity by clarifying its limits:

I refuse the call to fragment the national unity in an artificial form by means of creating parties. However, I also do not accept the theory of the single party which imposes its tutelage on the populace, oppresses the freedom of opinion, and effectively prevents the people from practicing their political freedom. Therefore, I desire the alliance to be the true limits for the national unity.[120]

The following spring, the ASU called a meeting to debate the limits of platforms. By March, President Sadat had endorsed the notion of fixed platforms reflecting the center, left, and right. On the 29th, this became official policy.

Anyone who had believed that there would be real debate had been sadly mistaken. Mark Cooper described this rather eloquently:

The action that could be taken within the regime's concept of democracy was rather restrictive. Not only would those in power not recognize freedom of organization, but they held back on freedom of publication and ruled out all forms of intermediary political activity – petitions, demonstrations, resignations on matters of principle, and so on, were all defined as undemocratic, if not anti-democratic. One was expected to speak one's piece at a specific time in a "controlled" context and nothing more. This was extremely meager fare for anyone with much of a political appetite.... Left and right had serious, even desperate, demands which the regime had not anticipated and had no idea how to satisfy.[121]

At the opening session of the People's Assembly on November 11, 1976, Sadat took a seemingly bold step, declaring that the platforms could become political parties. Although the elections had seen a high degree of tension and violence, the Center Platform remained firmly in control. It had gained 83 percent of the seats and held every leadership position in the Assembly.[122] Perhaps for this reason, Sadat thought the stakes were low enough that he could announce the formation of three political parties: the National Progressive Union Party (NPUP), a leftist party led by Khalid Muhyi al-Din;[123] the Arab Socialist Organization (ASO), a centrist party led by Prime Minister Mamduh Salim; and the Socialist Liberal Organization (SLO), a rightist party headed by Mustafa Kamel Murad. This was a dramatic change from the single-party, revolutionary regime that had dominated Egypt since 1952. Yet, the space for political activity would remain narrow.

Tensions were high in the Assembly and on the street, and they came to a head in the "food riots" of January 1977.[124] Under continued pressure from economic decline, the administration decided to reduce subsidies on January 17th without consultation, debate, or the vote of the Assembly. The following day, Egyptians awoke to increased prices on basic commodities (e.g., sugar, tea, and bottled gas), which represented nearly a 15 percent increase in the cost of living for the average person. Rioting spread rapidly from Aswan to Alexandria in two days of unrest that were reminiscent of the "burning of Cairo" that had sparked the overthrow of the monarchy almost exactly 25 years earlier. As the London *Observer* noted, "The long-suffering poor of Egypt last week rose up and shook President Sadat's bourgeois society until its teeth rattled."[125] Police stations and public property were prime targets, looting was widespread, and the human toll was high. By the end, the official count was 80 dead, 560 wounded, and 1,200 arrested, but most believed these numbers far underestimated the extent of the riots.

The riots were direct evidence of the deep dissatisfaction, and an increasingly mobilized, wide spectrum of Egyptians demanding both economic and political change. The government immediately blamed the leftists and foreign rivals – notably Libya and the USSR. On January 30th, for instance, Prime Minister Mamduh Salim accused these entities, adding that the legal, leftist (Nasirist) NPUP "had involved itself shamefully in this abominable national crime."[126] Yet, it was apparent that other groups were involved as well. Bearded youths were seen burning nightclubs and cabarets and smashing whiskey bottles.[127] In short,

> different people were on the streets expressing different discontents in different ways. Some would have taken to the streets for almost any reason. Others would have done so only under the most unique of circumstances. In all likelihood, the latter groups would have hesitated to engage in the kinds of activities that the former did. In a sense, each was out on the streets because the others were and all saw an opportunity to register their objections.[128]

The opposition was threatening not only because it was widespread, but also because it was organized. During the unrest, identical anti-regime pamphlets appeared simultaneously throughout the country; there were systematic attempts to cut internal communication, and there were apparently coordinated attacks on neighboring police stations, making it difficult for troops to support each other. Moreover, opposition forces had used their papers and links with the unions and student movements to mobilize the demonstrators. The NPUP appeared particularly threatening. It gained thousands of supporters, especially given its links with the unions, and mounted virulent attacks on Sadat's economic and foreign policies.[129] The government accused the party of instigating the 1977 bread riots, although the NPUP denied responsibility for the violence. Moreover, it was clear that the NPUP was not alone.[130] The government was clearly aware that it faced opposition, but the riots had demonstrated, to its apparent surprise, that there were many groups – on both the left and the right – that were willing to act.[131]

Despite the government's claims of leftist and foreign conspiracies, critics continued to point fingers at the government's policies as the primary cause of the riots. *Ruz al-Yusuf*, in a particularly pointed statement given Sadat's turn toward the west, stated that the U.S. Central Intelligence Agency was more likely to have been responsible for the riots than the Communists.[132] Speaking from the left, Assembly member Khalid Muhyi al-Din argued that hard economic times had led to unrest. From the right, Kemal al-Din Husayn – a parliamentary representative and an original Free Officer – charged that government policy, bungling, and stupidity had caused the riots, and he was promptly removed.[133] Even establishment papers such as *al-Iqtisadi* suggested that economic problems were severe and were the fundamental cause of the unrest.

Opposition forces demanded significant political reform. In a period of heightened discontent and with the absence of any significant integration into the regime, they were willing to mobilize in concert. The inclusion of opposition parties into the system was so limited, and so easily reversed, that political opposition elites increasingly turned to mobilizing forces outside the formal parties to make their demands.[134] As Hinnebusch notes:

on many basic issues, Sadat would not even permit the expression of opposition demands, much less accommodate them. Thus to a great extent, the opposition forces seemed increasingly to turn into counter-elites, trying covertly to build popular support at the expense of the regime, and, occasionally, resorting to "anomic" interest articulation – protests, demonstrations and, more rarely but especially on the part of Islamic groups, violence.[135]

There was no great love lost among many of these groups with their "historical rivalries and incompatible objectives."[136] But, in the absence of the integration of any of these forces into the regime, they increasingly formed an anti-regime front.

By February 1977, the regime had reversed its tentative liberalization. The government immediately established a platform and put it to the public in a referendum. Claiming 99 percent support, the government thereby established an eight-point program:

1. Conditions for forming parties would be governed by a new law from the Assembly.
2. Membership in clandestine or hostile organizations was punishable by up to life in prison.
3. Demonstrations intending sabotage or attacks on property were punishable by up to life in prison.
4. The payment of taxes was "a duty," and the limit for tax exemption was raised.
5. Registration of all personal wealth was required, and the failure to do so was penalized by the loss of political rights.
6. Rioters and the instigators of public disruptions – or those who disrupted the government, the public or private sector, or education, or who threatened to use violence – were potentially subject to penal servitude.
7. Workers using strikes that might harm the Egyptian economy would be subject to penal servitude.
8. Demonstrations that threatened public security would be punishable by penal servitude.[137]

In May, Sadat decided to put down NPUP opposition. He labeled all Communist and Nasirist opposition "haters"; he held a referendum aimed at banning "Communists" and "unbelievers" from political activity and barred them from obtaining public employment; and he gave a speech in which he told NPUP members, "You have no place among us." When the NPUP refused to disband, Sadat did not force its dissolution, but he did try to undermine it. He banned the party paper, forbade public meetings, repressed members, and encouraged the formation of the Socialist Labor Party (SLP) to counter its strength.[138]

At the same time, Sadat vowed to move quickly to resolve the Egyptian–Israeli conflict in an effort to secure aid and stabilize the economy.[139] According to Hasan al-Tohami – a friend of Sadat – the January uprising had convinced Sadat that if he did not reach a settlement with the Israelis soon, the future of his regime was in question. Yet, both the immediate restrictions set forth in the eight-point program and Sadat's decision to go to Jerusalem only fostered the collision between Sadat and his opponents.

Even before Sadat's November trip, the confrontation between the regime and Islamist militants had escalated. In July, militant Islamists from al-Takfir wa al-Hijrah kidnapped a former Minister of Religious Affairs in the hope of obtaining their comrades' release from prison. They threatened to kill him, and when the government refused to meet their demands, they did so. Violence followed. A series of crackdowns and shootouts left dead and wounded throughout the country, and the government arrested the group's top leaders and more than 600 of its members.[140] The government had shrugged off the Islamist participation in the January 1977 riots, maintaining the charade that Sadat – the "Believer President" – was firmly supported by Egyptian Islamists.[141] By summer, however, this was no longer possible.[142]

Regulations that followed sought to control the full political spectrum. New regulations essentially outlawed the Muslim Brotherhood and Nasirists, provided for tight control over the introduction of new parties, and allowed the regime to freeze the activities or resources of existing parties at will.[143] In short, Sadat liberalized, but he attempted to confine parties to a small set that would be "constructive," meaning in particular that they would refrain from attacking Sadat's foreign or economic policies. When they crossed these boundaries, as the NPUP and the liberal–right New Wafd Party did in 1978, they were effectively banned. In addition, Law No. 33 of 1978, which stripped individuals who "contributed to the corruption of political life before the July revolution" of all political rights, including the rights to vote and run for office, made it nearly impossible for the old Wafd Party to revive.[144] Indeed, by 1981, the regime tolerated only three parties – the government's NDP (the successor to the ASU) and two "loyal" opposition parties with leaders close to the regime, the Liberal Party from the center–right platform of the ASU and the Socialist Labour Party (SLP), which was created in 1978 as an alternative to the NPUP.[145]

Decrees in 1979[146] and 1980[147] further restrained the opposition. In particular, the "Law of Shame" (Law 95 of 1980), supported by the "Court of Ethics," provided a means for the regime to repress opponents. Purportedly charged with protecting "values from shame," the Court could pass judgments and impose sanctions, such as the suspension of civil and political rights, expellation from Egypt, or the sequestration of property.[148] Even members of the three legal parties feared to voice any criticisms up to the point where the majority of their members had defected. Finally, the month before the assassination, security forces arrested more than 1,500 government opponents and dismissed some professors and journalists from their jobs. At this time, Sadat warned that he had a list of 7,000 additional suspects.[149]

Thus, Sadat took measures toward liberalization, but because participation in the system was so limited for all opponents, he did not effectively
divide the opposition. Indeed, attacks continued, demands increased,
and room for maneuver within the formal political system was further
restricted.[150] Those arrested the month before the assassination represented nearly every political force, from Islamists to Marxists.[151] Within
the formal system, the three parties had become mere skeletons in which
even their members feared to participate. Political opponents, suffocating
under the current system, feared the states' actions, but they did not fear
each other. As in Jordan, the expectation that groups with very different
ideological stances might exploit instability to make their own demands
did not serve to restrain opponents.

It is important to note, before turning to the case of Egypt under
Mubarak, that the willingness of Islamists and secularist leftists to come
together on the streets of Cairo to demand reforms was not due to
the absence of an "Islamist threat." Al-Daʿwa, linked to the more moderate Muslim Brotherhood, proclaimed communism, secularism, Jewry,
and the Crusade to be the "four evils." More militant Islamists in al-
Jihad went beyond this, arguing that Christians and Jews were infidels
and thus legitimate targets of *jihad*. Moreover, the time for a peaceful
jihad had passed; the time had come for a violent struggle against Christians (particularly Egypt's Coptic population).[152] Such sentiments could
only frighten many Egyptians.

Moreover, Islamists were strong, and they demonstrated this through
both peaceful and violent means. By the late 1970s Islamists had gained
leadership positions at all levels in the student movement, prompting
Sadat to try to reassert control over the unions and return University
Guards to their campuses.[153] Sectarian violence had occurred in the
Minya village of Jad al-Sayyid in 1980 and in Cairo's al-Zaʿwiya al-
Hamrah neighborhood in 1981, presumably heightening the suspicion of
Islamists,[154] and Sadat had done his best to blur the distinction between
militant Islamists and the Muslim Brotherhood by suggesting that Takfir
wa al-Hijrah was the militant arm of the Brotherhood. Finally, in the aftermath of the 1979 Iranian revolution, Islamists demonstrated in support
of the revolutionaries,[155] and their confidence reached new heights. Saad
Eddin Ibrahim noted that the morale of the Military Academy and Takfir
wa al-Hijrah members he interviewed in 1979 was "soaring, boosted by
the initial success of the revolution in Iran."[156] Secularists viewing the
events in Iran during 1981 had as much reason to fear Islamists as they
did to fear them when reflecting on the Algerian crisis of the 1990s.

The opposition groups joined in pressuring the government because they were all equally repressed in the unified SoC. Hamied Ansari explains:

When he was finally convinced to act, Sadat made the fatal mistake of treating all the opposition as one monolithic entity bent upon destroying the regime. Sadat himself announced in the wake of the crackdown in September that there was no difference between the Muslim Brotherhood and the militant jama'at [Islamist groups]. Indeed . . . he said that the militant fraternities were the military arm of the Muslim Brotherhood. Sadat also made the serious mistake of treating the secular and religious opposition to his regime on [an] equal footing.[157]

Meiring concurs:

As one of Sadat's major opponents was to say when I interviewed him, Gallup Poll experts could not have done a better job. He had taken in top men from every conceivable nuance of political opinion other than his own. He had clamped the lid down on the whole wide range of political opposition, so that someone from in there was almost certain to blast it off; maybe it did not matter just who.[158]

CONCLUSION

In the unified SoC, political opponents become more willing to challenge incumbent elites as crises continue and the likelihood of success increases. Such was the case in Jordan and in Egypt under Nasir and Sadat. Although not examined here, it was also the case in Iran during the 1970s. Despite important differences among, and even competition between, opposition elites, they remained willing to mobilize and demand reforms. In return, the government either stepped up repression, as in Jordan, lost control, as in Egypt, or saw a total change of regime.

5

Opposition Dynamics in Divided SoCs

Divided SoCs foster very different dynamics of opposition during prolonged crises than do unified SoCs. In the divided system, legal opposition groups commit themselves to maintaining the stability of the regime, and incumbents punish them severely if they break this agreement. Thus, legal opposition groups are given an opportunity to express their political demands, but they are penalized if they mobilize "unruly" demonstrations. Thus, for them, the costs of joint conflict with excluded opponents are greater than those of isolated conflict. By contrast, as discussed in Chapter 3, illegal groups face lower sanctions if they mobilize in conjunction with legal opponents than they do if they act independently.

Consequently, the level and nature of the opposition to the regime varies over the course of prolonged crises. Because legal opponents have organizational structures and government acceptance that lower the costs of mobilizing an isolated protest, they are often able to exploit the early stages of crises to press their demands.[1] As the crises continue, however, the more radical, excluded opponents gain strength. Initially, this makes radical elites more likely to join an ongoing protest even if they are unwilling to mobilize independently. This, however, threatens the moderates – who face greater repression for destabilizing the system. As the crisis mounts and popular dissatisfaction increases, legal parties often choose to sit it out, reducing their challenges against the regime. In a divided SoC, opponents that have previously mobilized popular movements thus may become unwilling to challenge incumbents as crises continue, *even if their demands have not been met.*

To see more clearly why this is the case, this chapter extends the model presented in the previous two chapters to examine how the cost structures in a divided SoC affect opposition–government dynamics. It then applies these hypotheses to the cases of Morocco and Egypt during the late 1980s and early 1990s. In both cases, as the crises escalated in the mid-1990s, legal opposition elites became less willing to mobilize the masses in demanding reforms even as their capabilities increased.

OPPOSITION–GOVERNMENT INTERACTIONS IN A DIVIDED SoC

The dynamics of opposition found in the divided SoC are due to the different costs that legal and illegal opposition groups face in mobilizing unrest. For included opponents, the costs of Isolated Conflict are less than the costs of Joint Conflict with the illegal opposition. In contrast, for excluded elites, the costs of Joint Conflict are less than the costs of Isolated Conflict; thus, the expected utility of Joint Conflict becomes greater than the Status Quo before the expected utility of an Isolated Conflict does. As crises continue and the probability of success increases, radicals come to prefer Joint Conflict to the Status Quo but the Status Quo to Isolated Conflict. Later, they may come to prefer Isolated Conflict to the Status Quo, as was the case in Egypt. However, given high enough costs of mobilization, this need not be the case.

Table 5.1 demonstrates why moderate opponents may become unwilling to challenge incumbent elites as the probability of a joint conflict increases in the divided political environment. As in Table 4.2, the moderates' strategies move from left to right and those of the radicals' move from top to bottom as their probability of success increases. Initially, both included and excluded elites prefer the Status Quo to any conflict. However, as their probabilities of success increase, they both become more likely to prefer some form of conflict to the Status Quo. Because β and θ are greater than 1 in the divided SoC, moderates first come to prefer Isolated Conflict to the Status Quo, and later they may come to prefer Joint Conflict to the Status Quo. Excluded elites, however, come first to prefer Joint Conflict to no Conflict, and then later, as the probability of success continues to increase, they may come to prefer Isolated Conflict to the Status Quo. The greater the magnitudes of β and θ, the more likely that moderates who are willing to mobilize when radicals will not join become unwilling to do so as crises continue.

The outcomes of the model, given complete information, are shown in the corresponding cells of Table 5.1. As the probability of success increases, ceteris paribus, the expected utility of conflict increases. The

TABLE 5.1. *Dynamics of Protest in Divided SoCs*

Conditions for Radicals/ Moderates	$\pi_M < C_M$ (Moderates will not mobilize)	$\pi_M > C_M$ but $\pi_j < \beta C_M$ (Moderates will mobilize but only alone)	$\pi_M > \beta C_M$ (Moderates will mobilize jointly or alone)
$\pi_j|P_r| < C_R$ (Radicals will not mobilize)	Status Quo	Moderate Conflict	Moderate Conflict
$\pi_j|P_r| > C_R$ but $\pi_R|P_R| < \theta C_R$ (Radicals will mobilize jointly but not alone)	Status Quo	Status Quo	Joint Conflict
$\pi_R|P_r| > \theta C_R$ (Radicals will mobilize jointly or alone)	Radical Conflict	Radical Conflict	Joint Conflict

Note: Arrows show the direction of changing preferences as the probability of success increases.

moderates, will come to prefer Isolated Conflict to Joint Conflict if $\beta > 1$. They will continue to mobilize if they do not expect that the radicals will join in the conflict (i.e., as long as they believe that $\pi_j|P_R| < C_R$ for the radicals). However, as the radicals' probability of success increases, this condition becomes less likely. In this case, when moderates come to believe that the radicals will join if they mobilize, they may become unwilling to mobilize. As shown in Table 5.1, the equilibrium may move from the Status Quo (upper left corner) to Moderate Conflict (upper middle) and back to the Status Quo (middle second row). The greater the value of β and the smaller the difference between the probability of success if moderates mobilize independently versus jointly (i.e., the smaller π_R), the more likely that moderates become unwilling to mobilize when radicals will join in the conflict, even if they were willing to mobilize previously.[2] Thus, in the divided SoC, incumbent elites have an incentive to maximize the difference between the moderates' expected repression for Isolated and Joint Conflict. To do so, incumbents allow moderates to mobilize Isolated Conflicts with little repression while at the same time heavily repressing moderates who mobilize an exploited conflict. Consequently:

> In the divided SoC, moderates who previously challenged incumbent elites may choose not to do so when radical groups enter, even if incumbents have not accommodated their own demands. The larger the difference between the costs of mobilizing alone and jointly for both sides (i.e., the greater β and θ, when both are >1), the more likely that moderates will be deterred from mobilizing by the prospects of radicals joining.

This helps to explain why included opponents in Morocco and Egypt became less willing to challenge the regime as the crisis continued in the 1990s. In Morocco, the King created incentives for the included opponents to refrain from promoting a Joint Conflict. Thus, the legal opposition elites became more conciliatory as the radical elites became stronger and the likelihood that they would exploit unrest increased. Similar dynamics appeared in Egypt under Mubarak.

PALACE–OPPOSITION DYNAMICS IN MOROCCO

Challenge in the Nonexplosive Environment: The Early 1980s

In Morocco, the early economic crisis provided the legal opposition with an opportunity to demand the palace's attention. The economic crisis in 1981 intensified public dissatisfaction, increasing the probability that the opposition would successfully mobilize the populace to make demands. The year was particularly difficult. Drought cut cereal production nearly in half; people flooded into the cities from rural areas hoping to find work; and the cost of living rose quickly. Throughout the first part of the year, the opposition called a series of sectoral strikes, directed sharp criticism at the government, and highlighted the precarious situation in its papers. On April 1st, the government raised the minimum wages of industrial and agricultural workers and granted some social benefits to the agricultural sector. On May 28th, however, the government also raised prices on basic commodities between 14 and 77 percent.[3]

Opposition parties used the increased discontent to demand both economic and political changes. Although the government was willing to make some economic concessions, it rejected the political demands. Furthermore, it made clear that it was unwilling to engage in dialogue with the CDT. Instead, it allowed the Moroccan Labor Union (UMT), Morocco's oldest and largest union, which tended to be pro-government, to call a general strike on June 18th, while it prohibited the CDT from calling a similar demonstration. These decisions appeared to many to be an attempt to defuse the heightened popular hostility while containing the CDT,[4] but the attempt clearly failed.

The CDT called for a second nationwide general strike on June 20th. The strike was intended both to help remedy the economic situation and to knock loud and hard at the door of power. Not all in the party were agreed on the strike, but the majority could not ignore the economic predicament or the palace's intransigence.[5] The crisis gave them an opportunity to force the government to take account of the party and the union, making headway toward more institutional changes. Held on a Saturday and at a national level, the strike clearly challenged the government's ability to maintain control. An energized, angry populace considered this to be "their strike," and in quarters of Casablanca and Mohamedia the young and unemployed took to the streets in demonstrations and riots. They shouted slogans against the King, burned vehicles, and looted or demolished stores, gas stations, pharmacies, banks, and government buildings. The state's reaction was swift and firm. Armed forces entered, and by the end of June 22nd, many people were dead.[6] The police arrested thousands of rioters and demonstrators, suspended party newspapers, and jailed leaders of the opposition parties.[7]

Despite the repression, the socialist opposition continued its demands. On June 23rd, the parliamentary opposition accused the government of using "brutal violence" to put down the demonstrations and called for a parliamentary inquiry into the response.[8] Even the Istiqlal, participating in government at the time, said, "One can only regret the absence of dialogue between the government and the trade unions that could have permitted a direct and frank discussion."[9] Both the government and the opposition understood the high potential for violence, and the palace made economic concessions and took steps to increase its security. On July 9th, the King denounced the instigators of the riots and, blaming the CDT's abuse of the economic problems, announced the division of Casablanca into five administrative districts to strengthen local control.[10] Slowly, as the 1983 elections approached, the King also dangled the hope of greater political inclusion in front of the opposition, leading party members to expect future concessions if they avoided repeating the 1981 strikes.

Importantly, political contestation in the early 1980s remained primarily between the King and the parties. True, the masses had exploited the opportunity provided by the national strike and the overextended security forces to express their frustration. However, no other political opponents appeared to have mobilized in concert with the strikes. No other opposition groups were strong enough to press additional demands. In a nonexplosive political environment, then, the opposition took advantage of the lower mobilization costs accompanying the economic crisis to push its demands. This is the outcome that much of the literature on economic crises and reform would predict.

Morocco in the Mid-1980s: The Strengthening of Radical Opposition Groups

However, as the economic crisis continued, more radical Islamist opposition groups gained popular support. The costs of living continued to rise, particularly after the crisis of 1983. The prices of sugar, oil, and flour increased 30, 52, and 87 percent, respectively, between 1982 and 1985. The average cost of living grew 12.5 percent in 1984 alone, compared to 10.5 percent in 1982 and 6.2 percent in 1983.[11] Religious organizations distributed spiritual and physical resources to persons in need, thus strengthening their popular base. In contrast, the USFP and other legal opposition elites were unwilling to press demands, and their failure to address the economic crisis increased popular dissatisfaction with both the parties and the palace. As we would expect in a divided SoC, popular support for radical opponents increased faster than popular support for included opposition elites.

Two factors account for the legal opposition elites' failure to rally the workers in the mid-1980s. First, they remembered well the results of the 1981 general strike and had little desire to repeat the them. Second, the opposition had recently joined in the government in preparation for new elections, with the party leader ʿAbd al-Rahim Buʿabid assuming the portfolio of Minister of State. The Kingdom had held local elections in 1983, with pro-palace parties winning a significant victory and opposition parties calling "foul."[12] The opposition parties were in a difficult position. They wanted to mobilize the masses against the price increases, and yet they saw the upcoming elections as an opportunity to gain influence and were afraid to sacrifice this chance through confrontation with the King. Thus, they made angry statements against the adjustment policy and denounced rising prices, but they chose not to mobilize a general strike.[13]

Nevertheless, in January 1984, violent demonstrations and protests spread throughout the country. In December 1983, the government had reduced subsidies on basic commodities, increasing prices by 67 percent on butter, 33 percent on cooking oil, and 16 percent on lump sugar. In early January 1984, when the King announced more increases on petroleum products and rumors spread that the government was prepared to increase school fees as well, students took to the streets. Throughout January, they were joined by groups from other classes in approximately 50 cities across the country. Serious demonstrations took place in al-Hoceima, Nador, and Tetouan in the north between January 11th and January 21st.[14] At this time, nearly one-half of the 25,000-plus security force was located around Casablanca, where the Islamic Summit Conference was being held. Rioters took advantage of the lack of security in outlying areas, destroying property and looting government buildings. They also protested symbolically, shouting slogans against the King and carrying pink parasols to mimic the wealth they saw squandered by the palace and the government.[15] Security forces were regrouped and sent to restore order, and the penalties were harsh. On January 22nd, the King appeared on television, promising not to raise prices on staple goods such as bread, cooking oil, and sugar, which only weeks earlier he had argued was inevitable.[16] By January 23rd, all was quiet, but an estimated 100 persons had been killed. Among those arrested and prosecuted were many USFP members, but the party did not react.

While the activity in 1984 resembled the 1981 strikes, it was far more significant. Unlike the riots of 1981, these demonstrations began without the fanfare of negotiations and discussions between the unions and the government. The opposition parties' statements may have contributed to the rising public opposition, but the parties had not called a strike. The 1984 rioting lacked a clearly defined leadership and certainly a leadership in officially recognized channels. This was evident in the speech from the throne on July 7th. The King, waving a picture of Khomeini and tracts from the illegal opposition group Ila al-Amam, blamed Communists, Marxists, Leninists, and Islamists for the unrest. Yet, at the same time, he arrested a large number of activists from the legal opposition parties.[17] At a minimum, it was clear that the unrest extended beyond the control of the legal opposition parties. There was massive frustration strengthening social forces outside the official channels of power. Radical opponents had become capable of challenging the government, and they would do so when the costs of mobilization appeared very low.

The palace's first response was to threaten a new period of repression. In the same televised speech, the King reminded the people of the north that he had personally repressed revolts there when still crown prince. He warned that those who knew him as crown prince also knew what to expect from King Hasan.[18] He stepped up a campaign against hoarders and illegal traders[19] and took new measures to weaken the Islamist opposition. Shortly after the riots, the courts handed down long sentences on a group of Islamist activists. Although these activists had been arrested before the riots, the harsh sentences were said to reflect the palace's increasing fear of Islamists and to forewarn such groups against any future actions.[20]

Morocco's Opposition–Palace Interaction in an Explosive Environment

After 1984, it became clear to both the opposition and the palace that radical opposition groups could take advantage of public dissatisfaction to make demands that neither the palace nor the majority of the party leadership would like. The political environment had become explosive. Rather than considering the potential outcomes of conflicts solely between the palace and the parties, both sides began to consider the potential outcomes of conflicts that could be exploited by radical opposition elites. In this case, we would expect moderate elites to become unwilling to challenge the government if the costs of Joint Conflict are much greater than those of Isolated Conflict or if moderate elites expect that radicals will not mobilize independently.

The King took the offensive after the 1984 riots. Part of his strategy involved a change in foreign policy: the abrupt announcement of a union with Libya, Hasan's long-time foe, which was intended to raise popular support and to obtain economic benefits through low-cost access to Libyan oil that could stave off further unrest.[21] On the domestic front, Hasan II tried to increase his religious appeal by appointing a new, young Minister of Islamic Affairs and launching a campaign to strengthen his religious legitimacy.[22] He also tightened his control over various social sectors. In 1988, the palace also began creating or strengthening non-religious associations in each of the larger cities.[23] These associations were headed by important persons close to the King, supported by palace grants, and intended to stimulate and direct social, cultural, and economic events and projects that could not be undertaken by local communities. With their financial means and personal influence, they sought to ease economic problems as well as to fill the spaces of independent association. By giving individuals an alternative, and politically safe, venue to participate in the system, the associations eased popular pressure and made it more difficult for illegal opposition groups to operate.

In addition, the palace reinforced the role of the political parties. As Zartman notes:

After the 1981 and 1984 riots, the King required all candidates in the September 1984 elections to be members of a party. Henceforth, opposition was to be organized and organizations were to be responsible, thereby enlisting them in the government's job of control. With a common interest in avoiding anomie, government and unions bargain over demands in support of the polity.[24]

Initially, the legal opposition developed a fairly cooperative relationship with the King in the hope that this new partnership would lead to expanding political power. In part, this was surprising because the mid-1980s did not bring the increasing access to power that opposition elites had anticipated. During the 1984 elections, the nationalist parties, including the Istiqlal Party, had lost parliamentary seats to the Constitutional Union (UC), which formed one week before the local elections at the encouragement of the King.[25] At the same time, however, the parties suffered from their own internal weaknesses. The most obvious crisis existed within the USFP. With the decline of the USSR and the fall of the Berlin Wall, the appeal of socialism had diminished rapidly. The USFP thus lost the bases of its socialist alternatives to the economic reform programs. Consequently, the party continued to challenge the government through the media and in parliament, but its demands shifted quietly from strong, direct criticism of the plan as a whole to critiques of its implementation. Responding to popular demands, the unions still called for sectoral or regional strikes, but they refrained from calling the more disruptive and politically important general strikes.

Although the parties cooperated with the monarch, the opposition leaders still expected and demanded some political gains. At the end of the 1980s, some party leaders believed that without putting direct popular pressure on the King, they would remain in an unacceptably stifling political situation. The relationships between Prime Minister 'Izz al-Din Laraki and the opposition's union leaders were hostile. The leaders looked forward to new elections and a change in the government. Then, in 1989, the King asked the opposition parties to support a postponement of the elections for two years, giving time for the situation in the Western Sahara to improve. The USFP agreed, but only after intense internal debate and the promise of political concessions. When early 1990 failed to bring the promised political and economic changes, union-tied USFP leaders began to rally for a general strike.

With Morocco suffering from drought and an increasing economic crisis, the opposition pressured the government for political and economic change. By April 1990, the CDT called for a general strike. However, other opposition parties refused to join.[26] Consequently, the union leaders postponed the strike. A stalemate lasted until December, during which time debates within the parties and discussions between the CDT and the UGTM led to a decision to call a jointly sponsored strike. On December 14, 1990, the second general strike was called. The government circulated announcements warning public servants against participating. Security was tightened, particularly in Casablanca and Rabat, but this left other areas unprotected. In Fez, witnesses reported that security forces were spread throughout the city in the early morning as a show of force, but by early afternoon they had been rounded up and taken to the large coastal cities. Everything remained under control in Rabat and Casablanca, but parts of Fez went up in flames.

The violence of 1990 in Fez mirrored the earlier troubles. People from the shantytowns flooded into upper-class areas, pillaging and destroying signs of wealth. The police responded fiercely; death and arrest counts were high; and in the end, the government and the unions blamed each other for the devastation.[27] The real lesson for the palace was profound, however. In the current atmosphere, it was impossible to contain nation-wide popular strikes. Unlike 1981, when the level of discontent may have surprised both sides, or 1984, when the government was caught off guard with its security forces concentrated in Casablanca, the danger of the 1990 strike was well understood. The palace had ample time to prepare for the strike, and both opposition and government officials had expected it would remain under control.[28] The 1990 violence thus showed that even with adequate advance warning, the palace was unable to control all parts of Morocco at once. It had become clear that it was dangerous if the opposition used the streets to put pressure on the government.

At this time, the palace and the included opposition began to modify their positions, avoiding another unstable confrontation that radical opponents might exploit. Thus, the palace began to develop a more cooperative relationship with the opposition parties. The King formalized social pact negotiations with the major unions (the UMT, the UGTM, and the CDT) and set up advisory councils with opposition participation (e.g., the National Council of the Youth and the Future [CNJA]),[29] headed by USFP leader Habib al-Malki). The palace allowed the opposition to express its discontent with Morocco's position in the Gulf War through a well-organized, segmented demonstration in Rabat. Finally, in the throne speech of 1992, the King announced plans to revise the Constitution.

The opposition parties tried to exploit this political opening by organizing to press their demands. They formed the "Bloc," or Kutla, two months after the King's announcement. Composed of the Istiqlal, USFP,

UNFP, PPS, and OADP parties, the Bloc was intended to increase the opposition's bargaining power in the debate over constitutional revisions. Furthermore, by presenting a single candidate in each district, these parties expected to improve election results. Coordination faded quickly, however. The PPS alone supported the revised Constitution, and the idea of presenting a shared slate of candidates dissolved in disagreements over each party's relative power. Finally, only the Istiqlal and USFP parties presented a single slate.

The oppositions' demands were far from met. In campaigning for the upcoming elections, the parties continued to call for political reforms.[30] Furthermore, while the direct elections were a success for the opposition parties, the indirect elections were disappointing. In reasonably fair direct elections, the USFP, OADP, PPS, and Istiqlal parties won 100 of the 222 seats available. The Minister of Interior then allegedly stepped in to reverse this success. In the indirect elections, the nationalist parties and their associated unions won only 22 of 111 seats. The nationalist parties remained the parliamentary minority,[31] and they quickly and loudly called "foul."[32]

Nevertheless, King Hasan II wanted to draw the opposition closer to the palace. On October 8, 1993, he invited the opposition parties to join the government,[33] a move that would have implicated them in the government's policies and made it difficult for them to mobilize popular opposition to the government.[34] The following month, he announced that he had met with four leaders of the Bloc. He offered them cabinet ministries, with the exception of the portfolios of Justice, Interior, Foreign Affairs, Islamic Affairs, and Prime Minister. Through a series of negotiations, these exceptions were reduced to the Ministry of Interior and the Ministry of Islamic Affairs. The majority of opposition members refused these conditions, arguing that no real political change was possible as long as the current Minister of Interior remained in office.[35]

Although the King allowed the parties to refuse to participate in the government, he was unwilling to allow them to mobilize popular opposition to press additional demands. The postponed general strike of 1994 demonstrated this. In February 1994, the CDT called for a general strike, but the UGTM, the UMT, and the opposition parties were unwilling to agree. A UGTM leader explained, "we could smell trouble in the air." The prolonged economic crisis raised the level of frustration, and combined with Ramadan fasting, they feared a general strike would become an uncontrollable situation.[36] Instead, these parties offered to join the CDT publicly in a strike if the palace took an intransigent stance on the oppositions' demands. More significantly, the King announced that a general strike would be illegal. The argument was based on Article 14 of the Constitution, which said that a (yet undrafted) law would outline when strikes were legal. In the law's absence, the King argued, the palace had the right to declare the planned strike illegal. He did so, making it clear that if the CDT persisted in mobilizing opposition, the repercussions would be harsh.

However, if the unions cooperated, the King was willing to negotiate with them. Within 24 hours of the deadline, the CDT decided to delay the strike indefinitely. Consequently, the King responded publicly and directly to the union's demands in his throne speech of March 3rd.[37] Furthermore, on March 22nd the palace resumed social dialogue and promised the creation of an advisory council on economic and social problems. The King's wariness of a national general strike that could be exploited by unruly masses and more radical opposition meant that he was willing to negotiate with the opposition. The union leaders hoped that significant political concessions would be forthcoming.

By the mid-1990s, however, the opposition parties were leery of mobilizing the masses to push their demands. On the one hand, they faced increased internal difficulties. The potential ascendancy to power had split apart the Bloc and exacerbated serious schisms within each of the opposition parties. The cooperation between the Bloc parties slowly dwindled, with disagreements over the acceptance of the Constitution and the distribution of candidates in the upcoming elections. Still technically composed of all five parties, it had come to denote the incomplete, tenuous, and disintegrating cooperation of three: the USFP, the Istiqlal, and the OADP. Within each of the opposition parties, the question of whether or not to join the government under the given conditions has created vicious debate. The year 1994–1995 witnessed major changes in the OADP leadership, explosions within the USFP, and, for the first time, a fervently divisive congress for the PPS.[38] Although the Istiqlal Party appeared to have suffered less dramatic consequences, its leadership was nevertheless forced to check itself. The Central Committee, unanimously prepared to accept the King's offer, was surprised when the party membership was equally set against it. The chance to participate in the government, coupled with widespread fear of using popular mobilization to press further demands, divided the opposition parties.

More importantly, many included opposition elites had come to fear the demands and dissatisfaction of the masses themselves. This was evident during the train strike of 1995. Shortly before Eid al-Idha, train workers undertook a nationwide strike. Their dissatisfaction had been mounting, and at last the three major unions (the UMT, CDT, and UGTM) announced an indefinite strike. Union leaders expected the work stoppage to be relatively short, three to four days at most. Union members were prepared for a much longer, harsher struggle. For nearly one month, CDT leader Nubir Amaoui worked to end the strike. He was concerned that a prolonged struggle would lead to violence within the sector and that it could spread to, and be exploited by, other groups. Undoubtedly, this could result in repression of the union and the party. Within the party, it could also exacerbate already high tensions. Despite his concerns and his popularity as a union and party leader, the strike continued for 28 days, ending on June 6, 1995.[39]

The strike won the unions some of their demands,[40] but it weakened the USFP and CDT. It demonstrated the extent to which the legal opposition feared an uncontrollable mass movement. USFP elites clearly preferred backing down to escalating the palace–opposition conflict. The train strikes also exhibited the opposition's loss of control over the masses. Although they may have been able to mobilize people to go into the streets to press their demands, it was not clear that the opposition had the power to send them back to their houses. This was a major problem for the unions and the parties. Loss of control over popular forces would make them less valuable to the government as a partner in maintaining political stability.

The decision not to encourage strikes came despite the existence of serious opposition demands. The opposition parties had just experienced a difficult and frustrating series of negotiations with the government. Hoping to entice the opposition parties to join the government, the King had offered them portfolios after the 1994 elections. Yet, although Hasan II appointed 'Abd al-Latif al-Filali, who had good relations with the opposition, to head the new cabinet, he failed to achieve the opposition parties' cooperation. The sticking point was the removal of the Minister of Interior, Driss Basri.[41] While the opposition parties demanded that the heavy-handed Interior Minister leave his position, the King argued that to do so would "dangerously affect the good running of the sacred institutions."[42] After nearly one month of negotiations, on February 27th, al-Filali formed a 35-member cabinet of traditional loyalists.[43] The oppositions' demands were unmet. They continued to call for fair and impartial elections, with a distribution of government seats including the opposition.[44]

Ironically, the union's decision to thwart the strikes came despite a less repressive tone from the government. In contrast to the discussion of a general strike in 1994, when the palace prohibited mobilization, the palace took a less threatening tone. It argued publicly that the strikes would hurt the economy, particularly during the Eid, but it did not overtly repress the opposition.[45] It did not need to do so.

Rather, checking the opposition was their fear that the Islamist opposition could use disorder as a springboard for mounting a struggle to gain its own demands. The Islamist opposition in Morocco remained fragmented, but it was getting stronger every day.[46] Throughout the economic crisis, Islamists strengthened their ties with the people by providing social support services that the masses desperately needed. Moreover, the Islamists capitalized on the large, disgruntled segment of Morocco's population that felt that neither the government nor the legal opposition represented their interests. In contrast, the opposition parties had proven themselves unable to improve the economic situation and had focused on political debates in which the majority of Moroccans had little interest. Party members who competed with the Islamist groups in recruitment on college campuses and in city quarters were well aware of the Islamists' comparative strength.[47] Islamist activity on the campuses, and confrontations between Islamists and secularists, had become both more common and more violent. Islamists rioted at the University of Fez in February 1994, leaving five persons seriously injured.[48] In addition, Islamist groups had access to potentially dangerous resources, as the discovery of arms caches in and around Fez in the summer of 1994 demonstrated. Party leaders made some efforts to defuse the competition with the Islamists by drawing them into the party structure.[49] However, the division between the two camps was wide. Many Islamists viewed the party system as conservative and ineffective, and they rallied for a more radical departure from the status quo. Similarly, most opposition party elites considered the Islamists' agendas to be worse than the current system. Islamists' increasing strength, at the parties' expense, worried party elites. Legal opposition elites thus were unwilling to promote popular unrest, which could be harnessed by Islamist opposition elites to press their demands.

In addition, the parties feared increased repression if the situation exploded. Since 1990, the government appeared to have granted some concessions. The revision of the Constitution, public acknowledgment of the unions' demands following the proposed general strike in 1994, the removal of Prime Minister Mohammad Karim al-Lamrani, a long-time opponent of the unions, and the resumption of social dialogue were all small steps toward negotiation with the legal opposition elites. However, the palace also made it increasingly clear that it believed opposition attempts to mobilize the masses might be destabilizing, and this would not be tolerated. Included opponents knew that if they promoted unrest that challenged the fundamental political structure, they would pay very high costs. Party elites, who remembered the repression of the 1960s and the early 1970s under the then-current Minister of Interior, feared a return to the "Days of Basri."

The opposition parties were thus squeezed between two major threats: explosion from the bottom and repression from the top. Together, these threats narrowed the legal opposition's political space, limiting its willingness to use the prolonged economic crisis to demand political concessions. Legal opposition elites thus preferred to back down rather than to escalate conflicts with the palace.[50] As one Moroccan intellectual put it in 1995, "We look at Iraq, Algeria and Iran and know that we are much better off."[51]

DYNAMICS OF OPPOSITION UNDER MUBARAK

Regime–opposition relations during Mubarak's rule echoed those of Morocco but differed dramatically from those of the Nasir–Sadat period. Mubarak had fostered a divided SoC. In contrast to Sadat, he had allowed more opposition groups to participate in the formal system while simultaneously keeping important groups on the fringes. This turned the oppositions' attention to disputes over the finer rules of participation, and it increased their costs for destabilizing the regime. In the aftermath of Sadat's assassination, it was clear that there were strong, militant groups eager to demand political change, and from the outset, the existence of such groups tempered some of the included parties' demands. As the economic crisis continued and excluded radical groups – particularly the militant among them – became even stronger, the government made it exceedingly clear that parties would pay a high price if they facilitated such groups' actions. By the mid-1990s, even the legal party elites who in some ways supported the demands of excluded opponents found themselves less and less willing to challenge the government. Thus, although Egypt faced a desperate fight against the radicals, the moderates did not exploit the struggle to demand reforms; rather, fearing the radicals as well, they sided with the regime.

Egypt in the Early 1980s: The "Honeymoon Period"

In the early 1980s, Mubarak's presidency enjoyed favorable conditions. With increases in U.S. aid, oil revenues, and worker remittances from the

Gulf countries, Egypt's economy did well. Mubarak also implemented political reforms that improved relations between the government and the opposition. Fearing a return to the chaos that had preceded Sadat's assassination, both sides began "building bridges of good will."[52] Mubarak released political prisoners and lifted bans on opposition papers such as *al-Da'wa* and *al-Ahali*. He organized a National Conference on the Egyptian economy, inviting a diverse set of experts to join in the dialogue. He then held a series of 11 meetings with opposition leaders from October 1981 through December 1983. The NPUP, representing the left, rallied for the "correction" of Sadat's course, while on the right, the Wafd, which would win legal status in 1984, sought both economic and political liberalization.[53] It was a "honeymoon period" of dialogue and stability that contrasted starkly with the preceding years.

The mid-1980s thus saw important advances for the moderate opposition. Approaching the 1984 elections, opposition parties sought the abolition of Sadat's restrictive laws on political participation;[54] electoral reforms that would foster more proportional representation in the Assembly; free and fair elections; and competitive presidential elections. Some, but not all, of their demands were met in Law No. 114 of 1984 governing elections. The NDP still obtained 87 percent of the elected seats in the parliamentary elections, but the opposition won an unprecedented 13 percent. Importantly, it was a joint slate of Wafd and Muslim Brotherhood candidates that gained these seats. The regime refused to permit the Muslim Brotherhood formal admission to the system (a factor that had important consequences for opposition–government dynamics), but it allowed the Brotherhood to operate openly and contest the elections in conjunction with legal opposition parties. The Wafd, despite significant differences in ideology, had agreed to an alliance to take advantage of the Brotherhood's popular support. The regime also denied licenses to human rights organizations such as the Arab and Egyptian human rights organizations, but it allowed them to conduct their activities with a fairly high profile.[55]

The opposition made significant gains, but it was still dissatisfied. The Liberal, Action, and NPUP parties ran in the elections but failed to meet the high 8 percent national threshold required to obtain seats. Furthermore, opposition parties – particularly the NPUP – complained of electoral fraud. They once again rallied for reforms that would assure free and fair elections and reduce the NDP's dominance, and an independent lawyer, Kamel Khalid, took a case to the Supreme Court, declaring the exclusion of independent candidates in the electoral law to be unconstitutional.[56] When the Supreme Court issued an initial statement in his favor in January 1987, the opposition announced a rally to be held on February 5th, calling to abrogate the 1984 electoral rule, dissolve parliament, and conduct new elections. The government preempted them, however, with an announcement on February 4th of a referendum to dissolve parliament. One week later, they prepared a new electoral law, which allowed independents to run for 10 percent of the seats in the parliamentary elections. However, the government also stipulated that independent candidates had to win at least 20 percent of the vote to obtain seats, thus requiring a run-off election when this was not achieved in the first round. The condition favored independents with strong financial backing – and most probably connected to the NDP.[57]

The opposition parties were dissatisfied with these developments, which had not only completely excluded them from negotiations over new rules but had also taken only small steps toward rectifying what the opposition believed were major problems. Nevertheless, they chose to run. The government once again allowed the Muslim Brotherhood to participate in the April parliamentary elections, this time in an alliance with the Action Party and the Socialist Labor Party (SLP) under the slogan "Islam is the solution."[58] However, the results were not entirely satisfying for any party: the NDP gained 77 percent of the seats, while the Islamic alliance gained 14 percent of the seats and the Wafd obtained 9 percent.[59] The opposition parties continued to hold too few seats to challenge the ruling NDP, and the outcome of any parliamentary debate would be a foregone conclusion. In addition, the electoral rules had indeed favored NDP-backed independent candidates, who won 92 percent of the seats reserved for independents, including all nine that required a run-off election.[60] At the same time, from the incumbents' point of view, the elections were too close for comfort. The increasingly strong showing of the parties connected with the Muslim Brotherhood was unsettling. Moreover, the low turnout rate (approximately 25 percent of eligible Egyptians) and the high rate of invalid ballots, coupled with concurrent violence – some of which was instigated by radical excluded opposition groups – suggested that a large segment of the Egyptian population found the entire regime itself illegitimate.

Opposition–Regime Interactions in an Explosive Environment

Dissatisfaction increased as the economic crisis began in the late 1980s. With a fall in oil prices and high external debt, economic growth declined annually from 1986 to 1988, and per capita growth was negative.[61]

Unemployment rose. Official estimates put the unemployed at 1.46 million persons, 78 percent of whom had at least an intermediate degree,[62] but observers argued that total unemployment was nearly double the official figures, with an estimated 2.5 to 3 million Egyptians unemployed in 1991.[63] Even the employed fared poorly; the real wage for government employees plummeted to nearly half of its 1973 level in the late 1980s.[64]

The crisis gave the legal opposition an opportunity to demand reforms, but the government made it clear that doing so in a way that could destabilize the regime could cost them the gains they had made. In 1990, all opposition parties except the NPUP were still willing to confront the incumbents. As in 1987, the elections followed a Supreme Court ruling that found the previous electoral law, Law No. 188, unconstitutional. In response, the government had agreed to return to a simple majoritarian system with independent candidates in 222 districts, preparing for elections in December 1990. The opposition still balked, however, because the electoral reforms failed to guarantee free and fair elections.[65] Consequently, although the NPUP agreed to participate, other opposition parties boycotted the election.[66] This angered state elites. As Mustapha Kamel el-Sayyid explained, with mounting crises in the Gulf, President Mubarak wanted the international community to see Egypt as "observing the constitutional proprieties and . . . [remaining] a bedrock of political stability."[67] The boycott therefore appeared to be a deliberate attempt to embarrass the regime before both domestic and international public opinion.[68]

The conditions under which the opposition parties boycotted should be clear, however. The parties' decisions to boycott were made easier by the fact that they expected to do poorly in the elections. The Islamic Alliance and the Wafd all experienced leadership feuds at this time, and the Islamic Alliance in particular could not expect to run candidates in all 222 districts.[69] This made the decision to boycott easier. In addition, the new electoral law made it easier for opposition party members to run as independents; a good number of them did so, and four won parliamentary seats.[70] However, this does not fully explain the parties' decisions, for in their boycott, they were certainly challenging the regime's legitimacy. Moreover, as we will see, they were unwilling to boycott in 1995, despite similarly dismal expectations.

Even by the early 1990s, the legal opposition was unwilling to mobilize popular demonstrations that the excluded opposition could exploit. Their reticence was clear during the first Gulf War. The opposition parties considered a demonstration in which they would march to call for a "peaceful

solution." However, the march was called off, with Fu'ad Siraj al-Din of
the Wafd admitting that the security situation in Egypt at the time would
not allow such a demonstration. Similarly, the opposition parties considered marching to present a petition to President Mubarak requesting that
he not renew martial law. This demonstration, too, was withheld, and the
opposition presented the petition only on April 1st, after hostilities had
ended.[71] In short, the opponents demanded reforms, and they presented
their demands through conferences, statements, and in public committees. However, they avoided mounting public demonstrations when they
feared that these would turn unruly, destabilizing the regime and inviting
harsh repression.

In the atmosphere of prolonged economic despair, excluded opponents
became stronger.[72] Enjoying closer ties to the masses than the legal opposition elites, as described in Chapter 3, they capitalized on the popular discontent to widen their base of support. The increasing strength
of the Islamists was evident by 1991. The moderate Muslim Brotherhood drew support from its extensive social service organizations, and
during the early 1990s it gained a majority presence in the professional
associations.[73] More militant groups gained support as well. Academic
studies found that these groups drew support from unemployed and economically disadvantaged youth.[74] More striking evidence was found in
Imbaba, an enormous, depressing slum of nearly 800,000 people on the
outskirts of Cairo. By 1992, Imbaba included neighborhoods completely
under al-Jama'ah al-Islamiyah's control. Local leaders charged with maintaining Islamic law harassed women and young girls if they went out
without headscarves, forced Christian shopkeepers to pay "taxes," and
allowed groups of young men armed with guns and knives to "police"
the area. The neighborhoods in Imbaba were a state within a state.[75]

The pace and extent of violent attacks on the state and secular society
escalated in the early 1990s. Militants had used violence earlier, most
notably to disrupt the 1987 parliamentary elections,[76] but the early 1990s
found the number of militant groups growing rapidly.[77] The number of
casualties from violent confrontations between militants and the state rose
from 51 in 1990 to 322 in 1991, reaching 1,106 in 1992.[78] Clearly, not all
Egyptians supported the violence. Indeed, a poll conducted by *al-Ahram*
in Lower Egypt in 1994 found that 93 percent of Egyptians felt that
Islamist violence was not for the good of the people.[79] The results might
have been slightly different had the poll been taken before the violence
had escalated or in a different region. However, it undoubtedly would
remain true that the majority of Egyptians were not active supporters

of militant groups. Combined with the consistently poor voter turnout and the increased strength of the Muslim Brotherhood, however, the fact remained that opposition was growing.

The government was on the defensive. It responded to the immediate threat posed in Imbaba in December 1992, when it cordoned off the area and sent 15,000 troops to crush the militants in a five-week battle "unprecedented in its intensity, in its viciousness, in its length of time, and in the number of arrests." While this incident was unique in its scope, repression continued throughout the 1990s; by 1994, human rights groups estimated that over 20,000 Islamists were in Egyptian jails, although the hard-line Minister of Interior denied this, putting the estimate at 4,000. Moreover, as the crisis continued, simply the appearance of Islamist sympathies – wearing long beards, the *hijab* or *niqab* – put Egyptians under suspicion and sometimes carried sanctions.[80]

Mubarak attempted to thwart this opposition by usurping the space of political Islam. In the early 1990s, the state practiced informal favoritism toward Islamist associations, separating social from political demands.[81] Similarly, it gave clerics time on state-owned television and strengthened the role of senior *ulema* affiliated with *al-Azhar* as "guardians of the *shari'a*." Trying to outdo the political opposition, these clerics often advocated more radical social reforms than the political militants, but they did not try to mobilize popular political resistance.[82]

The government also sought to incorporate and control venues of opposition. It sought to extend control over Islamic organizations, bringing private mosques into the network supervised by the Minister of Religious Endowments. Apprehensive over Islamists' dominance in the professional associations, the government also passed Law No. 100, which required high voter turnout for elections to be valid. Where the candidates failed to obtain this (as they frequently had in the past), control of the syndicate would pass to a panel of judges to organize new elections.[83] The law was a pointed attack on the Islamists, who had gained a clear majority in the syndicates through elections with less than a 25 percent voter turnout.[84] However, it was also a strong blow against the opposition parties and technocrats more generally.[85] Opposition to the law was widespread, although syndicates were split over their reaction to the legislation.[86] As Ibrahim, Adly, and Shehata point out, it was Brotherhood control over the syndicates that led them to respond through demonstrations and work stoppages, petitions to the speaker of parliament, and special plenary sessions and joint conferences. Law No. 100 was the most controversial measure taken to control the formal political sphere, but the government also extended administrative control over the trade unions, universities, and local governments.[87]

Most importantly, the regime emphasized the institutional divisions between those who were legally admitted into the system and those standing in the shadows, sending clear messages to the legal opposition elites that they had much to lose and little to gain if they sought to destabilize the regime. Mubarak reminded them that their primary responsibility – and indeed, the price they paid for admission into the system – was to contribute to stability. Speaking at Alexandria University in June 1992, he argued:

> We are suffering from irresponsible political party activity. I understand that political party activity must be for the homeland's and the citizens' benefit. The party that does not act for the good of the citizens and to improve their living standards – to tell you the truth – does not deserve to live.[88]

The next month the government reinforced this message, passing legislation that broadened the definition of "terrorism" and provided for harsher sentencing.

Sharpening the distinction between legal and illegal groups, state elites emphasized that cooperation with excluded opponents – even the Muslim Brotherhood – would be heavily penalized. The goals of the Muslim Brotherhood were to be questioned; never having been brought into the system and in some respects close to more militant groups outside, it could not be trusted to uphold the system.[89] The Brotherhood repeatedly argued that it wanted to be admitted into the system, allowed to establish a legal political party,[90] not to overturn the regime. As the Brotherhood's spokesman, Ma'mun al-Hudaybi, put it, " 'we want to be ruled by Islam, not that we, the Muslim Brotherhood, rule by Islam.' "[91] Yet, the regime increasingly argued that the Brotherhood was only "a mainstream façade" of the militant Islamists.[92] Coordinating with them to put pressure on the regime would bring repression.[93]

In part, the regime repressed the Muslim Brotherhood because of its strength.[94] Allowed to operate openly but, in contrast to the legal parties, not perceived as wholly dependent upon the state, the Brotherhood made significant gains in the elections of parliament, student unions, and syndicate boards. The 1984 and 1987 elections had demonstrated the popular support for the Brotherhood; opposition parties that ran in alliance with the Brotherhood did the best in elections.[95] Islamists also gained control over the syndicates. Islamists won only 7 of 25 seats on the Doctors' Association Board in 1985, but they controlled 20 of its 25 seats by 1990.

By the early 1990s, they had also won clear majorities in the Engineers', Pharmacists', and Scientists' syndicates, and by 1992 they succeeded in taking over the Lawyers' Syndicate, traditionally a liberal stronghold.[96] Such strength, coupled with divergent perceptions of the Brotherhood's intentions, led one observer to warn in 1993 that the Muslim Brotherhood was "becoming a pole of power for a radical but non-violent Islamist alternative in Egypt," and that if free elections were held, a "repetition of the Algerian episode would be a serious prospect."[97]

Repression also stemmed from the Brotherhood's unwillingness to condemn the militants unconditionally. Some believed that the Muslim Brotherhood remained a real threat because it had never formally joined the political system or completely renounced violence; it gave moral (and, some argued, financial) support to the militants, and it seemed unwilling to take important steps to stabilize the regime. Brotherhood leaders constantly denied these allegations, arguing that they did not support terrorism.[98] At the same time, however, the Brotherhood blamed the regime ultimately for the violence and demanded political reforms.[99] It also continued to mobilize popular antigovernment demonstrations in the midst of an increasingly tense environment.

A 1994 demonstration by the Lawyers' association after the death of lawyer 'Abd al-Harith Madani was important in this regard. The lawyer, known for his defense of Islamists, had died at the hands of security forces, thus sparking a demonstration that witnessed antigovernment slogans and violence. The regime responded by arresting demonstrators, and although the Brotherhood denied responsibility and had not acted alone, cracking down on the Brotherhood.[100] The government emphasized that any actions taken to support the Islamists, by any means, were unacceptable. President Mubarak's response to the international controversy that surrounded the Madani case was telling. In an interview in the *New Yorker*, he retorted, "*Why* is there such a big fuss about Abdel Harith Madani? . . . What about the human rights of the women and children that these people kill? *Madani was a criminal!*"[101] There was little daylight between moderate and radical Islamists, between the illegal Muslim Brotherhood and more militant, illegal Islamist organizations, and activities that in any way fostered these groups' activities would be punished severely.

By the mid-1990s, the legal opposition could point to the popular discontent and increasing violence to demand reforms;[102] in fact, in the interest of retaining their legitimacy, they would be encouraged to do so. Yet, they had to tread carefully. They would face harsh sanctions if they mobilized popular unrest, challenging the regime or facilitating the radicals' ability to do so. In terms of our model, the incumbents emphasized that the costs of Joint Conflict were much higher than those of Isolated Conflict. In the divided SoC, in an environment where radicals were using all opportunities to challenge the government, moderate, legal opponents now sought not to increase, but rather to alleviate, pressure on the regime.

Thus, they abstained from pulling out all the stops just when the regime appeared weakest. Against the backdrop of violence and volatility, secular included opponents chose to cooperate with the regime rather than mobilize the discontented populace, demanding greater reforms. Mubarak was able to secure their support in his (uncontested) bid for the presidency during the fall of 1993.[103] The parties also agreed to participate in the National Dialogue, which the president announced in his first speech to the National Assembly following the presidential election. As in Morocco, the Dialogue was an overt effort to constrain the opposition. Mubarak explained in his opening speech:

> [the] major objective behind this dialogue is to ensure a basic condition of democracy without slipping into the chaos of ideas or conflict of stances which could threaten the supreme interests of the homeland. I also explained that the sound concept of democracy does not mean that there are no boundaries between the legitimate law-abiding forces and the illegitimate forces that provoke acts of violence and challenge law.... Stability is a guarantee for democracy and there can be no stability in a society overwhelmed by infighting and division.[104]

Explicitly excluding the Muslim Brotherhood[105] and other illegal opposition forces, Mubarak underscored the red line between acceptable and unacceptable opposition. The Dialogue had a rocky start as the opposition members and the government argued over the composition of its membership and, more importantly, over the agenda,[106] but the majority of moderate, legal opponents eventually chose to play the game, shoring up the regime.

Legal opposition elites from both the right and the left also turned a blind eye to the repression of Islamists. In some cases, they even appeared to welcome it. Opposition papers seemed to have a "blackout" on reports of human rights violations against Islamists, and in January 1993 secularists from both sides joined in the "intellectual monologue 'against terrorism'" at the Cairo Book Fair, proving "how far secular intellectuals of the right and left [were] ready to play into the hands of the government." Many in the opposition even welcomed the decision to exclude the Muslim Brotherhood from the National Dialogue. The Secretary General of the NPUP, Rif'at al-Sa'id, justified the government's decision, saying that it was "waking up to its 'danger'" of the Muslim Brotherhood. "There is no moderation in the Islamist current. The Brotherhood is an extremist organization that calls for the establishment of an Islamic state. The violent history of the Brotherhood speaks for itself."[107]

Opposition elites who were less enthusiastic about repressing the Brotherhood still found that the steps the government took to solidify the divided SoC undermined their ability to challenge the regime. Most notably, the government took harsh measures against the SLP, which had the closest ties with the Brotherhood. The SLP was the subject of continuous arrests and interrogations, although the government stopped short of revoking its status as a party.[108] In addition, the repression stimulated a debate within the party over its position vis-à-vis the Brotherhood and the regime.[109] On one side stood party members who argued that the SLP had long been an Islamist party, that cooperation with the Muslim Brotherhood was aimed at spreading Islamic culture, curing social and economic ills, and producing political reform, and that neither the SLP nor the Brotherhood supported terrorism.[110] Although they maintained publicly that the SLP maintained its own support base, they probably recognized that the SLP's alliance with the Brotherhood enhanced its popular support. On the other side stood those who, apparently with the government's encouragement, argued that the cooperation had led to an "Islamic takeover" of the SLP.[111] The SLP did not completely sever its ties with the Brotherhood,[112] but in the face of repression and internal dissension, cooperation declined and the SLP was weakened.

The extent to which the moderate, included opposition had become unwilling to confront the regime, despite the heightened discontent, was clearly demonstrated in the elections of 1995. Unlike 1990, when the opposition had boycotted the elections in an attempt to pressure the regime, the opposition accepted Mubarak's invitation to run in the 1995 contest.[113] The electoral law continued to be based upon independent candidates, and thus would have allowed members to run independently while the party challenged the regime. Furthermore, repression had increased, as the "law to assassinate the press" demonstrated,[114] and the National Dialogue had led to few concessions over the electoral procedures.[115] The opposition did not expect the polling to be free and fair, and they did not expect to make real gains in the elections.[116] As Judge Ma'mun al-Hudaybi, the Muslim Brotherhood's spokesman, explained, "There is nothing reassuring about the coming elections. Assuming that they will be honest is debatable. After all, there are no real guarantees.

The state owns the media and has total control over the tools and means of government."[117]

Nevertheless, the opposition participated, thus helping to legitimize the regime. Indeed, even the Brotherhood fielded candidates, hoping to demonstrate its willingness to play by the rules. The government, however, effectively refused this implicit petition, closing the Brotherhood's headquarters in Cairo, arresting more than 80 members in September alone, and trying detainees in the military courts. Discontent skyrocketed, and the violence surrounding the elections was unprecedented. Significantly, however, the opposition parties instigated few of the violent incidents.[118] Party elites had little reason to hope they would make any real gains, and they were quite right: The government manipulated the elections and, not surprisingly, gained 94 percent of the seats.[119] Yet, the opposition had not boycotted the government party, the NDP, as it did in 1990, and it did not take advantage of the highly flammable popular opinion to challenge the state elite.

In part, moderate secularists failed to mobilize because the "Algeria complex" led secularist opponents to fear the Islamists, and the government both shared and played upon these fears.[120] Indeed, in the early 1990s, the relationships between secularists and Islamists were extremely tense. In 1992, Islamists assassinated the secular journalist Faraj Fuda; in 1993–1994, they not only blocked the promotion of a professor of Arabic literature who worked on Islamist discourse, but they also tried to force him to divorce his wife on the charge that a non-Muslim man could not marry a Muslim (he, of course, claimed to be Muslim); in 1994, they attempted to assassinate the internationally renowned author Najib Mahfuz.[121] Certain leaders of the Muslim Brotherhood argued that some of these attacks were perpetrated by the state in order to turn secularists against them. However, their description of the "correct" solution for a case like that of Mahfuz – to bring him before a committee of *al-Azhar*, force him to repent if found guilty, and execute him if he refused – was not much comfort to secularists.[122] Such cases sent shock waves through the intellectual community, which otherwise advocated democracy and freedom.[123] Less newsworthy but equally important in shaping secularists' opinions were more everyday events such as the disruption of student meetings, assaults at book fairs, and attacks on weddings.[124]

Yet, the fact that moderate secularists chose to side with the government rather than to demand political change was not due only to the example of Algeria and the fear of Islamists. True, many feared the "real" intentions of even the most apparently moderate of these groups; however, such fears permeated discussions in Jordan, and yet, as we saw, there the opposition continued to demand reforms. Rather, in the divided SoC, the government was able to mark a clear line between the included and excluded opposition. It was also able to foster skepticism between the sides, continuously casting doubt upon the Brotherhood's true intentions if it were allowed to enter the system.

The opposition's reluctance to confront the state elites was also not simply due to the increased repression. More repressive measures were put in place during the early 1990s, despite proclamations of democratization, in what Eberhard Kienle described as the "Grand Delusion."[125] In the late 1970s, increased repression had only served to heighten the opposition, and it could have done so in the 1990s as well. Furthermore, most of the repressive measures put into effect in the early 1990s remained in effect after 1997, when, the Islamist radicals having been largely defeated, moderates once again demanded reforms.

Finally, the moderate secularists' silence was not just a function of their weakness vis-à-vis the Islamists. They were weaker than the Islamists, as demonstrated in subnational elections during the early 1990s, but this did not make it impossible for them to challenge the government. Indeed, their relative weakness could instead have compelled them to work in concert with Islamist forces to demand change, as it did earlier in Egypt and continued to do in Jordan.

Rather, in the divided SoC, the legal opposition elites realized that they enjoyed benefits of inclusion that could be quickly lost if they cooperated with those outside the formal political system. This served to divide the opponents, fostering different dynamics than existed in Jordan or in Egypt under Sadat. The legalized opposition elites, recognizing that they would pay a high price if they destabilized the regime and fearing Islamist ideology as well, moved closer to the state elite. Precisely when the state was weakest, the masses were most easily mobilized, and the opposition was most likely to succeed (i.e., when conditions for mobilization appeared most promising), they chose not to challenge the regime.

DYNAMICS OF OPPOSITION IN DIVIDED SoCs

Both in Morocco and in Egypt under Mubarak, the legal oppositions' unwillingness to challenge the state elite can only be understood as the result of a complex relationship between the incumbent elites, the excluded opponents, and the more moderate, legal opposition parties. In the late 1980s, when the economic crisis emerged and radical Islamists appeared weak, the moderates used the heightened discontent to demand political reform. Yet, after moderate Islamists made significant gains, the regime signaled strongly that cooperation with the Brotherhood, let alone more radical Islamist groups, was unacceptable. Thus, moderate secularists chose to cooperate with the regime.

Similar dynamics prevailed, despite some important differences between these cases. Political Islam was generally less threatening in Morocco than in Egypt, and yet manipulating the costs the legal opponents would pay for destabilizing the system led Morocco's moderates to cooperate with the palace, just as they did in the Egyptian regime. Similarly, the Muslim Brotherhood in Egypt was allowed to act much more openly than any similar forces in Morocco. Yet, the divided SoC still allowed the Egyptian regime to take advantage of the Brotherhood's status as an illegal organization in an effort to isolate it from the legal opposition parties. Formality mattered. Institutions governing the inclusion of opposition groups altered the nature of the opposition and the incentive structure within which they operated; thus, in contrast to Jordan and Egypt under Sadat, moderate opponents withdrew from challenging the regime as the crises continued, even as their grievances grew.

These cases have demonstrated that institutional structures create important divisions between political opponents. In the divided SoC, this can explain why opponents may become less willing to mobilize as crises continue. These institutional structures also affect the importance of ideological divisions in determining opponents' actions. Indeed, throughout the cases, the salience of ideological differences between opposition groups remains an important factor. The next chapter explores how state elites manipulate these divisions in the hope of reinforcing their regimes.

6

Formal SoCs and Informal Political Manipulation

The formal institutions that incumbents create to structure government–opposition relations also influence their choices of informal mechanisms through which they manage individual opposition groups. Authoritarian elites treat opponents differentially. They can allow some opponents to organize more openly, thus gaining political strength, while simultaneously repressing others. They also influence the choices of entrepreneurs by opening some political spaces while simultaneously closing others.[1] This chapter examines how incumbent elites attempt to minimize the challenges that they face by influencing the strength and weakness of opposition groups with different political preferences.

As we shall see, although the strategies of manipulation are equally available to all incumbents, the creation of unified or divided SoCs has important implications for which strategies they choose. In unified SoCs, incumbents attempt to limit challenges by strengthening moderates with competing ideological preferences. Furthermore, they want to strengthen moderates and co-opt radicals in order to keep the oppositions' demands close to the status quo. In divided SoCs, incumbents try to control the opposition by strengthening radical groups, but they do not co-opt these opponents.

OPPOSITION PREFERENCES, GOVERNMENT STRATEGIES, AND SoCs

Incumbents choose between two strategies to manage their opposition. They may try to fragment and moderate political opposition groups, promoting a balanced set of opposition forces with moderate, but diametrically opposed, political demands. Alternatively, they may try to reduce the threats to their regime by strengthening ideologically radical political opponents. The first, most commonly recognized tactic of divide-and-rule should be employed more frequently in unified SoCs, while the second is more likely in divided SoCs.

Before examining why this is the case, we need to distinguish between co-optation and the strengthening of opposition groups. When groups or individuals are co-opted, they receive some concessions in return for a change in their demands. For instance, incumbents may give opponents who previously advocated the overthrow of the regime important positions or extraordinary benefits; in return, the opponents abandon their calls for the regime's demise. Although less commonly recognized, incumbents can also foster the growth of some opposition groups as opposition. In this case, they allow – or even encourage – opposition groups to continue their activities and gain popular support. The incumbents and the opposition do not make any implicit or explicit agreements, however, and the opposition does not change its demands in response to the incumbents' favor. Thus, this strengthening of opposition is distinct from co-optation.

To understand when and why governments choose either to weaken or to strengthen different opposition groups, this chapter focuses on the Mobilization subgame of the model, considering how the policies that groups espouse influence their willingness to mobilize jointly and independently. As Table 6.1 demonstrates, ideological preferences have two effects on opponents' willingness to protest. First, they affect the extent to which opponents value concessions gained by the other opposition group. When moderates' and radicals' preferences are similar, concessions gained by the moderates also benefit the radicals and vice versa. Policy preferences also affect the expected utility of a Joint Conflict and, consequently,

TABLE 6.1. *Payoffs in the Mobilization Subgame*

Outcome	Moderates	Radicals	Incumbents
Moderate Conflict	$-|1 - \pi_M| - C_M$	$\pi_M (-|P_R - 1|)$ $+ (1 - \pi_M) (-|P_R|)$	$-\pi_M - C_G$
Radical Conflict	$-\pi_R(|P_R - 1|)$ $- (1 - \pi_R)$	$-(1 - \pi_R)(|P_R|)$ $-\theta C_R$	$-\pi_R(|P_R|)$ $- C_G$
Joint Conflict	$\pi_J[(1 - \alpha)$ $(-|1 - P_R|)]$ $-(1 - \pi_J) - \beta C_M$	$\pi_J[-\alpha (|P_R - 1|)]$ $- (1 - \pi_J)$ $|P_R| - C_R$	$\pi_J[-\alpha - (1 - \alpha)$ $|P_R|] - C_G$
Status Quo	-1	$-|P_R|$	0

opponents' decisions to mobilize. By strengthening groups that advocate some policies while weakening others, incumbents influence the likelihood that they face political challenges. The model and cases demonstrate three approaches that incumbents might take to weaken and control their opposition.

Fragmentation and Moderation

Incumbents may try to fragment and moderate the opposition. It should be immediately clear that radicals and moderates are unlikely to join in a coalition when they prefer the Status Quo to each other's preferred policy (i.e., when radicals' preferred policy lies to the left of -1, that is, $P_R < -1$). In this case, there is no policy that both groups could agree would be superior to the current policy.[2]

Consequently, incumbent elites can minimize political opposition by fostering opposition groups with divergent and incompatible ideological preferences. Doing so reduces the likelihood that each side chooses to confront the regime, and it also makes potential challenges less costly. Strengthening moderate groups with incompatible policy preferences makes opponents unlikely to join in a coalition to demand political change. This is particularly beneficial in the unified SoC, where both moderates and radicals face lower costs of mobilizing jointly than they do independently. Indeed, in a unified SoC, the existence of opposition groups with diametrically opposed preferences may make mobilization less likely even after one group becomes willing to mobilize. To see why this is so, first consider the moderates. They will prefer mobilization independently if $\pi_M > C_M$, where π_M is the probability that they succeed and C_M is their cost for mobilizing. However, in the unified case, radicals are more likely to join in because the costs of mobilizing jointly are lower than those of doing so independently and because radicals fear that the policies advocated by the moderates may be worse than the Status Quo.[3] The more likely the radicals believe the moderates will be successful in obtaining concessions, and the more they dislike the moderates' preferred policies, the more likely they are to go into the streets. Moderates, recognizing that their ideological adversaries may join in the unrest, may consequently be less likely to mobilize.[4] In the unified SoC, where both moderates and radicals face lower costs of Joint Conflict than of Isolated Conflict, an equivalent reasoning holds for the radicals.

Consequently, the incumbents can minimize the challenges they face by ensuring that both sides prefer to maintain the Status Quo rather than to risk a Joint Conflict, even after they come to prefer an Isolated Conflict to the Status Quo.[5] To do this, they need to maximize the distance between the two opposition groups' policies. They also need to ensure that both sides fear that the other group may succeed in gaining demands if it mobilizes, and yet believe that they have the ability to gain demands if they mobilize. The incumbents can do this by attempting to balance the political strength of both moderates and radicals and to balance the ideological distance between moderates and the Status Quo as well as between radicals and the Status Quo.[6] In short, incumbents may attempt to reduce their oppositions' demands by balancing the strength of competing groups with opposing policy demands.

This approach can be problematic, however. Political opponents who prefer the Status Quo to each other's position may change their minds if incumbents change the Status Quo, making it less palatable to both oppositions and leading opponents with very different political ideologies to come together and make political demands. Unable to agree upon any specific demands, they push for a change in the rules of the political game, after which they pursue their own political struggles. This was clearly the case in Egypt and Jordan, as discussed in Chapter 4. Similarly, the Nicaraguan coalition, National Opposition Union (UNO), brought together members ranging from the far left to the extreme right to challenge the Sandinistas, and the 1979 Iranian revolution saw a similarly broad set of actors bring down the Shah.

Neutralization Through Radicalization

Incumbents may also weaken their political opposition by strengthening much more radical, but weaker, opponents.[7] When radical elites are unable to mobilize successfully on their own but have the potential to exploit existing political instability, ideological divides can reduce the moderates' willingness to join in a coalition. In this case, the more extreme the radicals, the less likely opponents are to confront incumbent elites. In addition, as the potential for radical elites to exploit moderate conflict increases, the likelihood that moderates will challenge incumbents declines. Particularly in the divided SoC, as the radicals become stronger or their demands become more radical, the moderates become less willing to make political demands. The moderates refuse to join radicals in a coalition to press political demands, and they even become unwilling to challenge elites independently. These results are consistent with the dynamics of protest discussed in Chapter 4.

The reason for this is simple. The conditions set forth earlier hold for the divided as well as the undivided SoC. However, in this case, the moderates face greater costs for mobilizing jointly than they do for mobilizing independently. As a result, the likelihood that radicals gain their preferred position need not be as high as it is in the unified case in order for them to become unwilling to mobilize.[8] At the same time, however, the greater the distance between the radicals' preferred policy and the Status Quo, the more likely they are to join in the fray. This, in turn, makes the moderates less likely to mobilize. Consequently, the incumbents can benefit from weak illegal opponents holding radical positions. Incumbents benefit from the presence of radical elites poised on the sidelines to exploit an ongoing conflict.

A divided SoC encourages such a strategy. Although it is outside the scope of this book, it is worth noting that an institutional arrangement that prohibits some groups from participating in the formal political sphere encourages radical groups to form. Unable to participate no matter what policy position they advocate, radicals are unlikely to propose more moderate policies for strategic reasons. In addition, since legal opponents face severe penalties if they destabilize the regime, incumbents are expected to foster the belief that such instability is entirely possible. Thus, incumbents should promote the growth of extremely radical opponents; however, they do not want the radicals to become too strong. They want to ensure that the radicals remain a threat to the moderates but are not able to mobilize independently.

MANAGING POLITICAL OPPONENTS IN THE MIDDLE EAST AND NORTH AFRICA

Elites in the Middle East and North Africa have taken both approaches toward the political opposition. In Morocco, King Hasan II tried to weaken the opposition by fostering the growth of radical opponents. In Jordan and Egypt, King Husayn and President Sadat took the opposite approach. They attempted to limit opposition to the regime by strengthening and co-opting moderate opponents. As these cases remind us, the success of each approach is far from assured.

Before we examine these cases, it should be noted that it is often difficult to prove the methods by which incumbents attempt to manipulate opposition. Incumbents do not want to be seen as strengthening the opposition to their regime, either directly or indirectly. In addition, opposition elites avoid giving the impression that they rely on or benefit from the incumbent elites. Neither side explicitly acknowledges the support of or need for the other.

Strengthening the Radicals

Nevertheless, circumstantial evidence and interviews suggest that incumbents in Morocco attempted to weaken their opposition by ensuring that radical excluded elites fundamentally opposed to the regime remained on the fringes. Maintaining these radical movements weakened the opposition. As we saw in Chapter 5, the existence of radical opponents ready to capitalize upon political unrest served to make moderates less willing to mobilize. The irony for radical opposition elites is that the strengthening of their movements, which stand in direct opposition to the incumbent regime, helps to support the very regimes that they oppose.

Morocco. In Morocco, a growing Islamist movement helped to hold the moderates in check. Throughout the 1970s and 1980s, there were two main revolutionary Islamist movements in Morocco: Justice and Charity, led by ʿAbd al-Salam Yasin, and the Islamic Youth, led by ʿAbd al-Karim Mutiʿ.[9] During this period, the King allowed the Islamist movements to grow, in opposition to the leftists and secularists. After the mid-1980s, when it became clear that the Islamists might be able to challenge the King independently, King Hasan II played a delicate balancing game. He allowed these movements to remain strong enough to threaten the legal opposition, but he weakened them if they appeared capable of challenging the regime independently.

The King sought to weaken the most radical Islamist movement, the Islamic Youth, after it became willing to challenge the regime independently. Founded in 1969 by ʿAbd al-Karim Mutiʿ, the Youth was the most vitriolic and revolutionary of the Moroccan Islamist movements. An editorial published in the first issue of a review demonstrated their position well:

our present and our future are caught between the hammer of American imperialism and the anvil of its agents represented by the corrupt monarchical regime and those who support it....

Your review appears in these circumstances to be, God willing, in the vanguard of an authentic Islamic revolution in Morocco; a revolution that enlightens the horizons of this country and liberates its people to bring them back to the Islam of Muhammad and those of his people who have known how to follow him – not the Islam of the merchants of oil and the agents of the Americans.[10]

Muti's insistence on an Islamic state was as objectionable to the moderate secularists, however, as it was to the regime. Thus, in the early 1970s, clashes between Islamists and leftist students became common. At this point, the growth of the Islamists served to weaken the King's opposition.

However, in addition to using shrill language, Muti' was allegedly willing to use violent tactics that other revolutionary Islamists (most notably Yasin) did not employ. In 1975, the editor of the Socialist Party's paper and a leading Marxist was assassinated. The government claimed that Muti' was responsible. Although Muti' denied this claim, he left Morocco three days after the assassination and did not return. Similarly, there were rumors that Muti' had played a role in seizing the Great Mosque of Mecca in 1979.[11]

As the Youth became willing to challenge the King independently, the palace's tolerance for the movement declined. For the King, the difficulty was that, as the movement became stronger, it became a threat to the regime. Munson summed up the relationship between these Islamists and the King:

The Moroccan government initially favored the growth of al-Shabiba al-Islamiyya for the same reason Sadat initially supported the Jama'at al-Islamiyya in the universities of Egypt: to curb the Marxist groups that had dominated the student politics in the sixties. But like Sadat, Morocco's King Hasan II eventually realized that Islamic militancy could pose a greater threat to his regime than could the secular left.[12]

Instead, the government sought to neutralize the opposition by allowing the growth of such movements as 'Abd al-Salam Yasin's Justice and Charity. This movement was somewhat less militant, but it still advocated the overthrow of the monarchy. By allowing it to continue to grow, the King filled part of the vacuum left by Muti's exit from Morocco. The growth of support for Yasin, and for other Islamists in the same vein, could pose a threat to the moderates. It could also draw supporters away from more militant Islamist groups. Consequently, since the late 1970s, the King allowed the movement to grow, as long as it did not significantly challenge the regime independently.

Yasin had become a noteworthy political figure in 1974, when he wrote a startling "open letter" to King Hasan II entitled "al Islam aw al-Tufan: risalah maftuhah ila malik al-Maghreb" ["Islam or the Deluge: An Open Letter to the King of Morocco"]. The letter used unusually scornful and condescending language, reading, " 'My letter to you is not like all other letters for it is a letter that demands an answer'" and, frequently addressing the King with "Oh, my brother" ("ya akhi") and "Oh, my love" ("ya habibi"). In the letter, Yasin argued:

Islam gives him who spends the night hungry the right to bear arms against him who has deprived him of the bounty of God (*haramahu rizqahu*). . . . Your palaces, your properties, and the opulent class in the land all explain the presence of beggary and misery.[13]

The King asked ʿAbdallah Guennun, the head of the league of Moroccan *ulema*, how he should react, Guennun reportedly told him exactly what many other Moroccans may have believed as well: Only a lunatic would write such a letter. Thus, they admitted Yasin to a psychiatric hospital for three and half years, from 1974 to 1977. When he was released, Yasin continued his campaign against the King. In 1979, he began publishing an Islamic review, *al-Jamaʿa*. Although the authorities delayed its publication for nearly one year and refused Yasin permission to speak in the mosques, his organization was given the space to grow in the early 1980s. *Al-Jamaʿa* was published until 1983. Similarly, although Yasin did not speak in the mosques, mosque sermons became an important tool of Islamists from 1979 until 1984.

Yasin's movements were restricted, but the Moroccan regime allowed the Islamists to gain strength to the point at which they could be a threat to the legal opposition, and yet remained too weak to threaten the monarch independently. As Mohammed Tozy noted, the period before the 1984 riots could be thought of as the period in which Islamist movements "arose through official indifference and even complicity."[14] The King's complicity in allowing the Islamists to strengthen their movement was, quite understandably, difficult to prove. Yet, unless one accepts the hypothesis that the King benefited from a strong but constrained radical opposition, several facts remain difficult to understand.

The most difficult fact to explain is the continued presence of Yasin on the Moroccan political stage. One might expect that Yasin would have been removed from Moroccan politics permanently following the publication of his open letter. After all, such an open confrontation with the King was generally intolerable. Even if one accepts the argument that the King chose not to kill Yasin because he feared creating a martyr, several factors remain.[15] The most important is that, in the absence of any apparent political pressure, the government released Yasin from the psychiatric hospital in less than four years and allowed him to continue making the same demands (albeit in a more muted form) that he had previously.

Yasin was clearly not co-opted, and in releasing him, the King assured the strengthening of his movement.

Subsequently, the palace's control over Yasin's presence on the Moroccan political stage followed a predictable path. He was permitted to continue his work, strengthening the movement. As the movement became stronger, and when economic and political crises made Moroccans particularly volatile, Yasin was removed. Thus, the King permitted Yasin to spread his message, publishing *al-Jama'a* and mobilizing support for his movement. However, in 1983 Yasin's review was banned, and his attempt to publish a newspaper, *al-Subh*, was thwarted, just as the political and economic situations became particularly explosive. In December 1983, just days before the riots, the authorities arrested Yasin. He remained in prison until January 1986.

Upon his release, Yasin again mobilized opposition to the regime. His home became the center of his movement. Police guarded the house and questioned visitors, but supporters came. As Justice and Charity gained popularity, the movement became reminiscent of a Sufi order, and members referred to Yasin as their *murshid*, or guide. In December 1989, when the Moroccan situation again became particularly tense, the police stopped allowing visitors to Yasin's house. The following month, they arrested six leaders of the group as well as members, and their trial led to a demonstration of about 2,000 people in May 1990.

The King's relationship with Yasin cannot be explained by the simple need for the state to control political opposition. In the early years, it would have been relatively easy for the King to do away with Yasin's threat altogether. To explain the authorities' reluctance to do this, Munson has pointed to the potential martyrdom and popular backlash against killing Yasin.[16] That the King would have been so concerned about a backlash seems curious, since he apparently did not bar Muti', the more popular, stronger leader of the Islamic Youth, from operating within Morocco. Furthermore, Munson himself also notes that nearly 15 years later, despite the growth of the movement and the worsening economic situation, support for Yasin remained narrow enough that only about 2,000 persons participated in the demonstrations during the trial of 1990. While this is a substantial demonstration in a restrictive political system, the popular response to Yasin's arrest does not suggest that the death of the leader in the mid-1970s would have created a dangerous political opposition. Indeed, at that time, Yasin was less popular than he was by the 1990s, and the general political system was less explosive.

While it was not the fear of a popular backlash that led the King to release Yasin, it was also not co-optation of the Islamist movement that led the King to allow some growth of the Islamist opposition. Yasin had not changed his demands in the face of official pressure.[17] Nor had the authorities allowed him to mobilize unchecked. Indeed, since 1984, official control over areas pertaining to Islam had increased significantly. The state increasingly controlled movements that were previously tolerated and maintained tighter restrictions on the use of the mosques. Since the mid-1970s, the state used indirect means to control the use and proliferation of mosques, including zoning procedures and preliminary reviews of the construction of places of worship. In Decree 1-80-270 of May 6, 1981, the King created an institution for the clerics in which a regional council would supervise the *ulema*. The *ulema* were clearly not to work outside of the prescribed framework. Indeed, the King warned, "'Be careful, be careful! . . . Do not intervene in what does not concern you, like a rise in the price of gasoline or cigarettes.'" Finally, in the decree of October 2, 1984, the King regulated the building and use of mosques, requiring that the governor of each province issue permits for the construction of mosques, and that the Ministry of the Habbous and of Muslim Affairs appoint the *khatib* (preacher) and the *imam*.[18]

King Hasan II tolerated Yasin because he provided a threat to the included opposition as well as to the King. Yasin's contempt for the left was well recognized. Although he later argued that he would like to form an Islamist party,[19] he did not support a democratic government or envision a long-term role for secularist opponents. Instead, he called for a "'council elected in an Islamic manner,' *after all political parties have been banned*."[20] "'The party of Satan,' as Yasin called people who advocate a secular form of government, would not be allowed to participate in elections for this council."[21] Thus, his movement provided a useful counterweight to the secularist opposition. It was clearly against the leftists. The expectation that political instability might open the door for Islamists success threatened the left as much as the King himself.

In addition, Yasin's movement benefited the regime because it drew support away from more violent Islamist opposition groups that might have been willing to challenge the King independently. In fact, as Yasin's movement grew stronger, the Islamic Youth weakened. In part, its decline was due to the heavy-handed tactics of Muti' himself. Although overseas, he attempted to maintain tight control over the organization, at times even prohibiting members from marrying without his permission.[22]

Followers resented this, and the organization dissolved into competing, sometimes adversarial, splinter groups. After the mid-1980s, Moroccan incumbents also weakened the movement through repression and co-optation. In 1984, 71 members of the movement received sentences that ranged from four years' imprisonment to death.[23] As it became clear that membership in the organization was dangerous, some militants broke away to form new organizations, advocating a strictly Islamic state but refraining from direct attacks on the government. Others undoubtedly were drawn to Yasin's movement. By tacitly accepting the growth of radical Islamist movements, the incumbents neutralized the moderate secularists and weakened more radical Islamist groups as well.

Thus, the King supported the growth of radical Islamists, but only to the point where they could exploit instability, not mobilize independently. Indeed, incumbents are challenged with the need to balance the moderates' and radicals' strength. They need to ensure that the moderates remain strong enough to appear as a legitimate opposition force to the public at large, thereby limiting the public support of radicals and reinforcing the legitimacy of the regime. At the same time, the incumbents need radicals of sufficient strength to pose a threat to the moderates.

Incumbents want to balance the opposition forces, ensuring that the radicals are unable to challenge the state elites independently and that the moderates remain legitimate. As a result, if, or when, the radicals become capable of and willing to threaten the incumbents independently, they are repressed. When the moderates appear impotent, incumbents take steps to shore up their strength.

This was the case in Morocco. By the mid-1990s, it was clear to both opposition elites and the incumbents that the legal political parties were losing popular credibility. As discussed previously, this meant that the King acted to try to renew the "democratic" process in Morocco, most notably by revising the Constitution in 1996 and then appointing the first USFP Prime Minister, 'Abd al-Rahman Yusufi, in 1998. Both decisions were aimed at drawing the opposition closer to the regime while simultaneously giving it the appearance of greater power. For instance, the constitutional amendments of 1996 met opposition demands for full direct elections only partway: The King allowed direct elections of all representatives in the Chamber of Representatives (thereby replacing the one-third of indirectly elected representatives), but he simultaneously created a Chamber of Councilors with the ability to override the lower chamber. Thus, while the constitutional revision gave the appearance of greater power to the opposition, it continued to effectively constrain it. The apparent hope was to reverse the flow of popular support from the legal moderates to the more radical Islamists.[24]

Managing the Moderates

In Egypt and Jordan, incumbents sought to strengthen their political system by fostering moderate opponents with opposing policy preferences. Thus, the incumbents attempted to create a system in which opponents preferred the status quo to the potential success of their rivals. They also tried to co-opt opponents, moderating their demands. Thus, when opponents chose to mobilize independently, their demands would be restrained.

Egypt Under Sadat. Egypt provides an important contrast with Morocco precisely because many see the Egyptian and Moroccan incumbent elites as employing the same political strategies. Former President Sadat initially strengthened the Islamists against the leftists, just as King Hasan II did in Morocco. However, while their tactics appeared the same, their strategies were fundamentally different. President Sadat was not trying to strengthen the Islamists as an opposition force that would challenge his regime. Rather, he attempted to co-opt the more moderate Islamists, believing that their loyal opposition would help support his regime.

In 1970, Anwar Sadat reversed some of the long-standing repression of the Islamists and the liberal Wafd Party. That he chose to release the pressures on these opponents was not surprising. Unlike Nasir, Sadat entered office with a history of more congenial relations with the Muslim Brotherhood. Long before he became President, Sadat attended meetings and had long discussions with leading members of the Muslim Brotherhood. In addition, Sadat needed the Islamists' support. In 1970, he faced leftist and Nasirist opposition. If the Islamists could weaken these opponents, his own position would be more secure. Thus, Sadat reversed some of the long-standing repression of the Islamists and the liberal Wafd Party.[25]

When Sadat allowed the Islamists' return to the political stage, he was trying to co-opt the opposition. He released Islamists from prison and allowed them to hold meetings and distribute their publications. He also got the tacit agreement of the leaders of the Muslim Brotherhood that they would limit their demands and the means through which they made them. Indeed, they did. For instance, Salah Shadi, a leader of the Muslim

Brotherhood, argued in *al-Sha'b*, the official paper of the Islamic Alliance, that the Brotherhood had two goals:

1. An immediate goal of contributing to all that is good for the whole society through as much social service as possible.
2. A distant goal, i.e., the reform advocated by the Muslim Brotherhood and for which it is preparing itself. It is a complete and comprehensive reform (*islah*) carried out jointly by all forces of the nation and results in changing all existing condition.

   Until such a goal is achieved the Muslim Brotherhood offers its advice to all Egyptian governments, wishes them all success and wishes that Allah will mend this corrupt situation through it [Italics mine].[26]

In gaining the acceptance of the more moderate Brotherhood, Sadat had essentially clipped their wings. They were limited to demonstrations of disapproval of some government policies, most notably the peace treaty with Israel. In return, they received minor concessions, such as the well-publicized constitutional amendment in April 1980 stating that "Islam is the religion of the State" and the *shari'a* is "the main source of legislation." However, more radical groups emerged, arguing these minor demands and concessions were insufficient. Constrained from presenting stronger demands, the Muslim Brotherhood lost supporters to the more radical groups. Sadat inadvertently strengthened radical Islamist opponents by restricting the Muslim Brotherhood.

According to Gomaa, Sadat's mistake was that he believed the Muslim Brotherhood represented the mainstream Islamist tendencies and could control more radical opponents.[27] Under the leadership of Hasan al-Banna, the Muslim Brotherhood was able to control extremist elements. However, without this leadership, the 1970s saw a proliferation of more radical Islamist opposition groups. Sadat apparently failed to recognize early in his presidency that the Islamists continued to pose a serious threat to his regime. By the time he did, it was too late.

Jordan. In Jordan, King Husayn sought to maintain his regime by strengthening the moderate opposition against his more radical opponents and by exacerbating political divisions. The King allowed the most moderate Islamist and secularist voices space within the system, even during the periods of military rule. In addition, he reinforced the division between Palestinians and Transjordanians. Balancing the strengths of opponents with various political and social demands, the King created for himself a position as a mediator and stabilizer. As long as these alternate opposition groups appeared more threatening to each other than did the King himself, the King's position was secure.

The moderate secularist and religious opposition in Jordan challenged individual official policies, but never the legitimacy of the King's leadership; in return, King Husayn allowed them a limited role in the political system. The Muslim Brotherhood was the most moderate of the King's opponents. The Brotherhood's loyalty was clearly demonstrated during the power struggle between Prime Minister al-Nabulsi and the King. Unlike the leftist parties, the Brotherhood supported the King in this conflict with the Prime Minister.[28] Consequently, the King granted the Brotherhood a privileged position after 1957. Even when political parties were formally banned, the King allowed the Brotherhood to circumvent the law, operating as a charitable organization, and some members were appointed to influential positions in the government ministries.[29]

Secularist opponents gained similar access to the regime when they were willing to give up their more radical political demands. The Prime Minister's cabinet and, after 1979, the NCC, contained former Ba'thists and Communists who were willing to present only moderate political demands. The King regularly attempted to moderate opponents' demands, giving the strongest opposition leaders incentives to support the regime.

However, increasing opposition forced the King to create greater incentives to accept the regime. The creation and then expansion of the NCC was intended to co-opt increasing numbers of opponents. A review of the NCC's members showed that they included important political activists who participated in the underground parties and professional associations. In addition, the NCC promoted the acquiescence of potential opponents in the regime's policies. Nabil Khoury explains that the NCC was "another manifestation of a general political strategy on the part of King Hussein, ... which [aimed] to utilize the country's political institutions to co-opt intellectuals and businessmen, to appease traditional sectors of society and to mobilize support for royal policies."[30]

In addition to allowing both secularist and Islamist moderates to compete in the political system, King Husayn promoted communal and regional divisions among political opponents.[31] Several cleavages in Jordanian society were kept just below the surface of politics, to be exacerbated and emphasized whenever increasing societal tensions served to reduce political pressures. The most notable was the division between Jordanians of East Bank and Palestinian origin. Distrust between the two groups rose following Black September in 1970. Partially as a result, the palace allowed Transjordanians to dominate the military and bureaucracy, and more recently university positions as well. Palestinians came to resent Transjordanians' ability to benefit from their tribal connections in ways that were closed to them. On the other hand, a Palestinian elite continued to dominate the private sector. This elite threatened the Transjordanians, who feared they could take political positions as well.[32] The Palestinian elite also weakened the Palestinian resistance, since they continued to support the monarchy in return for a stable business climate. A second division remained between Transjordanians of Northern and Southern origin. The King emphasized this division by implementing an obvious and consistent balancing act between the two regions.

These divisions weakened the opposition, at least in the short run. The first parliamentary sessions following liberalization witnessed sharp conflicts between the Islamists and leftists. Immediately before the Madrid Conference, Islamists cooperated with the predominantly Transjordanian Constitutional Bloc to end the tenure of Prime Minister Tahir al-Masri, a Palestinian with ties to the leftists. It was an unusual coalition. The Islamists joined it largely to demonstrate their opposition to the peace process; the largely Transjordanian Constitutional Bloc cooperated with the Islamists because they opposed the appointment of a Palestinian prime minister associated with the leftists. Finally, leftists opposed to the peace process and frustrated with an increasingly restrictive political environment joined with the Islamists and the Constitutional Bloc in the no-confidence vote, forcing Tahir al-Masri out of office. As the peace process disappointed both groups, then, leftists and Islamists became willing to join in a coalition opposing the palace.

As leftists and Islamists emerged as allies, horizontal cleavages became increasingly important. The "Jordanian Likud," including Transjordanians generally, opposed a permanent and equal role for Jordanians of Palestinian origin in the political system and became more vocal as opposition to the process increased. Increased tensions between Jordanians of Palestinian and East Bank origin served to weaken the opposition against the regime. Laurie Brand argues that the state allowed these tensions to flare periodically in order to weaken the opposition:

The stoking of communal flames [was] a policy instrument to be used when there [was] a possibility that some challenge, generally, but not exclusively economic, could lead to a broad-based Jordanian–Palestinian opposition to the regime, perhaps along the lines of the nationalist wave that emerged in the 1950s.[33]

Indeed, as Marc Lynch notes, opposition elites from very different parts of the ideological spectrum were aware of this, and they actively worked against the monarch's attempt to divide Jordanian society.[34] In February 1997, Islamist opposition leader Layth Shubaylat released a public letter stating that " 'the state is collapsing and society is dividing.' " Similarly, Toujan Faisal, a leading member of the secularist opposition, accused the monarchy of promoting divisions between Jordanians of Palestinian and East Bank origin. In 1997, a broad coalition of opposition elites released a communiqué announcing similar concerns. Arguing for the importance of accepting the current Jordanian borders and population, the statement proclaimed: " 'We reject allowing parochialism and sectarianism to emerge with their evil manifestations. We should unite the people and not divide them. . . . The Jordanian national opposition parties call on everybody to halt this harmful debate.' "[35]

Fostering the existence of moderate opponents with competing political demands is risky, however. There are two threats. First, coalitions that span political divides become more likely as the opponents' preferences for the status quo declines. In addition, even when opposition elites become increasingly moderate, their supporters may not follow. In Jordan, Islamist opponents became increasingly unwilling to accept the Brotherhood's moderate position. The division among the opposition may yield more radical opponents, and these may be far less willing to uphold a deal with incumbents.[36]

CONCLUSION

As crises continue, incumbent elites are in a precarious position regardless of how they try to control their opposition. These threats differ, however, depending on the strategy of control. When incumbents attempt to maintain political stability by strengthening radical opponents, they risk fostering radical anti-government forces that can challenge the incumbents independently. When incumbents attempt to balance opposing forces, they risk adopting policies that so alienate both sets of opposition, leading them to cooperate in the struggle against the government. Incumbents create institutions and use informal strategies in their struggle to stay on top. The choices they make in doing so are important, but they are also risky. Institutions structure the logic of politics, but they do not fully determine the outcomes.

Conclusion

Authoritarian leaders not only make the rules, they play by them as well. This stands in contrast to conventional wisdom, which holds that formal institutions make little difference in autocracies. When kings, dictators, or presidents in closed regimes find themselves facing down their opponents, the expectation is that anything goes. The leaders can use a variety of means to stay in power: co-opting the willing; imprisoning, torturing, or killing their adversaries; diverting public attention to external conflicts with international rivals; and occasionally promoting political liberalization. Very little is said, however, of the formal mechanisms they use, particularly the creation of various institutional structures that spell out the rules of the game by which both opposition and incumbent elites should play.

Yet, these rules matter. Incumbent elites do try to repress, appease, and divide and conquer their opposition, as we have long known. They throw some into prison, only to release them decades later; they jail others in the hope of bringing them out much more quickly as changed men (and yes, usually men) who have gained a gloss of legitimacy that only imprisonment can bring, and yet have often lost their spark; and they appease others with ministerial portfolios, fine cars, and fancy wine. At the same time, however, they also make important choices over who is or is not allowed to play the formal game – forming opposition parties, opening offices, publishing newspapers, and calling conferences. Most simply, authoritarian elites can create formal rules that treat all opponents the same way, regardless of such identities as religion, ideology, geography, or ethnicity, or they can create institutions that distinguish among opponents, allowing some to play the game while refusing admission to others. These institutions not only affect the level of opposition that the leaders face, they also influence which opponents – both legal and illegal – these leaders try to eliminate and which they try to promote.

STRUCTURES OF CONTESTATION

SoCs are the outcome of elites' choices, independent of regime type. Morocco and Jordan demonstrate this nicely. Both are monarchies, and yet by the early 1990s, King Husayn and King Hasan II had fostered very different SoCs. Morocco had a divided SoC in which organized opposition based on Islam was strictly forbidden. Jordan, in contrast, allowed opposition parties to organize across the ideological spectrum, as long as they recognized the legitimacy of the monarchy. Egypt under Presidents Nasir, Sadat, and Mubarak provides further evidence that regime types and SoCs are not intimately linked. Under Nasir and Sadat, Egypt had a unified SoC, while under Mubarak it had a divided one. Authoritarian rulers in monarchies and presidential regimes can create institutions that either unify or divide their opponents.

These cases also demonstrate that SoCs are not the inherent and inevitable result of either historical experience or leadership styles. In Morocco and Jordan, King Husayn and King Hasan II both initially used the same strategy: creating a unified SoC. It was only in the 1970s, as both experienced increasing instability, that their choices diverged and King Hasan II chose a very different strategy. Similarly, Presidents Nasir, Sadat, and Mubarak all governed the same society. They also harkened back to the same revolutionary basis of legitimacy, although their interpretations of it differed somewhat. Nevertheless, the divergent strategies they chose again demonstrate that the institutional design of SoCs is independent of the many other important factors that can affect government–opposition relations.

CONSEQUENCES OF SoCs

SoCs have important consequences. In the unified SoC, all opposition groups are either allowed to or barred from participating in the formal political sphere. Opponents may have very different preferences concerning different policies; they may be stronger or weaker, more ideologically driven or less. However, all have an equal formal relationship with the regime. Even when some groups have been granted some informal privileges, as we saw in the case of the Muslim Brotherhood in Jordan, they are no more or less committed to maintaining the regime's stability than are their counterparts.

In contrast, in the divided SoC, some opponents are granted the privilege of participating in the formal political sphere, while others are excluded. Those who are allowed to join in authoritarian regimes have committed themselves to the maintenance of the regime. In return, they are allowed to express their demands and enjoy benefits of participation. They can even occasionally test the boundaries – leading demonstrations, calling strikes, and demanding reform. By doing so, the opposition seeks to demonstrate its independence from the regime and its position as a legitimate opposition force. This helps to shore up the regime, and it incurs little punishment as long as it is not destabilizing. Yet, when this mobilization crosses the boundaries – when strikes, demonstrations, and strident calls for reform threaten to shake the regime – legal opposition elites pay a high price. They not only face the same strong sanctions that illegal opponents face, they also may lose the gains they have made. They may lose their ability to play the game and all of the benefits that this provides.

Opponents standing on the sidelines see things very differently. They much prefer mobilizing in conjunction with legal opponents than going it alone. Joining in the strikes or demonstrations called by legal opponents, and particularly taking advantage of these to mount violent opposition against the authorities, is much safer than instigating such unrest independently. Doing so alone risks the immediate exposure of the leadership and its followers, and recognizing this fact makes adherents less likely to join. In contrast, publicly called strikes and demonstrations by legal opposition groups provide an important opportunity for illegal groups to join in, escalating the attacks against the regime while simultaneously hiding behind the cloak of the legal opposition. These opposition groups are consequently more likely to join in ongoing demonstrations than they are to mount such challenges independently.

Dynamics of Protest

The divergent incentives in unified and divided SoCs promote different dynamics of protest during prolonged crises. In the unified SoC, political demands increase as popular discontent rises. The coalitions they form to make demands also widen as the crises continue. Such was the case in

Jordan and Egypt under Nasir and Sadat. In these cases, opposition continued to mobilize as crises continued, eventually including opponents of very different ideological persuasions: Islamists, Marxists, Communists, democratic secularists, and, in Jordan, those of Transjordanian and Palestinian origin. Even the Muslim Brotherhood, which had been granted privileges in Jordan and in Egypt under Sadat, joined in demanding reform.

In the divided SoC, where incumbent elites have fostered a division between legal moderates and illegal radicals, moderates become less likely to mobilize the masses and demand reforms as the crises continue. Tied to the incumbent regime and thus unable to press for radical change, moderates cannot take full advantage of the increased discontent accompanying economic crises. In contrast, excluded political contenders capitalize on economic difficulties and expand their popular support. This opposition becomes an increasing threat to both incumbents and moderate opponents, and it nearly paralyzes the latter. Legal opponents, fearing that radical forces may exploit any political instability to press their own demands, become unwilling to mobilize against incumbents. They may occasionally mobilize an orderly strike to demand the expansion of political rights, and incumbents may accept this, even granting some of the legal opponents' demands. However, if they call a strike that more radical excluded elites exploit, turning it into unruly, violent demonstrations and demanding the overthrow of the regime, the incumbents repress them severely. For the moderates, it would then be better if they had remained silent. Thus, where a sharp division exists between included and excluded political opponents, moderates may become less likely to protest as economic crises continue.

Consequently, the dynamics of discontent were quite different in Morocco and in Egypt under Mubarak. In the early period of their crises, moderate, legal opponents took advantage of the discontent to demand reforms. Yet, as the crises continued, they became less willing to mobilize. Opponents outside the system capitalized on the discontent. As they became stronger, they were willing to exploit instability to demand their own reforms. King Hasan II and President Mubarak made it clear to the moderate opposition that creating such situations or joining with excluded groups to pressure the regime was wholly unacceptable. This was true even in regard to the Muslim Brotherhood. Mubarak had earlier granted the Brotherhood unique privileges, allowing it to organize openly while refusing to legalize it. However, by the mid-1990s, Mubarak took advantage of its illegal status to repress the Brotherhood as well as groups such as the SLP that were accused of cooperating with it. The institutional structure allowed Mubarak to divide the opposition, creating dynamics that were more violent but nevertheless mirrored those in Morocco. As the crisis continued, the moderate opponents became less and less willing to challenge the regime.

Informal Mechanisms of Rule

The formal institutions that govern the opposition also influence the informal mechanisms that incumbents use to manage the opposition. Incumbents try to manipulate the existence and strength of the many different opposition groups advocating a range of policies. They can alter the composition of the opposition by co-opting some actors or groups, giving them high positions or goodies in return for their moderating their demands. They can also alter the political scene by turning a blind eye to some opponents, severely repressing others, and encouraging still others to establish parties or organizations with given positions.

In unified SoCs, incumbents are more likely to use these mechanisms to promote the existence of moderate opponents with diametrically opposed preferences. In Jordan, for instance, the more moderate Muslim Brotherhood enjoyed some ability to organize and express demands even in the more repressive period from 1970 to 1989, largely in response to the greater strength of secularist opponents. Moderate secularists were also fostered, however. Thus, in the early 1980s, secular activists were invited into the NCC and Jamal Sha'ir was allowed to establish a pseudopolitical party. Members of more radical organizations associated with the PLO received much harsher treatment. Not surprisingly, the prison in Amman housing political prisoners was often referred to as "Funduq Filistin" ("Palestine Hotel").[1] President Sadat used a similar strategy in Egypt, releasing members of the Muslim Brotherhood in an attempt to counter the leftists.

In divided SoCs, incumbents actually benefit from the existence of radical ideological opponents poised to exploit political unrest. Because incumbents have manipulated the costs of opposition, these groups pose a threat to the moderates as well as to the incumbents. Moderates become unwilling to challenge incumbents when they believe that radical forces on the fringe are ready to exploit their activity to destabilize the regime, forcing them to pay high costs. Thus, in Morocco, King Hasan II benefited from the existence of radical Islamists, and while he took steps to clip their wings, he never fully caged them.

Considering how authoritarian leaders create institutions to manage competing opposition groups is both empirically accurate and theoretically fruitful. This work identifies different SoCs and the dynamics of opposition within them. It does not, however, answer the question of which structures incumbents choose to create. Nor does it examine how well these structures can withstand political pressures.

Institutional Formation

The first, and most difficult, issue is to discover why incumbents promote the institutional arrangements that they do. Why do incumbents choose to allow a wider or narrower portion of political constituencies to participate in the formal system? When do they create divided or unified SoCs? Understanding the creation of political institutions is much more difficult than examining how these institutions affect political behavior. Yet, it is extremely important.

The cases examined here provide some preliminary answers. Jordan and Morocco are distinguished most easily by their size and by the homogeneity of their population. In Jordan, the small size of the country made it relatively easy for the King to know and meet with the whole of his opposition. Morocco, in contrast, is much more expansive, and the political opponents were more numerous and widespread. Thus, allowing all of the opposition into the formal political system may not have been as difficult for King Husayn to manage as it would have been for King Hasan II. King Husayn could expect most of his opposition to be willing to negotiate with him and maintain their loyalty; given their numbers, he would know who did not. King Hasan II could have similar expectations of a segment of his opponents, and these he allowed to play the political game. That Egypt remained comparatively more stable under Mubarak than under Sadat lends some support to this hypothesis as well.

Divisions in the social structure also appear to affect whether or not incumbents promote divided or unified SoCs. In Jordan, King Husayn was both blessed and cursed by the Palestinian problem. Clearly, some opponents with Palestinian identities posed a political threat to the King. However, they were also a threat to the Transjordanians. Some Transjordanians grudgingly came to rely upon the King (also an outsider to some) to shield them from this threat. Similarly, many business entrepreneurs of Palestinian origin needed to rely upon the King for a secure and relatively unrestricted business climate. As discussed in Chapter 5, the King was able to exploit these fault lines. There was no need for him to create political divisions as well.

In Morocco, social divisions would not have been so easy to exploit. There were clear regional and ethnic distinctions among the Moroccan population (e.g., North vs. South, Amazigh vs. Arab), and these distinctions had political implications. Yet, these groups did not pose such clear threats to each other, nor did they rely as much on the King. It is unlikely that these groups' fear of each other would have made political opponents unwilling to confront the palace. Yet, differences in social structures do not fully explain the choices of SoCs. Indeed, that King Hasan II chose to reconfigure the Moroccan system in 1996, allowing the Islamist Party of Justice and Development to participate in 1997, demonstrated once again that leaders actively and strategically structure contestation. These institutional arrangements are a result of strategic decisions. Even in the same country, a leader can choose different SoCs over time. That the domestic debate over Amazigh identity,[2] along with debates over the role of religion in society, has since risen on the agenda suggests that formal structures and informal strategies of rule may be closely related. It also means that the question of when such strategies – both formal and informal – are used remains an important area of study.

Resilience of Structure

The related set of questions that remain unanswered is how well incumbents in these institutional arrangements withstand severe political challenges. Incumbents' strength (as measured by such factors as popular support and military resources) plays an important role in determining whether or not regimes can withstand political opposition. However, their strategies are important as well. Does repression help to thwart or further mobilize political opponents? When does a degree of political liberalization limit opponents' demands, and when does it provide fuel for greater mobilization?

Preliminary work suggests that the relationship among various opposition groups, as well as between the government and opponents, is important in determining how resilient political regimes can be. It suggests that a weak security system, in which opposition groups can exploit some level of political unrest, may actually help reduce opposition in the divided SoC. No such phenomenon appears in the undivided environment. Similarly, a limited amount of political liberalization may reduce the maximum demands made in the divided SoC, but such an opening is only likely to lead to greater demands in the undivided system. The strategies used to reduce conflict in the two systems are likely to differ. The effects of these strategies on states' abilities to withstand conflict also depend on the type of political environment in which they are used.

Recognizing competing opposition groups and considering how incumbents manipulate SoCs to restrain these opponents is important in understanding government–opposition relations. It helps explain when opponents choose to press demands, as well as how successful they may be. Much more work is needed, however, for the reasons for the emergence of various institutional structures, and their importance, to be fully understood.

Appendix

Political Forces in Egypt, Jordan, and Morocco

Major Moroccan Political Forces in the 1970s and 1980s

	Dates Founded and Disbanded	Prominent Leaders and Predominant Constituency	Ideological Tendency and Party Platform	Additional Notes
Legal Parties				
Constitutional Union Party l'Union Constitutionnelle Hizb al-Ittihad al-Dusturi	1983–	Founded by Muʿti Buʿbid when he was serving as Prime Minister. Umbrella party of royalist independents with significant support from the King.	Royalist pro-government party. Proposed a progressive agenda, emphasizing responsiveness to both cities and the countryside, and support for medium-sized private sector enterprises.	Became the largest party in parliament after the 1984 elections due to Hasan II's strong support. Published *Risalat al-Ummah*.
Democratic Constitutional Party le Parti Constitutionnelle Démocrate Hizb al-Dustur al-Dimuqrati	1959–	Muhammad al-Wazzani, with support from his personal followers.	Pro-government nationalist party. Largely motivated by a personal conflict between al-Wazzani and Istiqlal's al-Fasi.	Emerged from Democratic Party of Independence, founded in 1946. In 1993, readopted old PDI name. Published *al-Raʾi al-ʿAmm*.

Party	Date	Leaders	Platform	Notes
The Istiqlal (Independence) Party le Parti de l'Istiqlal Hizb al-Istiqlal	1944–	Early leaders included ʿAllal al-Fasi and Ahmad Bellafrej. Later leaders include Muhammad Boucetta, Muhammad al-Yazidi, and ʿAbd al-Haq Tazi. Began as a small party of urban merchants and French-educated intellectuals. After the 1940s, attracted urban poor and new urban migrants.	Nationalist party. Initially, aimed at achieving independence. Later, concerned with economic reform and Islamic socialism.	Younger leaders split from party and formed the UNFP in 1959. Oscillated between periods of participation in and opposition to government. Associated with the General Union of Moroccan Workers. Published al-ʿAlam and L'opinion.
National Democratic Party le Parti National Démocrate Hizb al-Watani al-Dimuqrati	1981–	Arsalane al-Jadidi, ʿAbd al-Hamid Qasimi, and other rural landholding notables from the RNI who were frustrated with the leadership of Ahmad ʿUsman.	Royalist pro-government party. Advocated governmental aid for large-scale commercial agriculture, food subsidies, and protectionist agricultural law.	Obtained four government portfolios in 1981, but power declined after 1983 due to competition from Royalist UC. Founded a student organization, the National Union of Democratic Students (UNED), in 1983. Published al-Dimuqrati.

(continued)

	Dates Founded and Disbanded	Prominent Leaders and Predominant Constituency	Ideological Tendency and Party Platform	Additional Notes
National Rally of Independents le Rassemblement National des Indépendants al-Tajammuʿ al-Watani lil-Ahrar	1978–	Ahmad ʿUsman and independent royalists.	Royalist pro-government party. Lacked a coherent ideology or program but favored rapid modernization, a pro-Western stance in foreign policy, and Morocco's bid for sovereignty over the Western Sahara.	Formed as a means of organizing independent royalists. Enjoyed renewed royal patronage in early 1990s since the UC (formed in 1983 to play the same role as RNI) was not more successful. Published al-Mithaq al-Watani.
National Union of Popular Forces Union Nationale des Forces Populaires al-Ittihad al-Watani lil-Quwwat al-Shaʿbiyah	1959–	Mahdi Bin Barakah and then ʿAbdallah Ibrahim, with support primarily in urban areas from labor, merchants and the French-educated intelligentsia. Supported by the only organized labor syndicate, the UMT (led by Mahjub Bin Sadiq), until 1963, and by the only student union (UNEM).	Leftist opposition party. Less Islamist than the Istiqlal Party. Adopted an anti-royalist line with pan Arab nuances, frequently boycotting elections.	Founded by a radical breakaway group of the Istiqlal. Bin Barakah was exiled from Morocco in 1960, and the party was frequently repressed. In 1975 a faction led by Buʿbid left to found the USFP. By 1984 most UNFP supporters had moved to the USFP or to clandestine radical groups such as the Movement of March 23. Published al-Ittihad al-Watani.

Organization of Democratic and Popular Action l'Organisation de l'Action Démocratique et Populaire Munazamat al-ʿAmal al-Dimuqrati al-Shaʿbi	1983–	Mohammed Bin Saʿid with followers from the Movement of Mars 23 willing to accept Morocco's bid for the Western Sahara. Leftist opposition party. Based on Marxist-Leninist principles, adopted more socialist populist agenda than other legal opposition parties. Brought to legal status in part when it supported King's Western Sahara policies.	Emerged from the underground Movement of March 23, which had come from a split with the UNFP in 1970. Published *Anual*, edited by ʿAbd al-Latif ʿAwad.
Party of Action le Parti de l'Action Hizb al-ʿAmal	1974–1984	Founded by ʿAbdallah al-Senhaji (formally a member of Istiqlal and a founding member of both MP and UNFP), with support from intellectuals, administrators, and businessmen, primarily from the Sous plain and Middle Atlas. Rural, largely Amazigh party. Tried to provide rural elites with a more leftist and innovative alternative to the MP.	Won only two seats in 1977. Published *al-Maghribi*.

(continued)

(continued)

	Dates Founded and Disbanded	Prominent Leaders and Predominant Constituency	Ideological Tendency and Party Platform	Additional Notes
Party of Progress and Socialism le Parti du Progrès et du Socialisme Hizb al-Taqaddum wa al-Ishtirakiyah	1974–	'Ali Ya'ta with a following primarily of urban students and teachers.	Leftist opposition party. Advocated Eastern European–style communism with nonrevolutionary tactics. Supported nationalization, price controls, and an anti-Western orientation of foreign policy.	PPS was a new organizational name for the former Moroccan Communist Party (1948–1968) and the subsequent, unsuccessful Party of Liberation and Socialism (1968–1970). Published al-Bayane.
Popular Democratic and Constitutional Popular Movement le Mouvement Populaire Démocratique et Constitutionnel al-Harakah al-Sha'biyah al-Dusturiyah al-Dimuqratiyah	1967–	Founded by 'Abd al-Karim al-Khatib, with a small group of personal followers, particularly from urban areas.	Pro-government, urban-oriented party. Platform similar to that of the Popular Movement, from which al-Khatib had split.	al-Khatib split from the Popular Movement when long-held personal tensions between al-Khatib and al-Mahjubi Ahardan exploded over reactions to the emergency law following the 1965 riots. Won no seats in 1984 elections. Published al-Maghrib al-'Arabi.

Popular Movement le Mouvement Populaire al-Harakah al-Sha'biyah	1957–	al-Mahjubi Ahardane, Secretary General until 1986, with a primarily rural Amazigh constituency, particularly strong in the northern and central mountainous regions.	Pro-government, rural-oriented party. Outcome of rural resentment of the urban orientation of the then-dominant Istiqlal. Advocated austerity, nonalignment, and minimization of rural inequalities under the motto "Islamic socialism."	Formed with support of King to counter Istiqlal and joined the pro-monarchy alignment, FDIC, in 1963. Participated in every government from 1961. Published *al-Harakah*.
Socialist Union of Popular Forces l'Union Socialiste des Forces Populaires al-Ittihad al-Ishtiraki lil-Quwwat al-Sha'biya	1972–	'Abd al-Rahman Yusufi replaced 'Abd al-Rahim Bu'bid following Bu'bid's death in 1992. Primarily urban-based support, particularly from young, low-level state employees, workers, and intellectuals.	Leftist opposition party. Considered the most important legal opposition party, it was ideologically close to Western European social democratic parties. Called for civil liberties, land reform and limited nationalization, and human rights. Supported Morocco's bid for the Western Sahara.	Emerged from the Rabat branch of the UNFP headed by 'Abd al-Rahim Bu'bid. Won 14.6% of the votes in the 1977 parliamentary elections and became the leading opposition party in Morocco. Linked to the Democratic Labor Confederation (CDT). Published *al-Ittihad al-Ishtiraki* and *Libération*.

(continued)

	Dates Founded and Disbanded	Prominent Leaders and Predominant Constituency	Ideological Tendency and Party Platform	Additional Notes
Illegal Opposition				
Islamic Community le Groupe Islamique al-Jamaʿah al-Islamiyah	1977–	Founded by ʿAbd al-Ilah Benkirane with support of moderates from the Islamic Youth movement after the 1977 repression.	Islamist opposition movement. Most moderate Islamist opposition group, it attempted from the mid-1980s to participate in the legal political system.	Changed its name to Reform and Renewal (al-Islah wa al-Tajdid), then in 1996 to Movement of Unity and Reform (Harakah al-Tawhid wa al-Islah) in an attempt to gain legal recognition. When King Hasan II reconfigured the political system in 1997, it participated in elections as the Party of Justice and Development.
Islamic Youth Association Mouvement de la Jeunesse Islamique Jamʿiyah al-Shabibah al-Islamiyah	1969–	Led by ʿAbd al-Karim al-Mutiʿ and ʿAbd al-Salam Naʿmani, primarily with support of the urban poor, secondary and university students, technical workers, and professionals. Strong in major cities.	Islamic opposition group. Heavily influenced by Hasan al-Banna's Muslim Brotherhood, sought to spread Islamic morals and values, and officially rejected the use of violence.	Legalized as a cultural association in 1972. Repressed by the government after accused of the murder of a USFP leader, ʿUmar Bin Jelloun, in 1975. Split into four factions in the late 1970s and early 1980s.

Justice and Charity Movement Justice et Bienfaisance Harakat al-ʿAdl wa al-Ihsan	1974–	Led by ʿAbd al-Salam Yasin, primarily with support of students.	Islamist opposition movement. Sought total restructuring of the government along Islamic lines. Was seen as tactically less violent than the Islamic Youth.	Emerged from the Islamic Youth, initially as Usrat al-Jamaʿah but changed its name in 1987. Yasin became a symbol of anti-establishment Islam. Government crackdown on the movement in the 1990s led to riots in Moroccan universities.
Movement of March 23 Mouvement du 23 Mars Harakah 23 Mars	1970–	Muhammad Bin Saʿid, with support of more radical UNFP members.	Leftist opposition party. Based on Marxist-Leninist principles but divided in its position over the Western Sahara.	Emerged from split within the UNFP and took its name from a day of anti-government riots that erupted as a result of massive discontent with the government. By the end of the 1970s, most members had returned to the UNFP or joined the newer OADP. Published 23 Mars.

(continued)

	Dates Founded and Disbanded	Prominent Leaders and Predominant Constituency	Ideological Tendency and Party Platform	Additional Notes
Mujahidin Movement Harakah al-Mujahidin	Early 1980s–	ʿAbd al-ʿAziz Naʿmani, supported primarily by youth and students.	Islamist opposition movement. Sought to overthrow the Moroccan monarchy and establish a leftist regime based on Islam.	Considered the most active movement emerging from al-Shabibah al-Islamiyah. Closer to Iran than Morocco's other Islamist groups.
Ila al-Amam (Forward) Organization Munazamat "Ila al-Amam"	1970–	Led initially by Ibrahim Serfaty with small group of followers.	Leftist opposition party. Supported a leftist agenda and self-determination in the Western Sahara.	Emerged from the Party of Liberation and Socialism. Outlawed largely due to its support for self-determination in the Western Sahara. After its leader and many members were imprisoned, most members reaffiliated with the PPS.

Major Jordanian Political Forces in the 1970s and 1980s

	Dates Founded and Disbanded	Prominent Leaders and Predominant Constituency	Ideological Tendency and Party Platform	Additional Notes
Legal Group				
Muslim Brotherhood Jama'at al-Ikhwan al-Muslimin	1946–	'Abd al-Latif Abu Qurrah, 'Abd al-Latif 'Arabayat with support in urban areas (i. e., Amman, Irbid, Madaba, Karak, Aqaba) and among rural women and Jordanians of Palestinian origin.	Islamist organization. Desired implementation of *shari'a* law and maintenance of "Islamic morals" but accepted democratic institutions. Called for the liberation of Palestine. Known for social and charitable work.	Allowed to operate legally as a charitable association, not a political party.
Illegal Opposition				
Progressive Arab Resurrection (Ba'th) Party Hizb al-Ba'th al-'Arabi al-Taqaddumi	1951–	'Abd al-Rahman Shuqayr, Munif al-Razzaz, and Bahjat Abu Gharbiyah, with support of intellectuals, students, and liberal professionals.	Leftist opposition party. Proposed Arabization of the army, total independence from Britain, nonalignment, and Arab unity.	Published *al-Ba'th*.

(continued)

(continued)

	Dates Founded and Disbanded	Prominent Leaders and Predominant Constituency	Ideological Tendency and Party Platform	Additional Notes
Communist Worker's Party in Jordan Hizb al-ʿUmmal al-Shuyuʿi fil-Urdun	Late 1970s–1992	Hisham al-Hijazi, Nizar al-Qayid, and Yusuf Hamid.	Leftist opposition party. With Marxist–Leninist orientation, demanded greater democratic freedoms and respect for constitution.	Split from Palestinian Communist Worker's Party. In 1992, merged with the Jordanian Democratic Party.
Constitutional Arab Front al-Jabhah al-ʿArabiyah al-Dusturiyah	1975–	Milhim al-Tall with support of tribal leaders.	Jordanian nationalist party. Promoted Jordanian and Palestinian national identities. Sought liberation of Palestine, unity of Greater Syria, and adherence to the constitution as the basis of politics.	First won parliamentary seats in 1989.
Democratic Front Organization in Jordan Munazamat al-Jabhah al-Dimuqratiyah fi al-Urdun	1974–	Nayif Hawatmah.	Leftist opposition party. Based on Marxist principles and dedicated to the liberation of Palestine through revolution of the masses.	Split from the PFLP in 1974. Jordanian branch of the Democratic Front for the Liberation of Palestine (al-Jabbah al-Dimuqratiyah li-Tahrir Filastin), which was established in 1969. Received logistical support from Syria.

Party	Dates	Founders/Support	Description	Notes
Unionist Democratic Unionist Bloc al-Tajammuʿ al-Dimuqrati al-Wahdawi	1983–	Jamal al-Shaʿir with support of ex-members of the Baʿth party, professors, civil servants, intellectuals, and lawyers.	Center-left party. Sought return to parliamentary life and reform of the political party law. Demanded pan-Arab unity on a confederal basis, unity of the East and West Banks, and adoption of neutralist foreign policy	Semiunderground party. Openly held party meetings in period of martial law.
Jordanian Communist Party al-Hizb al-Shuyuʿi al-Urdunni	1951–	Fuʿad Nasir and Yaʿqub Ziyadin, with strong West Bank support.	Leftist opposition party. Sought a communist state in Jordan.	Formed from merger of the Palestinian Communist Party (Palestinian League of National Liberation) and the Jordanian Marxists.
Jordanian Revolutionary People's Party Hizb al-Shaʿb al-Thawri al-Urdunni	1970s–1992	Burayq al-Hadid and Ahmad Mahmud Ibrahim	Leftist opposition party. Promoted Arab culture and intellectual advancement.	Jordanian branch of Arab Socialist Worker's Party, which merged with the Baʿth Party in 1993.

(continued)

(continued)

	Dates Founded and Disbanded	Prominent Leaders and Predominant Constituency	Ideological Tendency and Party Platform	Additional Notes
Liberation Party Hizb al-Tahrir	1952–	Shaykh Taqi al-Din al-Nabhani with breakaway members from the Muslim Brotherhood.	Islamist opposition party. Called for the comprehensive application of Islam in Jordan. Rejected the monarchy.	Split from the Jordanian Muslim Brotherhood.
Popular Front for the Liberation of Palestine al-Jabhah al-Shaʿbiyah li-Tahrir Filastin	1969–	George Habash, Abu Mustafa, and, later, Ahmad Sadat.	Leftist opposition party. Based on Marxist principles, sought to liberate all of Palestine and establish a democratic socialist Palestinian state.	Received logistical support from Syria.

Major Egyptian Political Forces under Sadat, 1970s

	Dates Founded and Disbanded	Prominent Leaders and Predominant Constituency	Ideological Tendency and Party Platform	Additional Notes
Legal Parties				
Arab Socialist Union al-Hizb al-ʿArabi al-Ishtiraki	1961–1977	Rifʿat Mahjub, Husayn Shafʿi, and ʿAli Sabri with a heterogeneous constituency including professionals, state bureaucrats, workers, and peasants. A 1962 law stated that all union members must be ASU members.	Government party. The only legal party of the early 1970s, promoted the Nasirist agenda, including strengthening pan-Arabism and socialism. Under Sadat, increased calls for democratic reforms and economic liberalization.	Became virtually irrelevant after 1975, when Sadat split the left, right, and center wings of party into three separate platforms. Disbanded in 1977, when platforms were legalized as parties.
Liberal Socialist Party Hizb al-Ahrar al-Ishtiraki	1976–	Mustafa Kamel Murad and Mustafa Bakri with support of the business class. Estimated membership 50,000.	Rightist conservative party. Called for economic liberalization, private sector development, lower taxes, pro-Western foreign policy. Supported a multiparty system but called for a ban on the Communist Party.	Grew out of right-wing platform of the ASU and was legalized in 1977. Published daily newspaper *al-Abrar* and weeklies *al-Haqiqah* and *al-Nur*.

(continued)

(continued)

	Dates Founded and Disbanded	Prominent Leaders and Predominant Constituency	Ideological Tendency and Party Platform	Additional Notes
National Democratic Party al-Hizb al-Watani al-Dimuqrati	1977–	Husni Mubarak, Yusuf Amin Wali, ʿUbayd Mansur, and Mustafa Khalil with support of the business class, professionals, and some limited rural support after 1981. Estimated 2.5 million party members.	Centrist pro-government party. NDP succeeded the ASU as the government party; supported economic *infitah*, multiparty democracy with a strong state, turn toward the West, Camp David Accords, and normalization of relations with Israel.	Grew out of center platform of ASU. Published state newspaper *al-Mayu*.
National Progressive Unionist Front Party Hizb al-Tajammuʿ al-Watani al-Taqaddumi al-Wihdawi	1977–	Khalid Muhyi al-Din, Kemal al-Din Rifʿat, Muhammad Ahmad Khalf-Allah, and Rifʿat al-Saʿid with support of trade unionists, leftist intellectuals, rural sector and former Communist Party members. Estimated membership 150,000.	Leftist, social democratic party. Pro-labor, called for increased public sector support and greater democratic freedoms. Opposed normalization of relations with Israel and Egyptian reliance on the United States.	Grew out of leftist platform of the ASU. Blamed for 1977 IMF riots. Published *al-Ahali*, with circulation of approximately 100,000.

Socialist Labor Party Hizb al-ʿAmal al-Ishtiraki	1977–	Ibrahim Shukri, ʿAdil Husayn, Naji al-Shihabi and Majdi Ahmad led party of socialists, liberals, and Egyptian nationalists. Estimated membership 350,000.	Leftist nationalist party. Sought economic development but with social welfare protection. Called for multiparty democracy.	Legalized to check the NPUP after 1977. Disbanded but reemerged in 1983. Published biweekly *al-Shaʿb*.

Illegal Parties

al-Jihad	1978–	ʿAbd al-Salam Faraj, Khalid al-Islambuli, with support from Shabib Muhammad and lower-class students drawn primarily from Upper Egypt, especially Asyut and Minya.	Islamist opposition party. Advocated *jihad* as an armed struggle to establish an Islamic state. Accused more moderate groups of having been co-opted. Saw Christians and Jews as infidels and legitimate targets of *jihad*.	Responsible for the assassination of Sadat. Planted explosives in Coptic churches in 1980.
Egyptian Communist Party Hizb al-Shuyuʿi al-Masri	1920–	Husni al-ʿArabi, with support of Marxists and other dissidents of NPUP.	Leftist opposition party. With Marxist basis, opposed Sadat's economic reforms and relations with the United States and Israel. Sought to preserve Nasir's legacy.	Published small newspapers (irregularly).

(continued)

	Dates Founded and Disbanded	Prominent Leaders and Predominant Constituency	Ideological Tendency and Party Platform	Additional Notes
Muslim Brotherhood Jamaʿat al-Ikhwan al-Muslimin	1928–	Founded by Hasan al-Banna. Later led by Muhammed Abu al-Nasr, Mustafa Mashhur, Maʾmun al-Hudaybi, and Sayf al-Islam Hasan al-Banna with support of the urban classes, especially professionals.	Islamist opposition party. Called for the extension of *shariʿa* law and sought social reforms to safeguard "Islamic morality." Opposed implementation of the *infitah* and normalization of relations with Israel after 1979 and opposed U.S-Egyptian relations.	Improved relations between government and the Brotherhood under Sadat, who released Brothers from prison after 1970 to counter Nasirists. Published *al-Daʿwa* and *al-ʿIttisam*.
New Wafd (Wafd) Party Hizb al-Wafd al-Jadid	1978–	Fuʿad Siraj al-Din and Hilmi Murad with support from professionals, landowners, and bureaucrats in liberal upper-middle classes and others who wanted a base to oppose Sadat (including some Marxists, Islamists, and independents).	Center-right opposition party. Denied that Nasir's revolution was a popular revolution, claiming it was a coup. Called for parliamentary-cabinet system, greater economic liberalization, and restricted public sector of economy. Ambiguous foreign policy position.	Formed from prerevolutionary Wafd party. Not legally recognized in 1978. Published *al-Wafd*.

Mohammad's Youth Shabib Muhammed (aka Military Academy Group)	Early 1970s–	Poor recent migrants to Cairo, Alexandria, and Asyut.	Islamic opposition party. Religious fundamentalist party that advocated an Islamic caliphate. Called upon members to integrate into society (i.e., normal dress, lifestyle) to avoid attracting attention.	Responsible for 1974 attack on Technical Military Academy. Allegedly supported by Libya.
(Excommunication and Emigration) Takfir wa al-Hijrah	1960s–	Led by Shukri Mustafa, with support of religious conservatives disillusioned with the Muslim Brotherhood, particularly poor recent migrants to Cairo, Alexandria, and Asyut. Estimated support of 3,000–5,000 members.	Conservative Islamist opposition party. More radical than the Muslim Brotherhood, it denied the legitimacy of the regime and of society as a whole, including the religious establishment. Advocated total withdrawal from society in order to prepare to "restore" the political order through force. Engaged in paramilitary training.	Offshoot of the Muslim Brotherhood. Charged with 1977 assassination of Minister of Religious Affairs Muhammad al-Dhahabi.

Major Egyptian Political Forces under Mubarak, 1980s and 1990s

	Dates Founded and Disbanded	Prominent Leaders and Predominant Constituency	Ideological Tendency and Party Platform	Additional Notes
Legal Parties				
Arab Democratic Nasirist Party al-Hizb al-ʿArabi al-Dimuqrati al-Nasiri	1990–	Hamdi Sabahi and Amin Iskander, with middle-class support. Limited support among university students.	Leftist-oriented opposition party. Called for government-led economic development, including a large role for the public sector, greater freedom, and multiparty democracy. Sought Arab unity and preservation of the Nasirist legacy. Strongly anti-Zionist and anti-U.S bias.	Legalized in 1992 after court battle. Led opposition to Mubarak's third term in the 1993 national referendum. Boycotted the National Dialogue Conference in 1994. Poor showing in the 1995 elections. Published *al-ʿArabi*.
Liberal Socialist Party Hizb al-Ahrar al-Ishtiraki	1976–	Mustafa Kamel Murad and Mustafa Bakri, with support of the business class. Estimated membership of 50,000.	Rightist conservative party. Called for economic liberalization, private sector development, lower taxes, pro-Western foreign policy. Called for a multiparty system but a ban on Communist Party.	Grew out of right-wing platform of the ASU and legalized in 1977. Published *al-Ahrar* and the weeklies *al-Haqiqah* and *al-Nur*.

Party		Leadership and support	Platform	Notes
National Democratic Party al-Hizb al-Watani al-Dimuqrati	1977–	Husni Mubarak and Yusuf Amin Wali, with support primarily from the business class and professionals. Estimated 2.5 million party members.	Centrist, secularist pro-government party. Supported *infitah*, a strong state with multiparty democracy, the Camp David Accords, and normalization of relations with Israel.	Grew out of center platform of ASU. Published *al-Mayu*.
National Progressive Unionist Party Hizb al-Tajammu' al-Watani al-Taqaddumi al-Wahdawi	1977–	Khalid Muhyi al-Din, Kemal al-Din Rif'at, Lufti al-Khawli, Muhammad Ahmad Khalf-Allah, and Rif'at al-Sa'id, with support of trade unionists, the rural sector, intellectuals, and former Communist Party members. Estimated membership of 150,000.	Leftist social democratic party. Pro-labor, the party called for increased public sector support and greater democratic freedom. Opposed normalization of relations with Israel and Egyptian reliance on the United States. Party slogan: "Against corruption. Against terrorism. For more democracy. For more bread."	Grew increasingly weak with legalization of the Socialist Labor Party and complaints of harassment by the Mubarak government. Did not win any seats in the 1984 or 1987 elections but was one of the few parties to run in the elections of 1990.

(continued)

(continued)

	Dates Founded and Disbanded	Prominent Leaders and Predominant Constituency	Ideological Tendency and Party Platform	Additional Notes
New Wafd Party Hizb al-Wafd al-Jadid	1978–	Fu'ad Siraj al-Din, Mumtaz Nasr, and Ibrahim Faraj, with support from professionals, landowners, bureaucrats in the liberal upper middle classes, and others who wanted a base to oppose Sadat (including some Marxists, Islamists, and independents). Estimated 2 million members.	Center-right opposition party. Denied that Nasir's revolution was popular, claiming that it was a coup. Called for parliamentary-cabinet system, greater economic liberalization, and a restricted public sector. Became increasingly anti-Western and anti-Israel, and began to adopt Islamic overtones.	Lost Coptic support after the 1984–1987 alliance with the Brotherhood, then lost Muslim supporters to the Brotherhood. Boycotted the 1990 elections, although some members ran as independents. Published *al-Wafd*.
Socialist Labor Party Hizb al-'Amal al-Ishtiraki	1977–	Ibrahim Shukri, 'Adil Husayn, Naji al-Shihabi, and Majdi Ahmad led a party of socialists, liberals, and Egyptian nationalists. Estimated membership 350,000.	Leftist nationalist party. Opposed Sadat's economic reforms. Sought economic development but with social welfare protection. Called for multiparty democracy. Took on increasingly Islamic overtones and was the mainstream party most critical of Mubarak.	Disbanded but reemerged in 1983. Allied with the Brotherhood after 1987. Boycotted elections of 1990. Published biweekly newspaper *al-Sha'b* and biquarterly periodical *Manbar al-Sharq*, but regularly closed by government after 1991.

Umma Party Hizb al-Ummah	1984–	Ahmad al-Sibahi ʿAwad Allah with Islamist followers. Estimated membership 250,000.	Islamist opposition party. Formed primarily to allow the Muslim Brotherhood members to stand for election under the guise of a legal party. Called for implementation of *shariʿa* law, legalization of all religious parties, and economic and political liberalization. Made some demands for economic and political liberalization	Little activity after Muslim Brotherhood made an alliance with the Wafd Party and then the SLP. Published weekly newspaper *al-Ummah*.

Illegal Groups

Egyptian Communist Party al-Hizb al-Shuyuʿi al-Masri	1920–	Founded by Husni al-ʿArabi, with support of Marxists and those dissatisfied with NPUP. Little popular support.	Leftist opposition party. Opposed economic liberalization and called for defense of Nasir's legacy. Anti-Israel and anti-U.S. bias.	Published small newspapers sporadically.
Takfir wa al-Hijrah Excommunication and Emigration	1960s–	Led by Shukri Mustafa, with support of religious conservatives disillusioned with the Muslim Brotherhood, particularly poor recent migrants to Cairo, Alexandria, and Asyut.	Conservative religious opposition group. Splintered between those who call for immediate Islamic law and those who favor a more gradualist approach.	Charged with attacks on video and alcohol stores and nightclubs in 1987.

(*continued*)

	Dates Founded and Disbanded	Prominent Leaders and Predominant Constituency	Ideological Tendency and Party Platform	Additional Notes
Islamic Community al-Jama'ah al-Islamiyah	Founded around 1992	Jamal Farghaly Haridi with previous members of al-Jihad.	Conservative religious opposition group. Sought Islamic regime in Egypt through militant means.	Charged with terrorist attacks against the government, tourists, and Christians in Upper Egypt.
Islamic Jihad	Late 1970s	Muhammad 'Abd al- Salam Faraj, 'Abbud al-Zummar, and 'Umar 'Abd al- Rahman, with rural support.	Conservative religious opposition party. Called for overthrow of regime and extension of *shari'a* law throughout Egypt.	Charged with killing of President Sadat. Linked with 'Umar 'Abd al-Rahman and the 1993 bombing of the World Trade Center. Had links with other terrorist groups.
Muslim Brotherhood Jama'at al-Ikhwan al-Muslimin	1928–	Muhammad Abu al-Nasr, Ma'mun al-Hudaybi, and Sayf al-Islam Hasan al-Banna with followers from urban areas.	Religious opposition party. Called for the extension of *shari'a* law. Opposed normalization of relations with Israel after 1979 and criticized U.S.–Egyptian relations. Opposed cooperation in U.S.-led allied coalition against Iraq in 1990–1991.	Boycotted 1990 elections. Called on the government to legalize the party, although many members ran as independents or on other party slates. Allied at different times with Wafd Party and SLP.

| New Islamic Jihad | 1990– | Shawki Rizq al-Shaykh | Conservative religious opposition group. Called for implementation of Islamic law throughout Egypt. | Charged with assassination of National Assembly Speaker Rif'at al-Mahjub in October 1990. Allegedly responsible for Muslim–Christian riots in 1990. |

Sources: al-Sayyid, *Ahzab al-muʿaradah wa siyasat al-infitah al-iqtisadi fi Misr*; Ansari, "The Islamic Militants"; Ayubi, "The Political Revival of Islam"; Bayat, "Revolution without Movement"; Dagharni, *al-Intikhabat wa al-ahzab al-siyasiyah al-Maghribiyah*; East and Joseph, *Political Parties of Africa and the Middle East*; Hinnebusch, "The Reemergence of the Wafd Party"; Hurani, *al-Ahzab al-siyasiyah al-Urduniyah*; Kassem, *Egyptian Politics: The Dynamics of Authoritarian Rule*; Mustafa, *Intikhabat al-barlamaniyah fi Misr 1995*; Paz, "The Global Jihad Brotherhood"; Rubin, *Islamic Fundamentalism in Egyptian Politics*; Sarah, *Ahzab wa al-quwwa al-siyyasiyah fi al-Maghrib*; Sullivan and Abed-Kotob, *Islam in Contemporary Egypt*; Tachau (ed.) *Political Parties of the Middle East and North Africa*.

Notes

Introduction

1. Diamond "Thinking About Hybrid Regimes"; Levitsky and Way, "The Rise of Competitive Authoritarianism"; Levitsky and Way, "Autocracy By Democratic Rules."
2. Walton, "Debt, Protest and the State in Latin America": 308.
3. For a review, see Walton and Ragin, "Global and National Sources of Political Protest." It should be noted, however, that economic growth and prosperity may also be destabilizing, depending on how the benefits are distributed. Mason, "Modernization and Its Discontents Revisited."
4. Chaudhry, "Economic Liberalization in Oil-Exporting Countries"; Lawson, "Divergent Modes of Economic Liberalization in Syria and Iraq"; Remmer, "The Politics of Economic Stabilization"; Richards and Waterbury, *A Political Economy of the Middle East*; Waterbury, "The Political Management of Economic Adjustment and Reform"; Skidmore, "The Politics of Economic Stabilization in Postwar Latin America"; Collier (ed.), *The New Authoritarianism in Latin America*; Haggard and Kaufman, "Economic Adjustment in New Democracies"; Haggard and Kaufman, *The Political Economy of Democratic Transitions;* Bienen and Herbst, "The Relationship Between Political and Economic Reform in Africa"; Geddes, "Economic Reform and Democracy"; Pool, "The Links between Economic and Political Liberalization"; Bermeo, "Sacrifice, Sequence and Strength"; McFaul, "State Power, Institutional Change and the Politics of Privatization in Russia."
5. There were economic protests in 16 of the 30 countries analyzed by Bratton and van de Walle in "Popular Protest and Political Reform in Africa": 421.
6. Ibid.: 429–430.
7. It is important to note from the outset that I use the term "government" to mean "an organization which controls the principal concentrated means of coercion within the population" (Tilly, *From Mobilization to Revolution*: 52). "Regime" denotes the "rules of the game."

8. Initially, modernization theorists hypothesized that the new states would eventually become democracies (e.g., Lerner, *The Passing of Traditional Society*; Deutsch, "Social Mobilization and Political Development"; Almond and Verba, *Civic Culture*). When this expectation failed to materialize, and particularly when nascent democracies were overturned, dependency (e.g., Wallerstein, *Modern World-System*) and bureaucratic authoritarian (e.g., O'Donnell, *Modernization and Bureaucratic-Authoritarianism*; Collier, *The New Authoritarianism in Latin America*) theorists sought to explain this failure. While dependency theory was less optimistic about the prospects for democratization, bureaucratic authoritarianism held, for instance, that the middle classes would support military rule as long as it helped to dampen popular demands and promote economic development; however, once sufficient "capital deepening" had taken place, demands for democratization could surface again.

9. Przeworski, *Democracy and the Market*: 58.

10. Pye, "Political Science and the Crisis of Authoritarianism."

11. O'Donnell and Schmitter, *Transitions from Authoritarian Rule*: 10.

12. See also Przeworski, "Democracy as a Contingent Outcome of Conflict": 74–75; Karl, "Dilemmas of Democratization in Latin America": 1–21; Dahl, *Polyarchy*: Chapter 3.

13. Przeworski, "Democracy as a Contingent Outcome of Conflicts": 61. Also on the instability of partial liberalization, see Bova, "Political Dynamics of the Post-Communist Transition": 113–138.

14. Heydemann, "Taxation without Representation: Authoritarianism and Economic Liberalization in Syria." See also Perthes, "States of Economic and Political Liberalization": 44–71.

15. Khrouz, "De l'endettement à l'ajustment": 80.

16. Satloff, *Troubles on the East Bank*: 12.

17. Central Bank of Jordan, *Monthly Statistical Bulletin*, March 1983, cited in Alougili, "Comparative Study of Jordan's Foreign Policy": 261.

18. American Embassy in Amman, report made for the U.S. Department of Commerce, "Foreign Economic Trends and Their Implications for the United States": 3, cited in Shami, "A Study of Marketing": 45.

19. World Bank figures from 1988 cited in Ben Ali, "La politique économique marocaine de l'indépendence à nos jours": 5.

20. Sinclair, *Middle East Economic Handbook*: 286.

21. Direction de la statistique, *La population active urbaine* (1990, 1993).

22. Smadi, *The Unemployment Problem in Jordan*.

23. Abdullah Malki, "Returnees – How Much of a Burden?" *Jordan Times*, July 22, 1992: 1.

24. International Monetary Fund, "Supplement to the Staff Report for the 1990 Article IV Consultations with Jordan," cited in Fathi, *Jordan: An Invented Nation?* 171.

25. For data on Morocco, see Royaume du Maroc, *Annuaire statistique du Maroc*, 1979–1994.

26. For a discussion of economic policies and development in the past decade from various viewpoints, see Berrada and Saadi, "Le grand capital privé marocain"; Malki, *Trente ans d'économie marocaine*; Larbi and Sbihi, *Économie marocaine 1960–1990*; Leymarie and Tripier, *Maroc: Le prochain dragon?*; Malki, "L'endettement international du Maroc"; Payne, "Economic Crisis and Policy Reform"; Benazzou, *Panorama économique du Maroc 1969/1985*; Khrouz, *L'économie marocaine*; Benazzou and Mouline, *Panorama économique du Maroc 1985/1990*; Morrisson, *Equity and Adjustment in Morocco*.

27. This was revealed only after 1989. George D. Moffett, "Jordan: Impetus for Change Grows." *Christian Science Monitor*, June 15, 1989: 3.

28. Unable or unwilling to risk a domestic backlash by joining the allied coalition, Jordan withheld its support from the international community during the Gulf War. In return, the United States and Saudi Arabia, two of its most important financiers, withheld aid. In addition, with the Gulf War, Jordan once again found itself the host of refugees. This time the refugees arrived with capital, which eased slightly the economic troubles. However, they also needed employment and services; 44 percent of the returnees were less than 15 years old, and 55 percent were between 15 and 59 years of age. School enrollment alone increased by 42,500 pupils in 1992. *Jordan Times*, January 20, 1992: 3. The Ministry of Planning estimated that Jordan needed a $7 billion investment in infrastructure to accommodate the refugees. Carroll, *Business as Usual*: 58.

29. It should be noted that whether it is the reforms or crises that cause unrest is a subject of a debate that will not be addressed here. See Gersovitz and Bienen, "Economic Stabilization, Conditionality and Political Stability"; Haggard and Kaufman, "The Politics of Stabilisation and Structural Adjustment."

30. Handoussa, "Crisis and Challenge:" 4.

31. CAPMAS, 1960 and 1976 Population Censuses in Fergany, "A Characterization of the Employment Problem in Egypt": 44.

32. Wickham, *Mobilizing Islam*: 32.

33. Handoussa, "Crisis and Challenge": 3.

34. The fall in oil prices coincided with a steep rise in Egypt's debt service obligations. By 1986, the IMF estimated Egypt's debt service payments to be no less than $5.5 billion, almost twice the debt service of 1981 and more than 50 percent of the value of all exports and services in 1985–1986. If the debts had been paid, debt service payments would have taken all income from oil exports, Suez Canal fees, and tourism, as well as about one-third of labor remittances. Ibid: 3–5. See also Amin, *Egypt's Economic Predicament*: 12–21.

35. Debt rose from $30 billion to $37.8 billion. Amin, *Egypt's Economic Predicament*: 14.

36. Richards, "The Political Economy of Dilatory Reform": 1724.

37. Fergany, "A Characterization": 27–29, 45–46.

38. Wickham, *Mobilizing Islam*: 43.

39. Assaad and Commander, *Egypt: The Labour Market Through Boom and Recession*: app. Table 1 cited in Wickham, *Mobilizing Islam*: 47.
40. Assaad and Rouchdy, *Poverty and Poverty Alleviation Strategies*: 9.
41. Kienle, "More Than a Response to Islamism": 221.
42. It should be noted that not all components of civil society are, by definition, oppositional. Stepan distinguishes civil society from "political society" (political parties, elections, legislatures), which engage in contestation over state power, and notes that political society "is frequently absorbed by dominant groups into the state." *Rethinking Military Politics*: 3–4.
43. For examples, see Harbeson, Rothchild, and Chazan, *Civil Society and the State in Africa*; Bernhard, "Civil Society and Democratic Transition in East Central Europe"; and Norton, *Civil Society in the Middle East*, Vols. I and II.
44. Tilly, *From Mobilization to Revolution*: 16–29; Zald and Berger, "Social Movements in Organizations": 823–825; McCarthy and Zald, "Resource Mobilization and Social Movements": 1216.
45. Loveman, "High-Risk Collective Action": 477–525.
46. A 1995 survey found that 51 percent of Jordanians believed that the parties have little success in expressing public demands. Only 42.6 percent of those surveyed had heard of the most popular political bloc, the Islamic Action Front. See CSS, *Istitla'a lil-ra'i hawla al-dimuqratiyah fi al-Urdun 1995*.
47. The estimated number of associations can be found in Ghazali, "Contribution a l'analyse," cited in Korany, "Monarchical Islam": 174.
48. al-Sayyid, "A Civil Society in Egypt?" 273; Ibrahim, Adly, and Shehata, "Civil Society and Governance in Egypt": 24; Makram-Ebeid, "Democratization in Egypt": 120.
49. Nelson, "Linkages Between Politics and Economics": 56.
50. Geddes, "Economic Reform and Democracy": 104–118.
51. Ibid.: 111.
52. Specifically, hierarchical military structures can hinder a full transition because military leaders try to negotiate safeguards; sultanism and totalitarianism impede consolidation; posttotalitarianism is less of a hindrance because it allows some civil society; and civilianized authoritarianism is best for consolidation. Linz and Stepan, *Problems of Democratic Transition and Consolidation*.
53. Geddes, "The Breakdown of Authoritarian Regimes."
54. Gandhi and Przeworski, "Dictatorial Institutions and the Survival of Dictators" and Przeworski and Gandhi, "An Institutional Theory of Development."
55. Interview with Zayd al-Rifa'i as quoted in Mutawi, *Jordan in the 1967 War*: 9. Rifa'i emphasized this point more harshly in 1995, when he argued that "[t]he government executes the policies of His Majesty and any talk of the government having a different view from his Majesty is complete nonsense" (*Jordan Times*, November 15, 1995: 1). For further discussions on King Husayn's political support, see Brand, *Jordan's Inter-Arab Relations*; Satloff, *Troubles on the East Bank*; Jureidini and McLaurin, *Jordan: The Impact of*

Social Change on the Role of the Tribes; and Fathi, *Jordan: An Invented Nation?*

56. For more detailed discussions of the Moroccan system, see Sehimi, "Les élites ministérielles au Maroc"; Korany, "The Magreb"; Zartman, "Opposition as Support of the State"; and Ben Ali, "Changement de pacte sociale et continuité de l'ordre au Maroc."

57. See, for example, Crowley, "Barriers to Collective Action," and Treisman, "Political Decentralization and Economic Reform."

58. Tutunji, "Planning a Workforce for the Future."

59. Davenport, "'Constitutional Promises' and Repressive Reality."

60. Indeed, the early 1980s, after Mubarak came into power, were notable for allowing greater freedom and restraint from the use of military courts. This trend increased during the deliberalization of the 1990s. Yet, more freedoms remained than at the end of the 1970s. Kienle, *Grand Delusion*: 48.

61. For a discussion of the lack of real political reform in Moroccan politics, see Hermassi and Vandewalle, "The Second Stage of State Building": 32–33.

62. Richards and Waterbury (*A Political Economy of the Middle East*: 297–298) note that monarchs have a particular interest in creating a set of divided, competing political groups. This is true, but as we shall see, the manner in which kings undertake this role may differ across monarchies. For further discussion of this difference, see Lust-Okar and Jamal, "Rulers and Rules": 353–356.

63. Bryen, Korany, and Noble, "Conclusion": 276.

64. Dahl, *Polyarchy*.

1. The Manipulation of Political Opposition

1. Aristotle, *The Politics*: 1316b.

2. Tilly defines "contentious politics" as "all situations in which actors make collective claims on other actors, claims which, if realized, would affect the actors' interests, when some government is somehow party to the claims." This concept covers a set of theories that are often considered independently: social movement theories, theories of political protest and revolution, and even some theories of political development. There is considerable debate over the relationships between various outcomes and the definition of contention, but I do not enter into it here. McAdam, Tarrow, and Tilly, "Toward an Integrated Perspective": 143–153; Lichbach, *The Rebel's Dilemma*; essays in Jenkins and Klandermans (eds.), *The Politics of Social Protest*; and Tarrow, *Power in Movement*: 1–9.

3. Francisco, "Coercion and Protest"; Karmeshu and Mahajan, "A Dynamic Model of Domestic Political Conflict Process"; Moore, "Dissent and Repression"; Moore, "The Repression of Dissent"; Ginkel and Smith, "So You Say You Want a Revolution."

4. Lohmann, "The Dynamics of Informational Cascades"; Kuran, "Now Out of Never"; Chong, *Collective Action and the Civil Rights Movement*; Tilly, *From Mobilization to Revolution*: 84–90. For many studies of social movements,

scholars further assume that activists can be distinguished from nonactivists on the basis of some set of factors, as noted in McAdam, "Gender as a Mediator of the Activist Experience": 1211. As Jennings and Anderson argue, this assumes homogeneity among various social or political groups. Jennings and Anderson, "Support for Confrontational Tactics Among AIDS Activists": 312.

5. See Maxwell and Oliver, *The Critical Mass in Collective Action*; Hardin, *Collective Action;* Hardin, *One for All*; and Lichbach, *The Rebel's Dilemma* for very different understandings of solutions to the collective action problem. Classic debates have arisen over the relative importance of selective incentives for movements. See esp. Gurr, *Why Men Rebel;* Popkin, *Political Entrepreneurs and Peasant Movements in Vietnam*; Scott, *The Moral Economy of the Peasant*; and, more recently, Posusney, *Labor and the State in Egypt.*

6. Paige, *Coffee and Power*; Midlarsky and Roberts, "Class, State and Revolution in Central America"; Migdal, *Peasants, Politics and Revolutions.*

7. Tilly, *From Mobilization to Revolution*; Tarrow, *Power in Movement.*

8. McAdam, Tarrow and Tilly, "Toward an Integrated Perspective": 164.

9. Reising, "United in Opposition?" Kuran, "Now Out of Never"; Chong, *Collective Action*; Tarrow, *Power in Movement*: 144–145, 186–187.

10. Tilly, *From Mobilization to Revolution*: 106–115; Gamson, *The Strategy of Social Protest.*

11. Meyer and Staggenborg, "Movements, Countermovements, and the Structure of Political Opportunity"; Glenn, "Competing Challengers and Contested Outcomes"; Kowalewski and Hoover, *Dynamic Models of Conflict and Pacification.*

12. DeNardo, *Power in Numbers.*

13. Gavious and Mizrahi, "Two-Level Collective Action and Group Identity."

14. Evans, Rueschemeyer, and Skocpol (eds.), *Bringing the State Back In*. See also Migdal, Kohli, and Shue, *State Power and Social Forces*. For an interesting debate over how much understanding the role of the state aids in explaining political opposition in the Arab world, see Anderson, "Lawless Government and Illegal Opposition"; Leca, "Opposition in the Middle East and North Africa."

15. See, for instance, work focusing on opponents' ability to mobilize resources or their attempts to frame issues to form broad coalitions: Tilly, *From Mobilization to Revolution*; Tarrow, *Power in Movement*. To a lesser extent, scholars have considered what factors would lead to openings, rare moments in which the state became temporarily weaker than the opposition, or when regimes split, leading some incumbent elites to call upon and be willing to make pacts with opposition groups in order to counter other incumbent elites. See most notably Skocpol, *States and Social Revolutions*, and Huntington, *The Third Wave.*

16. Rational choice theorists have been most explicit about the role of selective incentives in promoting mobilization. Implicitly, these theories provide the most room for incorporating state-provided negative incentives to participation. See Coleman, *Foundations of Social Theory*; DeNardo, *Power*

in Numbers; Hardin, *Collective Action*; Popkin, *The Rational Peasant*. For a review of this literature, see Moore, "Rational Rebels."

17. There is a large literature examining how and when repression increases or decreases the level of mobilization. See DeNardo, *Power in Numbers*; Wintrobe, "The Tinpot and the Totalitarian"; Francisco, "The Relationship Between Coercion and Protest"; Gellner, "The Impact of Political System Structure on Probability Patterns of Internal Disorder"; Gupta, Singh, and Sprague, "Government Coercion of Dissidents"; Opp and Roehl, "Repression, Micromobilization, and Political Protest"; Lichbach, "Deterrence or Escalation?" Tarrow, *Power in Movement*: 149–150.

18. Ghadbian, *Democratization and the Islamist Challenge in the Arab World*; Robinson, "Can Islamists Be Democrats?" For a closer study of Islamist opposition in Saudi Arabia, see Fandy, *Saudi Arabia and the Politics of Dissent*.

19. Tarrow, *Power in Movement*: 21.

20. Scott, *Weapons of the Weak*; Wiktorowicz, *The Management of Islamic Activism*; Tarrow, *Power in Movement*: 30–42.

21. Lichbach, "Deterrence or Escalation?"

22. Schwedler, "Framing Political Islam"; Bachelani, "Mobilization and Electoral Success."

23. Skocpol, *States and Social Revolutions*. See also Goldstone and Useem, "Prison Riots as Microrevolutions." See also Skocpol and Goodwin, "Rentier State and Shi'a Islam in the Iranian Revolution"; Kowalewski and Hoover, *Dynamic Models of Conflict and Pacification*; Tilly, *From Mobilization to Revolution*: 209–211.

24. Przeworski, "Some Problems in the Study of the Transition to Democracy"; Bova, "Political Dynamics of the Post-Communist Transition"; Crescenzi, "Violence and Uncertainty in Transition"; Zielinski, "Transitions from Authoritarian Rule and the Problem of Violence." Social movement theorists have long recognized the importance of splits in elite coalitions. See Piven and Cloward, *Poor People's Movements*.

25. *New York Times*, February 21, 1989: A3.

26. DeNardo, *Power in Numbers*; Kowelewski and Hoover, *Dynamic Models of Conflict and Pacification*.

27. Geller, "The Impact of Political System Structure on Probability Patterns of Internal Disorder."

28. Gurr, "War, Revolution and the Growth of the Coercive State."

29. Geddes, "The Breakdown of Authoritarian Regimes"; Posusney, "Multi-Party Elections in the Arab World"; Bratton and van de Walle, *Democratic Experiments in Africa*: 242–255.

30. Coppedge, "District Magnitude, Economic Performance, and Party-System Fragmentation"; Neto and Cox, "Electoral Institutions"; Taagapera, "The Number of Parties as a Function of Heterogeneity and Electoral System"; Ordeshook and Shvetsova, "Ethnic Heterogeneity, District Magnitude, and the Number of Parties"; Siavelis, "Continuity and Change in the Chilean Party System."

31. Mainwaring and Shugart, "Juan Linz, Presidentialism and Democracy"; Stepan and Skach, "Constitutional Frameworks and Democratic

Consolidation"; Eaton, "Parliamentarism vs. Presidentialism"; Linz, "Presidential or Parliamentary Democracy"; Przeworkski, Alvarez, Cheibub, and Limongi, *Democracy and Development*; Mainwaring, "Presidentialism, Multipartism"; Cheibub and Limongi, "Modes of Government Formation."

32. Widner, "Political Reform in Anglophone and Francophone African Countries": 74–75. See also essays in Jenkins and Klandermans (eds.), *The Politics of Social Protest*.

33. Although the concept has made a notable comeback in recent years, it is not new. Peter Eisinger used the term "structure of political opportunities" to denote the "degree to which groups are likely to be able to gain access to power and to manipulate the system." He argued that "the incidence of protest is . . . related to the nature of the city's political opportunity structure." See Eisinger, "The Conditions of Protest Behavior": 11.

34. Kitschelt, "Political Opportunity Structures and Political Protest"; Kriesi, "The Political Opportunity Structure of New Social Movements"; Klandermans, Kriesi, and Tarrow, *From Structure to Action*. For cycles of protest explained as the result of opportunity expansion and contraction, see Koopmans, "The Dynamics of Protest Waves"; Tarrow, *Power in Movement*.

35. McAdam, "Conceptual Origins:" 27.

36. Tarrow, *Power in Movement*.

37. Gamson and Meyer, "Framing Political Opportunity."

38. Meyer and Staggenborg, "Movements, Countermovements."

39. See overview in Loveman, "High-Risk Collective action."

40. Kowlewski and Hoover, *Dynamic Models of Conflict and Pacification*.

41. McAdam, Tarrow, and Tilly, "Toward an Integrated Perspective."

42. Important recent contributions from scholars focusing on the Middle East include Schwedler, *Faith in Moderation*; Wickham, *Mobilizing Islam*; Wiktorowicz, *Management of Islamic Activism*; and contributions in Wiktorowicz (ed.), *Islamic Activism*.

43. Meyer and Staggenborg, "Movements, Countermovements."

44. I thank Jose Cheibub for this insight. A similar argument is found in Greenwood, "Business Regime Loyalties in the Arab World."

45. See Scott, *Weapons of the Weak*; Singerman, *Avenues of Participation*; Wiktorowicz, *The Management of Islamic Activism*.

46. See Lust-Okar and Jamal, "Rulers and Rules."

2. Structures of Contestation

1. Social and political factors may affect how well incumbents can implement policies in response to opposition demands, but this chapter will not examine this issue. See essays in Jenkins and Klandermans (eds.) *The Politics of Social Protest*, particularly Kriesi, "The Political Opportunity Structure of New Social Movements."

2. The level of moderation or radicalness of an opposition group is defined as the distance between the opposition group's ideal policy position and the status quo. This is similar to the distinction made by DeNardo, *Power in Numbers*, Chapter 6.

3. Dahl, *Polyarchy*.
4. Ibid.
5. According to Tilly's classic formulation, all opposition groups are *contenders*, groups that "during some specified period, [apply] pooled resources to influence the government." Opponents who are allowed to enter the formal political sphere (polity) are "members," and those who are excluded are "challengers." The "polity" is formally defined as "the collective action of the members and the government." Tilly, *From Mobilization to Revolution*: 52.
6. As Shwadran notes, "The Amir was inclined to rule in an autocratic manner;... he preferred the paternal rule of the sheikh of the desert which he knew so well... to any system of self-rule by the population, no matter how limited." Shwadran, *Jordan*: 166.
7. On political parties and their relations with the Amir during this period, see Amawi, "State and Class in Transjordan"; Mahawin, *al-Ahzab wa-al-quwwah al-siyasiyah fi al-Urdun*; Musa and al-Madi, *Tarikh al-Urdun fi al-qurn al-'ashrin*; al-Husayn, *My Memoirs Completed*; Amawi, "Jordan"; Kirkbride, *From the Wings*.
8. On relations between King 'Abdallah and the Palestinians, see al-Husayn, *My Memoirs Completed*; Nevo, *King Abdallah and Palestine*; Mishal, *West Bank/East Bank*; Cohen, *Political Parties in the West Bank Under the Jordanian Regime*; and Plascov, *The Palestinian Refugees in Jordan*.
9. Socioeconomic statistics reflect some of this perceived difference. For instance, 22 percent of Transjordan's population was urban in 1946, compared to 34 percent of Palestinians; the number of schools had risen from 299 to 406 in Palestine between 1932 and 1944, while it had declined from 186 to 155 in Transjordan from 1935 to 1944. (Konikoff, *Transjordan*: 18 and *Government of Palestine, A Survey of Palestine*: 137–139, 148–151 both cited in Aruri, *Jordan: A Study in Political Development*: 34.)
10. Voters elected 20 members from the East Bank and 20 from the West Bank.
11. Shwadran, *Jordan: A State of Tension*: 287.
12. For discussions of this period, see 'Abidi, *Jordan*; Aruri, *Jordan*; Musa and al-Madi, *Tarikh al-Urdun fi al-qurn al-'ashrin*.
13. There are two versions of this story. In the official one, Talal was believed to have psychological problems and therefore to be an unfit ruler. In the second, he was believed to be too liberal, and therefore was not acceptable to the British and conservative loyalists.
14. Mishal, *West Bank/East Bank*: 34.
15. Defense Regulation No. 1 allowed the Prime Minister to revoke the license of periodicals preaching ideologies against the Constitution. Defense Regulation No. 5 gave the Prime Minister the authority to prohibit owners of public restaurants and cafes from tuning into stations that were considered hostile to the government. The Defense Regulations also allowed the Prime Minister to issue injunctions against strikes and to punish anyone urging workers to strike. Finally, they provided for the exile or arrest without trial of any citizens believed to be dangerous to national security.
16. Dann, *King Hussein and the Challenge of Arab Radicalism*: ix.

17. Isma'il was well known for his brutality. Europeans described him thus: "With his own sword he would strike off the head of the slave who held his stirrup as he mounted his horse, or several heads of his own Black Guards as he rode down their ranks; he disemboweled the living and organized displays of torture for the titillation of his senses." Gavin, *Lords of the Atlas*: 29.
18. Ibid: 17–18.
19. Ibid: 21.
20. Many Moroccans of Amazigh origin prefer "Amazigh" to "Berber" because the latter term was initially coined by Romans who, upon meeting fierce resistance in North Africa, considered them "Barbarians." On the debate, see Zerhouni and Maghraui, "Between Religion and Secularism."
21. After the fall of the Mawlay Isma'il, for example, the *makzhen* could not use roads linking Fez to Marrakesh via Tadla or the Fez-Tafilat route. Waterbury, *Commander of the Faithful*: 328.
22. As Eugene Etienne, the first Undersecretary of State for the Colonies and member of the Comité du Maroc, argued to the French Union Coloniale in 1903, "My friends! What a wonderful field for your activity! It is in Morocco that you will find phosphate deposits and iron mines, wheat fields and olive plants! It is there that you will find markets for the cotton goods of Rouen and the Vosges! Wool to supply our weavers in Roubaix and Tourcoing! Railroads to build, harbors to develop!" The French Socialist Jean Jaures' premonition was correct, however: "Once the financiers have become masters of Morocco, France [would] be pushed into a war of occupation.'" Goldberg, *The Life of Jean Jaures*: 343.
23. In 1901 the Franco–Italian agreement gave Italy a free hand in Tripoli (Libya) and France control in Morocco. In the Anglo–French Entente of 1904, the British accepted French influence in Morocco as long as Britain gained a free hand in Egypt.
24. It should be noted that after the reign of Mawlay Hasan (1873–1894), the Sultan faced resistance in the Bilad al-Siba (the uncontrolled territories).
25. Quoted in Hoffman, *A History of Morocco and the Land of the Moors*: 213.
26. For discussion, see Maxwell, *Lords of the Atlas*: 181.
27. al-Fasi, *Independence Movements of Arab North Africa*: 132.
28. A French advisor to the Sultan told al-Fasi, "'Your demands consist of three parts: the first can be implemented now; the second may be implemented, but only after a while; as for the third, it can never be implemented because we have no intention of voluntarily pulling out of Morocco.'" al-Fasi, *Independence Movements of North Africa*: 138.
29. Estimates from ibid., 193.
30. For detail, see Maxwell, *Lords of the Atlas*.
31. Ashford, *Political Change in Morocco*: 65.
32. Khalil, *Arab States and the Arab League*: 218.
33. Ling, *Morocco and Tunisia: A Comparative History*: 128.
34. Landau, *Moroccan Drama*: Appendix ix.
35. Ibid., Appendix x.
36. Zartman, *Man, State and Society in Contemporary Maghrib*: 116.

37. See, for instance, Hart, "Rural and Tribal Uprisings in Post-Colonial Morocco, 1957–60": 84–104.
38. By 1959, the first split in the Istiqlal appeared. ʿAllal al-Fasi continued to lead the Istiqlal, the more conservative wing of the party, which accepted King Muhammad V's snail-like pace toward political reform. Younger leaders – Muhammad Basri, Mahdi Bin Baraka, and Mahjub Bin Sadiq – left to form the UNFP in September 1959, arguing for limiting the monarch's power as a first step toward more radical change. The *makhzen* promoted such fragmentation by actively intervening in party affairs, helping establish new organizations to counterbalance the Istiqlal and co-opting rural and local notables.
39. Hodgkin, *African Political Parties*: 79; Sarah, *Ahzab wa-al-quwwa al-siyasiyah fi al-Maghreb*: 18–19.
40. On the role of Islam in supporting the regime, see Leveau, "Religion et état: Islam et contrôle politique au Maroc"; Tozy, *Monarchie et Islam politique au Maroc*; Combs-Schilling, "Performing Monarchy, Staging Nation." In contrast, see Munson, *Religion and Power in Morocco*; Bourqia, "The Cultural Legacy of Power in Morocco."
41. The 1962 Constitution is available in Hassan II, *The Challenge: The Memoirs of King Hassan II of Morocco*.
42. See Rousset, "La difficile conciliation entre l'idéologie unanimitaire et l'idéologie democratique," as quoted in Korany, "Monarchical Islam with a Democratic Veneer": 159.
43. This article reads: "The person of the King shall be sacred and inviolable."
44. Richards and Waterbury, *Political Economy of the Middle East*: 297–298. Similarly, with regard to Morocco, "The king today is at the center of a [number of] concentric [circles]. He is the chief of the small clan of Alawites. He directs those families [the *makhzen*] that have longstanding ties with the reigning family. Then dressed in white with a red fez he is the 'shadow of God' on earth. But if he appears in suit and tie, he is the head of the modern state bequeathed to Morocco by Napoleon via Lyautey. It is often said that this modern state, composed of technocrats, runs the matters [of the kingdom] while the makhzen manages its people through the controls of matrimonial exchanges and through the distribution of wealth. Clément, *Maroc: Les menaces et les composantes internes de la securité*, cited in Hermassi and Vandewalle, "The Second Stage of State Building": 36.
45. Both kings established reputations as more tolerant rulers than their authoritarian counterparts, but they were willing to repress those who remain unconvinced of the king's legitimate right to rule. Their subjects were well aware of the extensive and well-established internal security establishments (*mukhabarat*), and human rights records demonstrated the monarchs' willingness to use them. See, for instance, Munson, *Religion and Power in Morocco*; Perrault, *Notre ami le roi*; Waltz, *Human Rights and Reform*. For a somewhat different, although compatible, periodization of the Moroccan regime, see Ben ʿAli, "Changement de pacte social et continuité de l'ordre politique au Maroc."

46. The 1950s and 1960s saw critical shifts across the Arab world. While Kings Husayn and Hasan II remained in power, their counterparts in Iraq, Libya, and Egypt lost their thrones in a series of coups.
47. *Times* (London), May 26, 1953: 4.
48. The amendments allowed parliament to overturn the government with a simple majority vote, as opposed to the two-thirds majority required before the constitutional revision, and it required the King to dissolve the government whenever he dissolved parliament, forming a caretaker government in its place.
49. *al-Jaridah al-Rasmiyah*, December 16, 1953, cited in Aruri, *Jordan*: 110.
50. The government could revoke the license and dissolve any party that held views contrary to the Constitution or party regulations, presented false information about its goals, or relied upon foreign support. Initially, the parties could appeal to the High Court of Justice if their license was denied. A 1955 amendment made the Minister of Interior's decision final. See ibid.: 110–114.
51. The distribution of seats at this time was: 16 opposition parties (Baʿth Party 3, Communist Party 2, Nationalist Socialist Party 11); 10 pro-government parties (Arab Constitutional Party 9, Community (Ummah) Party 1); and 14 independents. Ibid.: 112.
52. On August 16th, Abu al-Huda revived the Defense Regulations. Once again, the government gave the Minister of Interior authority to prohibit assemblies deemed detrimental to "public interest" and to ban hostile newspapers. Banned newspapers included *al-Ra'i* (*Arab National*), *al-Yaqzah* (*Baʿth*), *al-Kifah al-Islami* (*Muslim Brotherhood*), *al-Jabhah al-Watani* (*Communist*), *al-ʿAhd al-Jadid*, and *Sawt al-Shaʿb*. The government rejected petitions by the Baʿth and National Front (Communist) parties to participate in elections and jailed opposition candidates and political activists. Sulayman al-Hadid, head of the Baʿth Party, and Sulayman al-Nabulsi, of the National Socialist Party, were among those arrested. ʿAbd al-Rahman Shuqayr (a National Front candidate) and M. A. Khalifah (head of the Muslim Brotherhood) fled to Damascus. Aruri, *Jordan*: 111. According to John Glubb, Abu al-Huda also attempted to rig the elections, using official persuasion to get all soldiers to vote for his candidates. Glubb, *A Soldier with the Arabs*. 350–351.
53. Only the three National Socialist and Communist representatives dissented. This stood in stark contrast to parliament's vote of confidence in Abu al-Huda's government on March 7, 1953, when 18 members withheld confidence.
54. Allocations for the three ministries related to social services accounted for only 50 percent of the allocation for public security. There was one doctor for each 23,300 people but one policeman for each 320 citizens. *Proceedings of the House, First Emergency Session*, cited in Aruri, *Jordan*: 119.
55. "Many Casualties in Jordan Rioting," *Times* (London), December 17, 1955: 6.
56. Glubb, *A Soldier with the Arabs*. 410
57. Glubb had never trusted ʿAli Abu Nawwar, but Husayn did. He had met Abu Nawwar in France, where Glubb had sent the officer in order to minimize the

threat to the throne. Later, Husayn insisted on bringing Abu Nawwar back to Jordan, acting against Glubb's advice.

58. National Socialists held the portfolios of Defense, the Interior, and Foreign Affairs as well as three other posts. Ba'thist and National Front deputies, as well as two independents, held the remaining portfolios.

59. *Proceedings of the House*, December 9, 1956, cited in Aruri, *Jordan*: 2.

60. The Soviet news agency, Tass, appeared in Jordan, and Communist China sent a labor delegation to meet the Prime Minister. On December 19th, the government also signed the Solidarity Agreement with Egypt, Syria, and Saudi Arabia by which the Arab states would pay the £12.5 million subsidy currently provided by Britain. This paved the way for Jordan's abrogation of the Anglo–Jordanian Treaty.

61. Shwadran, *Jordan*: 343.

62. "We perceive the danger of Communist infiltration within our Arab home, as well as the danger of those who pretend to be Arab nationalist while they have nothing to do with Arabism. We will never allow our country to be the field for a cold war which may turn into a destructive hot war, if the Arabs permit others to infiltrate their ranks.... No gap must be left to allow the propaganda of Communism to ruin our country. These are our views which we convey to your Excellency as a citizen, and as our Prime Minister. We hope that you and your colleagues, the Ministers, will adopt an attitude which ensures the interests of this country and stops the propaganda and agitation of those who want to infiltrate through to the ranks of the citizens." Snow, *Hussein*: 115. See also Shwadran, *Jordan*: 346.

63. Snow, *Hussein*: 115

64. See Farzali, "Inhisar al-tawazunat al-urduniyah," *Suraqiya*, May 1, 1989: 8–9.

65. Dann, *King Hussein and the Challenge of Arab Radicalism*.

66. L'Union Marocaine du Travail.

67. These included the Constitutional Democratic Party (PDC), the Popular Movement (MP) and Independent Liberals (PLI).

68. Union Nationale des Étudiants du Maroc.

69. The government instituted a Moroccanization policy, including an investment policy whereby at least 50 percent of the capital in enterprises had to be domestic. In addition, land from foreign settlers was restored and distributed. Both policies had the effect, however, of shoring up the old elite. See Berrada, "Le marocanisation de 1973 éclairage rétrospectif"; Swearingen, *Moroccan Mirages*.

70. The Tripartite Agreement divided the colony into Mauritanian and Moroccan provinces, with three provinces – Boujdour, Es Smara, and al-Ayound – under Moroccan control.

71. Korany, "Monarchical Islam with a Democratic Veneer": 160.

72. For a review of the political parties, see also El Benna, "Les partis politiques au Maroc."

73. This identity grants him legitimacy in the eyes of the people, particularly the rural peasant classes. The king also exploits this role to limit others' ability to challenge his position. See Munson, *Religion and Power in Morocco*; Leveau,

"Islam et contrôle politique au Maroc"; Lamchichi, *Islam et contestation au Maghreb*; Ben 'Ali, "Émergence de l'espace socio-politique et stratégie de l'état au Maroc."

74. See *Middle East International*, December 17, 1989, 17–19; Carroll, *Business as Usual*: Chapter 5.
75. Dekmejian, *Egypt Under Nasser*: 38, 150–152. See Chapter 3 for a discussion of internal struggles.
76. Bernard-Maugiron, *Egypt and Its Laws*: 316.
77. *Al-Ishtiraki*, December 24, 1966, cited in Baker, *Egypt's Uncertain Revolution*: 94.
78. On this battle, see Bianchi, *Unruly Corporatism*: 92; Posusney, *Labor and the State in Egypt*: Chapter 1.
79. Brown, *Rule of Law*: 77–81.
80. Posusney, *Labor and the State in Egypt*: 76.
81. al-Ittihad al-ʿAm li Niqabat al-ʿUmmal fi Misr.
82. Springborg, "Professional Syndicates in Egyptian Politics, 1952–1970"; Barraclough, "al-Azhar: Between the Government and the Islamists."
83. Harik, "The Single Party as a Subordinate Movement": 102.
84. Cooper, *The Transformation of Egypt*: 32.
85. Baker, *Egypt's Uncertain Revolution*: 99.
86. Speech before Parliament on October 8, 1970; see *al-Ahram*, October 9, 1970: 1. and Cooper, *The Transformation of Egypt*: 66–67.
87. Sabri's base of support was in the ASU, and Gomaʿa's base of support was in the security branches. Cooper, *The Transformation of Egypt*: 65.
88. Rutherford, "Struggle for Constitutionalism": 263–264.
89. Baker, *Egypt's Uncertain Revolution*: 124.
90. "UAR," *Africa Contemporary Record*, 1971: B74; *al-Ahram*, November 20, 1970: 1.
91. Cooper, *The Transformation of Egypt*: 70–71.
92. Posusney, *Labor and the State*: 94–95; Rutherford, "Struggle for Constitutionalism": 266; Waterbury, *Egypt of Nasser and Sadat*: 352; Baker, *Sadat and After*. For full text, see *al-Ahram*, May 1, 1971: 1, 3–4. Sadat echoed this again in the October Working Paper. See Ministry of Information, *The October Working Paper*: 97: 1.
93. *al-Ahram*, November 26, 1970, see also *al-Ahram*, December 18, 1970: 1, 3.
94. Kepel, *The Prophet and the Pharaoh*: 104–106; Ibrahim, "An Islamic Alternative in Egypt," in Ibrahim, *Egypt, Islam and Democracy*: 35–51.
95. Zaki, *Egyptian Business Elites*: Chapter 5.
96. Cooper, *The Transformation of Egypt*: 145; Dekmejian notes, however, that there was a similar change in the cabinet immediately following the defeat in 1967. In the March 1968 cabinet, 39.4 percent of the members were military officers compared to 65.4 percent in June 1967. Dekmejian, *Egypt Under Sadat*: 129, 259.
97. Rutherford, "Struggle for Constitutionalism": 275–276.
98. Ayubi, "Government and the State in Egypt Today": 3.
99. Makram-Ebeid, "The Role of the Official Opposition": 24. See also Soltan, "Taming the Elite": 7–8.

100. el-Sayyid, *Ahzab al-mu'aradah wa siyasat al-infitah al-iqtisad fi misr*: 7.
101. Wickham, *Mobilizing Islam*: 66.
102. el-Sayyid, "Civil Society in Egypt?" 281.
103. Major parties include the National Democratic Party (the regime party), New Wafd Party, Socialist Labor Party, National Progressive Unionist Party, Liberal (Ahrar) Party, and Arab Democratic Nasirist Party. For discussions, see Wickham, *Mobilizing Islam*: 240–241; Kienle, *Grand Delusion*: 69.
104. See CHRLA, "Section II: Legal Restrictions Imposed on the Right to Form Political Parties in Egypt" (March 9, 1999), available at www.chrla.org/reports/poltix/poltix.htm
105. CHRLA, "Egyptian Politics: The Fiction of the Multiparty System," available at www.chrla.org/reports/poltix/poltix.htm
106. Kienle, *Grand Delusion*: 29.
107. Wickham, *Mobilizing Islam*: 64.
108. Soltan, "Taming the Elite": 5.
109. Kienle, *Grand Delusion*: 95.
110. This was seen as well in Mubarak's 1989 May Day speech, in which he argued for "all democratic parties and groups to put aside, even momentarily, their differences over public work so that all patriotic efforts could be focused on positive cooperation to achieve the undisputable national goals, over which people should not differ." Cited in Wickham, *Mobilizing Islam*: 67.

3. Playing by the Rules

1. In terms of Tilly's classic model, excluded opponents are *members* of the polity and excluded opponents are *challengers*.
2. Tilly suggests this as well in *From Mobilization to Revolution*: 126.
3. Dekmejian, *Egypt Under Nasir*: Chapter 11; Zaki, *Egyptian Business Elites*.
4. Amawi, *State and Class*; Anderson, *State and the Opposition*; Fischbach, *State, Society and Land*; Greenwood, *Business Regime Loyalties in the Arab World*; Massad, *Colonial Effects*.
5. See Salayman al-Farzali, "Inhisar al-tawazunat al-urduniyah,"; *Suraqiya*, May 1, 1989: 8–9; Bailey, "Cabinet Formation in Jordan"; Brand, *Palestinians in the Arab World*.
6. Author's interviews with Muhammad Njadat, Hani Hourani, and 'Abdallah Radwan. See also the interviews in Fathi, *Jordan: An Invented Nation?* and *Christian Science Monitor*, November 8, 1993: 2.
7. For instance, of 131 ministers in office from 1952 to 1968, only 2 had positions in the party organization before becoming minister, while 83 held such positions either during or after their terms as minister. Dekmejian, *Egypt Under Nasir*: 192–199.
8. Kotob, "The Accommodationists Speak": 321–339.
9. Ayubi, "The Political Revival of Islam"; Ibrahim, "Egypt's Islamic Militants."
10. Sagiv, "Judge Ashmawi and Militant Islam in Egypt": 531.
11. By 1975, the two most important Moroccan parties were the Istiqlal Party, which had an important role in the Independence Movement, and the USFP,

a socialist offshoot of the Istiqlali splinter party, the UNFP. Of these parties, the USFP was the stronger opposition party, particularly by the early 1980s. The Istiqlal Party lost a certain amount of its following because it agreed to participate in the government. The USFP would eventually join the government in 1997, when its Secretary General, ʿAbd al-Rahman Yusufi, became its first Prime Minister. This is discussed in more detail in Chapter 5.

12. For discussion of the Jordanian National Movement, see Anderson, *State and the Opposition*.

13. See for example, al-Ittihad al-maghrebi lil-shaghal (UMT), "Min ajli rafʿa al-dimuqratiya"; al-Ittihad al-ʿam lil-shaghalin (UGTM), "Tadakhul al-akh"; al-Ittihad al-maghrebi lil-shaghal, "Min ajli rifaʿa tahadi al-taqhir al-dimuqrati."

14. In all interviews, members of political parties, both including and outside of the Istiqlal Party and the USFP, independent observers, and government officials agreed that general strikes and cooperation between the CDT and UGTM were politically motivated.

15. On a more active period of Jordanian workers' unions, see "Thalathin ʿamann ʿala nashu al-harakah al-naqabiyah al-ʿamaliyah al-urduniyah: 1946–1970"; "Thalathin ʿamann ʿala nashu al-harakah al-naqabiyah al-ʿamaliyah al-urduniyah: 1971–1976." On the current relationship between professional associations and political parties, see Brand, " 'In the Beginning Was the State," and Hamarnah, *al-Urdun*. For examples of the relationships between politics and the unions, see Jordanian Engineers Association, "La li al-Tatbiʿa"; Keilani, "Time to Rein in Associations, Tabloid Press," *Jordan Times*, December 2, 1995: 3. This is not to suggest that the relationship between associations and parties is purely cooperative. Competition between the two forces increased, particularly after the liberalization. See *Jordan Times*, August 5, 1998: 3.

16. Tilly, *From Revolution to Mobilization*: 171.

17. The level of violence that groups are willing to perpetrate and the extent to which they are willing to make concessions are also important dimensions, but they will not be explicitly discussed here.

18. Social and political factors may affect how well incumbents can implement policies responding to opposition demands, but this chapter will not examine this issue. See essays in Jenkins and Klandermans (eds.), *The Politics of Social Protest: Comparative Perspectives on States and Social Movements*, particularly Kriesi, "The Political Opportunity Structure of New Social Movement."

19. For discussion of the state's role in promoting political interest groups in the United States, see Walker, *Mobilizing Interest Groups in America*. Chapter 5 examines incumbents' roles in shaping individual opposition groups in greater detail.

20. See, for example, Riker, *The Theory of Political Coalitions*.

21. Waltz, "Interpreting Political Reform in Morocco": 285.

22. Interviewees in both Morocco and Jordan argued that strong radical groups were more likely to be repressed than equally radical weak groups.

23. Kotob, "The Accommodationists Speak": 328–329. *al-Usrah al-ʿarabiyah*, May 9, 1993 in FBIS, NES-93-095, May 19, 1993: 11–12.

24. Juan Linz has made similar observations about the relationships between what he calls "semi-opposition" with the masses and the government. For him, however, these relationships make the semi-opposition unable to challenge the government. While I agree with him on the distinctions and character of semi-opposition and excluded opponents, I disagree with him over whether or not they become *unable* to challenge the government. Rather, as we shall see in Chapters 4 and 5, they become *unwilling* to do so. See Linz, "Opposition to and Under an Authoritarian Regime."

25. Opposition elites frequently argue that the charter is more binding on them than it is on the regime. See, for example, comments by Khadir and Madanat (members of the National Charter Committee) at the Seminar on Democracy and the Rule of Law – Assessment and Outlook, Royal Cultural Center, Amman, November 19, 1995.

26. For discussion of the Tunisian pact, see Anderson, "Political Pacts, Liberalism and Democracy."

27. Perthes, "Stages of Economic and Political Liberalization": 50. Both sides note the codependency of government and opposition in maintaining political stability informally as well. Opposition party leaders, members and observers noted this in interviews. That the palace tried to convince Fikq Basri to return to Morocco that year in the hope of breathing some life into the parties suggests that the regime saw the situation similarly. At a very different time in Iran, an advisor to the Shah expressed a similar concern, that the parties were becoming too weak to provide an outlet of popular frustration. See Alam, *The Shah and I*: 429–430, 453.

28. Shukrallah, "Political Crisis and Political Conflict in Post-1967 Egypt": 84.

29. Korany, "Monarchical Islam with a Democratic Veneer."

30. Both regimes are defined in their constitutions as parliamentary hereditary monarchies. This principle is restated as the first principle in the Jordanian National Charter: "Adherence by all to legitimacy and to respect of the letter and spirit of the Constitution shall enhance the union between the people and their leadership." Regarding Morocco, see ibid.

31. For details on restrictions in the Jordanian case, see Hashemite Kingdom of Jordan, *Political Parties Law No. 32 for the year 1992*. For a more detailed discussion of the state's ability to restrict the legal opposition, see Wiktorowicz, *Management of Islamic Activism*; regarding increased limitations on Jordanian parties, see Lust-Okar, "The Decline of Jordanian Political Parties: Myth or Reality?"

32. Author's field notes, Rabat, Morocco, June 1995.

33. Denoeux, *Urban Unrest in the Middle East*: 95.

34. Makram-Ebeid, "Egypt's 1995 Elections."

35. Interview, ʿAziz Muhsin, Chambre de commerce et d'industrie de la wilaya du grand Casablanca, Casablanca, May 30, 1995. On the monarch's manipulation of elections to distribute political power, see Korany, "Monarchical Islam with a Democratic Veneer"; Claisse, "Les systèm de légitimité a l'épreuve": Rousset, "Le système politique du Maroc."

36. See also Dahl, *Polyarchy*; Krane, "Opposition Strategy and Survival in Praetorian Brazil, 1964–79."

37. For reviews of arbitrary detention, censorship, and other human rights abuses, see U.S. State Department, "Morocco Human Rights Practices," March 1996; U.S. State Department, "Jordan Human Rights Practices, 1995," March 1996.

38. Korany, "Monarchical Islam with a Democratic Veneer": 172. See also Claisse, "Les systèmes de légitimité a l'épreuve"; Rousset, "Le système politique du Maroc."

39. Karawan, "Political Parties between State Power and Islamist Opposition"; 22; El-Mikawy, "State/Society and Executive/Legislative Relations"; 28–29.

40. Brynen, "The Politics of Monarchical Liberalism: Jordan"; interviews with the author note this as well.

41. El-Mikawy, The Building of Consensus.

42. Hinnebusch, "The Formation of the Contemporary Egyptian State from Nasser and Sadat to Mubarak": 200–201.

43. Tamimi (ed.) Power-Sharing Islam? cited in Kramer, "Good Counsel to the King": 274. These are also major points of the Islamic Action Front Electoral program.

44. El-Mikawy, The Building of Consensus: 115.

45. Krane, "Opposition Strategy": 31, 38.

46. Interviews with ʿIsa Madanat; Munson, Religion and Power in Morocco.

47. Interview with Jamal Shaʾir, April 1997.

48. Reportedly, both Sadat and Mubarak offered the Muslim Brotherhood legal status as a charitable association but it refused, demanding legal recognition as a political party instead.

49. This is particularly true of legal opponents when illegal groups exist. This is noted, for example, in interviews with Dr. ʿAbd al-Majid Bouzoubaa (Adjoint Secretary General and Secretary of Information of CDT, Council Member of USFP), Rabat, July 14, 1995; M. Chirat (UGTM and Istiqlal Party leadership); Najib Akesbi (Professor of Economics, Mahad Ziraʿi (Agricultural Institute) and Member of USFP), Rabat, July 13, 1995; Driss Ben ʿAli (Professor, Mohammad V University), July 19, 1995. That these concerns exist was also noted by a western diplomat in Rabat, June 27, 1995.

50. Wickham, Mobilizing Islam: 209–210. See also Ayubi, Political Islam: 73.

51. Ernest Gellner, "Patterns of Rural Rebellion in Morocco," Archives européenes de sociologie, 3, 1962: 297–311, cited in Denoeux, Urban Unrest in the Middle East: 202. Similarly, see Waterbury, Commander of the Faithful.

52. Saaf, Chroniques des Jours de Reflux; Moore, "Political Parties"; Tessler, "Alienation of Urban Youth."

53. CSS, Istitlaʿa al-raʾi hawla al-dimuqratiya fi al-Urdun 1998.

54. Suleiman, "Attitudes, Values and Political Process in Morocco": 115. See also Tessler, "Alienation of Urban Youth"; Suleiman, "Socialization to Politics in Morocco"; Nedelcovych, "Determinants of Political Participation." Formal and informal interviews with the author, graduate students of economics and political science, May–June 1995 in Rabat and Casablanca.

55. The Istiqlal reportedly had 200,000–250,000 members, the USFP had an estimated 100,000, and the MP and RNI had approximately 50,000–100,000

members each in the early 1980s. The remaining parties were weak and declining. Ihrai, *Pouvoir et influence*: 226.

56. Khalil al-Shubaki, "Nata'ij istijiwab waqi' al-hayat al-siyasiyah fi al-Urdun," *al-Ra'i*, January 14, 1995: 1.

57. To the first question, 73% responded "yes," 14% "no," and 13% had no opinion. To the second, 48% responded "no," 36% "yes," and 16% had no opinion. "Charting Untrodden Ground," December 29, 1994–January 4, 1995, *al-Ahram Weekly*, Issue 201. Available at weekly.ahram.org.eg/archives/1994 poll.yesss.htm.

58. Ibid.

59. Soltan, "Taming the Elite": 2, 6.

60. *Christian Science Monitor*, November 26, 1990: 8. See also El-Mikawy, "State/Society and Executive/Legislative Relations": 22.

61. The Istiqlal Party alternated between government (in power 1960–1963, 1976–1983) and opposition. See Zartman, "Opposition as Support of the State," and El-Mossadeq, "Political Parties and Power-Sharing."

62. Hendriks, "Egypt's New Political Map." Similar sentiments are noted in Posusney, *Labor and the State in Egypt* and in personal correspondence with the author.

63. Kienle, *Grand Delusion*: 27, 55.

64. Bernard-Maugiron et. al (eds), *Egypt and Its Laws*.

65. Economist, *Book of Vital World Statistics*, 1990.

66. For a discussion of Jordanian political parties, see Lust-Okar, "The Decline of Jordanian Parties: Myth or Reality?" Interviews with political party leaders and observers, April–June 1998, 1995, 1994. On Egypt, see Wickham, *Mobilizing Egypt*: 178; El-Mikawy, *The Building of Consensus*: 67.

67. Kienle, *Grand Delusion*: 9.

68. Regarding Egypt, see Makram-Ebeid, "Egypt's 1995 Elections": 130; El-Mikawy, *The Building of Consensus*: 46.

69. Roussillon, "Islam, islamisme, et démocratie": 332; Langohr, "Tentative Propositions on NGOs and Democratization in the Arab World": Langohr, "Too Much Civil Society"; al-Ahram, "Taqrir al-istiratizhi al-'arabi, 1991": 390.

70. el-Sayyid, "A Civil Society in Egypt?"

71. Chai, "An Organizational Economics Theory of Antigovernment Violence"; Denoeux, *Urban Unrest in the Middle East*.

72. Abdalla, "Egypt's Islamists and the State": 30.

73. Ibrahim, "Egypt's Islamic Militants": 13; Ayubi, *Political Islam*: 164.

74. See Fandy, "Egypt's Islamic Group: Regional Revenge?" 607–625; Ayubi, *Political Islam*: 83.

75. As Timur Kuran notes, the revolutions in the former Communist states surprised observers because the majority of those who sympathized with the opposition took great pains to keep their sympathies private. Kuran, "Now Out of Never."

76. Weaver, "The Novelist and the Sheikh": 66.

77. Korany, "Monarchical Islam with a Democratic Veneer"; Lamchichi, *Islam et contestation au Maghreb*; Combs-Schillings, "Performing Monarchy, Staging Nation": 200.
78. Tessler, "Alienation of Urban Youth": 93.
79. Denoeux, *Urban Unrest*: 130.
80. It should be noted that this does not suggest that the repression will be less than that of a demonstration consisting of only legal opponents. For legal opposition groups, the inclusion of excluded participants heightens repression.
81. Relaxing the assumption of perfect information, the moderates can expect that the radicals will exploit the conflict with probability λ and that they will not exploit it with probability $(1 - \lambda)$, where $\lambda \in [0,1]$. In the case of perfect information, λ is known and is either 0 or 1.
82. This is because radicals are defined as those having policy preferences that are farther from the status quo than the moderates' preferences. Thus, it follows that $P_R < -1$ or $P_R > 1$.
83. For a discussion of ideologues and pragmatists, see DeNardo, *Power in Numbers*: Chapter 4.
84. The value of the obtained policy outcome in a conflict with actor j, π_J, depends upon the opposition's policy preferences and its strength relative to that of the incumbents. These factors determine which policy demands they make and how likely the opponents are to obtain these demands.
85. I compared the following outcomes to the outcomes of models in which the utility of policy changes is increasing or diminishing as the policy change approaches the opposition's preferred policy. In the case of increasing returns to policy changes (in a language similar to DeNardo's, the preference function of ideologues), the expected payoffs for policy outcomes were $-|P_I - \pi_J|^{1/2}$, and in the case of diminishing returns (again, in DeNardo's language, the preference function of pragmatists) the expected utility for policy outcomes was $-(P_I - \pi_J)^2$. Again, there were no significant differences between the results of these models and the results presented here.
86. $R_M > R_R$ and R_G, and all are greater than or equal to 0. In other words, the loss of significant popular support for the legal opposition is divided into two parts. The first is a transfer of support from the moderate opposition to the government; the second is a transfer of support from the moderate to the radical opposition. Thus, the gains to radicals and the incumbents cannot be greater than the loss incurred by the moderates.

4. Dynamics of Opposition in Unified SoCs

1. Formally, Auxiliary Assumption 1 is $\pi_M + \pi_R = \pi_J$ if $\pi_M + \pi_R < 1$ and $\pi_J = 1$ otherwise. I use this rather than the joint probability of success $(\pi_M \pi_R)$ since the probability that either succeeds in mobilizing is partially dependent upon the likelihood that the other mobilizes in conjunction. I expect that the conditional probability that either succeeds with the presence of the other mobilizing is greater than the probability of success independently. To simplify, I am simply using the sum of the independent probabilities.

2. Formally, Auxiliary Assumption 2 is P_R is infinitely close to 1, approaching from above.

3. Simply, the increased probability of success in conjunction with the policy gains is greater than the discount rate of future returns if the opposition mobilized in the previous period.

4. Editors of the magazine were Murawayd al-Tall, brother of the former Prime Minister, Wasfi al-Tall, and head of Jordan's Cooperative Organization, and Tariq Marsawa, a leading columnist. Yorke, "Hussein's Bid to Legitimize Hashemite Rule": 18; interview with Murawayd al-Tall, Amman, Jordan, November 1995.

5. Interview with Jamal Sha'ir, April 27, 1997.

6. The NCC was established in 1978 as an appointed advisory council to the government. The council had no power to set or reject legislation and served primarily to "co-opt intellectuals and businessmen, to appease the traditional sectors of society and to mobilize support for the regime." Khouri, "The National Consultative Council."

7. Some suggest that opening parliament also was intended to help prepare the kingdom to engage in tripartite (Palestinian–Israeli–Jordanian) peace talks. See Rami Khouri, "Jordan's Parliament Approves Elections," *Washington Post*, January 10, 1984: A10. However, it is clear that popular pressure played a role as well. See Fathi, *Jordan: An Invented Nation?* 103.

8. *Washington Post*, December 27, 1985: A21.

9. Throughout the late 1970s and early 1980s, King Husayn and President Hafez al-Asad had a decidedly cool relationship. This was due in part to Jordan's reliance upon Iraq, Syria's nemesis in the region, for economic relations. It was also partly a result of Jordan's general willingness to allow its own Islamists, as well as the Muslim Brotherhood of Syria, to operate in Jordanian territory. For a discussion of Syrian–Jordanian–Iraqi relations during this period, see Brand, *Jordan's Inter-Arab Relations*.

10. *Le monde*, February 26, 1980: 9.

11. Letter from King Husayn to Prime Minister Zayd al-Rifaʿi, published in the *Jordan Times*, November 11, 1985: 1.

12. In the education ministry, where the Muslim Brotherhood could have the most influence, the government "retired" seven members from their posts.

13. Brand, *Jordan's Inter-Arab Alliances*.

14. *Washington Post*, December 27, 1985: A1. See also interviews cited in Mazen Ahmad Alougili, "Comparative Study of Jordan's Foreign Policy": 122.

15. "The King and the Campus," *The Middle East*, 141, July 1986: 12.

16. *Christian Science Monitor*, May 13, 1988: 9.

17. First noted in an interview with Muhammad al-Masri (Researcher, CSS), Amman, November 10, 1995, and confirmed by other Jordanians and Western observers.

18. Economic studies showed a decline from $1,800 per capita in 1982 to $900 in 1988. *Christian Science Monitor*, May 1, 1988: 4.

19. For details, see *Washington Post*, April 24, 1989: A11.

20. Unofficial estimates were as high as 10 killed and 72 injured. *Washington Post*, April 21, 1989: A22; *Washington Post*, April 25, 1989: A11.

21. See *Washington Post*, April 20, 1989: A 29, 31; interview with Saʿad Silawi, journalist, *al-Raʾi*, November 20, 1995.
22. See, for example, the author's interviews with Radwan ʿAbdallah, November 1995; ʿIsa Madanat, November 20, 1995; also *Washington Post*, April 22, 1989: A1, 20.
23. First noted to the author in an interview with ʿIsa Madanat (founding member of the Jordanian Communist Party), Amman, Jordan, November 20, 1995.
24. *Washington Post*, April 22, 1989: A1, 20.
25. For discussion of the disturbances, see *Washington Post*, April 22, 1989: A1, 20.
26. Anonymous former senior official, cited in *Christian Science Monitor*, May 1, 1989: 4.
27. Jordanian journalist, cited in *Christian Science Monitor*, June 15, 1993: 3. Similarly, see *Washington Post*, March 14, 1989: A21.
28. Bin Shakir, a former army commander and, at the time of appointment, Chief of the Royal Court, was an important choice. As a distant cousin of the King, he was less likely to receive criticism from Jordanians who feared that criticizing him might be perceived as unacceptably criticizing the King himself.
29. Opposition to Zayd Rifaʿi centered on calls of corruption. This corruption affected many ministries; Zayd Rifaʿi was called by one official the "Chief Thief."
30. For further discussion of the factors surrounding the 1989 elections, see Abu Jaber and Fathi, "The 1989 Jordanian Parliamentary Elections"; Mufti, "Elite Bargains and the Onset of Political Liberalization in Jordan," *Comparative Political Studies*, 32, February 1999: 100–129; Robinson, "Defensive Democratization in Jordan."
31. In this election, 22 Muslim Brotherhood adherents, 15 Islamists with other affiliations, and 10 secularist antigovernment candidates were elected. The King then named Mudar Badran Prime Minister because of his better ties with Islamists. He included two independent Islamists and two leftist nationalists from the democratic bloc in his cabinet.
32. The King first publicly mentioned the National Charter on May 10, 1989, but preparations for it began only after the elections.
33. Thus, a survey conducted by the CSS at the Jordanian University found that popular opinion would be based upon how well the economic grievances were met, not the political demands. The masses saw political liberalization primarily as a step toward economic progress. CSS, *Public Opinion Survey on Democracy in Jordan*: 3.
34. On the debate, see Mufti, "Elite Bargains and the Onset of Political Liberalization in Jordan"; interviews cited in Fathi, *Jordan: An Invented Nation?*
35. *Washington Post*, October 3, 1989: A25.
36. Hawatmeh, "The Changing Role of the Press."
37. Ahmad Obeidat, "Democracy in Jordan and Judicial Control."
38. Fahed Fanek, cited in Salim al-Zouby, Ahmad al-Momany, and Mahmoud Kilani, "Discussion to the Report of the Committee or Formulation of Conclusions," 92–121 in Dobers et al. (eds.), *Democracy and the Rule of Law*: 92–121.

39. Radical groups that refused to recognize the system remained on the fringe. These included the Islamist Jihad al-Bayt al-Muqaddas, led by Shaykh As'ad al-Tamimi, and Hizb al-Tahrir, founded in 1952 by Shaykh Taqi al-Din al-Nabhani. Milton-Edwards, "A Temporary Alliance with the Crown"; Taji-Farouki, *A Fundamental Quest.*

40. Interview with 'Izz al-Din in "Democratization Is a Continuous Process...," *Jordan Times*, July 27, 1993: 1.

41. Milton-Edwards, "A Temporary Alliance with the Crown."

42. For discussion of the internal debate over liberalization, see Mufti, "Elite Bargains and the Onset of Political Liberalization in Jordan"; Lucas, "Institutions and Regime Survival Strategies."

43. Murad Nermeen, "Not Simply a Welcome But a Resounding Oath of Allegiance." *Jordan Times*, September 25, 1992: 1.

44. Abu Jaber, "The 1989 Jordanian Parliamentary Elections."

45. Prime Minister Badran offered the Muslim Brotherhood the Ministry of Higher Education, while the Brotherhood demanded the Ministry of Education and the Ministry of Religious Affairs and Endowments. The gap between the power afforded the Brotherhood in the Ministry of Higher Education, which had no real effect on the national education, and the Ministries of Education and Religious Affairs, which controlled the curricula in all public schools and every mosque in the country, was extremely wide. However, six independent Islamists were offered portfolios, including the Ministers of Justice, Labor, Health, Social Affairs, Religious Affairs and Endowments, and a Minister of State for Government Affairs.

46. Milton-Edwards, "A Temporary Alliance with the Crown."

47. Portfolios held by the Muslim Brotherhood included those of the Minister of Social Development (Yusuf al-'Azm), Minister of Religious Affairs and Endowments (Ibrahim Zayd al-Kilani), Minister of Health ('Adnan al-Jaljuli); Minister of Justice (Majid al-Khalifah), and Minister of Education ('Abdallah al-Akaylah).

48. See Jillian Schwedler, "Framing Political Islam in Jordan and Yemen": 139.

49. *Christian Science Monitor*, November 16, 1989: 4.

50. The previous voting scheme allowed voters to cast ballots for as many candidates as there were seats in the multimember districts. The opposition argued that frequently one ballot was cast according to traditional tribal loyalties and the second according to ideological preferences. Thus, removing the option of casting multiple votes led voters to choose their candidates according to tribal loyalties and patronage ties and weakened the prospects for less traditional, ideologically based candidates. In addition, the opposition objected to the gerrymandering of districts by which more traditional rural districts were disproportionately represented in comparison to urban and camp areas. al-Urdun al-Jadid Research Center, *Post-Election Seminar*. For a discussion of the relationship between kinship ties and politics in Jordan, see Anis Khassawneh, "The Social Setting of Administrative Behavior in Jordan"; Claremont Graduate School, Ph.D. Thesis, 1987; Amin Awwad Muhanna, "Modernization: Political Stability and Instability"; Fathi, *Jordan: An Invented Nation?*

51. In addition to the author's interviews, see interviews cited in Bachelani, "Mobilization and Electoral Success": 178–187.

52. "On the Parliamentary Elections of 1993 CE," a press release from the Media Relations Department of the Islamic Action Front, November 21, 1993: 1–4 cited in: ibid. 187.

53. In general, the King and the palace came to dominate the executive branch after liberalization. This was stated first to the author by Radwan ʿAbdallah (Professor of Political Science, University of Jordan) on November 19, 1995 and confirmed by other Jordanian activists and nonactivists as well as Western observers.

54. Jordan Media Group, *Jordan: Keys to the Kingdom*: 94. On expectations of the economic dividend, see Carroll, *Business as Usual*: 65–68.

55. For an overview of the Anti-Normalization Campaign, see Kornbluth, "Jordan and the Anti-Normalization Campaign."

56. Popular opposition to the Israeli–Jordanian peace process was extraordinarily high. One study conducted after the agreement in 1994 found that 80 percent of Jordanians opposed the peace treaty. Economic Intelligence Unit, *Country Report: Jordan, 4*, 1994: 8.

57. *Jordan Times*, May 29, 1995: 1.

58. As a result of the ban, Ibrahim ʿIzz al-Din resigned from the government. See Economic Intelligence Unit, *Country Report: Jordan, 3*, 1995: 9–10.

59. "Sharif Zayd: Constructive Criticism Is Welcome, But Not ʿImported Principles,'" *Jordan Times*, November 19, 1995: 1; author's notes from ʿAbal-Karim Kabariti (Minister of Foreign Affairs), "Opening Remarks" at the Seminar on Democracy and the Rule of Law, November 19, 1995.

60. *Jordan Times*, December 11, 1995: 1.

61. Lamis Andoni, "Jordan: Democratization in Danger," *Middle East International*, 116–17. The most notable immediate repression was the arrest of the Islamist leader Layth Shubaylat on December 9, 1995. He was ostensibly arrested on the charges that he had slandered the royal family, undermined the welfare of the country and incited sectarian strife. He had previously been arrested in 1992 (see *Jordan Times*, September 2, 1992: 3), but this arrest was widely perceived, as a strong signal to opponents of normalization with Israel. *Jordan Times*, December 10, 1995: 3.

62. Prime Minister Yitzhak Rabin, who had been King Husayn's partner in the signing the Jordanian–Israeli Peace Treaty and with Yasser Arafat on the Oslo Accords, was assassinated by a young Israeli on November 4, 1995. The author witnessed Jordanians watching as the official television station carried a live broadcast of clearly distraught King Husayn and a crying Queen Nur attending the Israeli Prime Minister's funeral. Jordanians, many of whom sympathized more with the Islamist paper's headline, "Death of a Murderer," than they did with what they perceived as the King's view of the leader, were shocked. It reminded them of the casual manner in which the King had aided the Prime Minister in lighting his cigarette in a previous meeting. Both events, signaling the extent to which the chasm between the King and his people had widened, were talked about widely.

63. See Kamal, "Bread Subsidy to Go." *Middle East International*, August 2, 1996: 11.
64. See Ryan, "Peace, Bread and Riots.
65. For details of the debate, see Lucas, "Institutions and Regime Survival Strategies."
66. See Omar, "A Changed Landscape." *Middle East International*, December 5, 1997: 12–13.
67. Boycotting parties included the Islamic Action Front; the secularist-leftist Jordanian People's Unity Party and the Jordanian People's Democratic Party (HASHD), both with ties to Palestinian liberation groups (the PFLP and DFLP, respectively); and the Constitutional Front Party, the Jordanian Arab Partisans Party and the Nationalist Action Party (al-Haq). Notably, however, the Future (Mustaqbal) Party (led by former Minister of the Interior Sulayman 'Arar) and independents such as the Tahir al-Masri and Ahmad Obeidat also joined the boycott. Tahir al-Masri was a former Prime Minister and House Speaker, and Ahmad Obeidat was a former Prime Minister and Chief of Security.
68. Protesters were prepared to attempt a similar demonstration in Irbid, but the large numbers of police deterred them. Economist Intelligence Unit, *Country Report*:, 12; Kamal, "Protests Turn to Violence."
69. "al-Nakbah" is the Palestinian, and more generally Arab, description of the Israeli Declaration of Statehood.
70. Included among these were also former Prime Ministers Ahmad Obeidat and Tahir al-Masri.
71. The conference was timed to coincide to the day with the 70th anniversary of the First National Congress (*al-Mu'tamar al-Watani*), in which nationalist opposition forces came together in the aftermath of 'Abdallah's heavy-handed repression of parliamentary opposition and issued a "National Pact" (al-Mithaq al-Watani) expressing their grievances to Amir 'Abdallah.
72. *Jordan Times*, October 1, 1995: 1; *Jordan Times*, November 20, 1995: 1; *Jordan Times*, October 26–27, 1995: 6.
73. 'Abd al-Karim al-Kabariti (Minister for Foreign Affairs), "Opening Remarks" at the Seminar on Democracy and the Rule of Law, Royal Cultural Center, Amman, Jordan, November 19, 1995.
74. *Christian Science Monitor*, November 2, 1989: 4; interviews with Toujan Feisal, November 1995 and 'Isa Madanat, November 20, 1995.
75. Personal observations at party meetings, and interviews, 1995 and 1997.
76. Divisions within parties are also problematic. Interviews with Radwan 'Abdallah, Sa'ida Kilani, 'Isa Madanat, and other party leaders and observors, 1995 and 1997; *Jordan Times*, June 17, 1992; 1, 5.
77. The Communist Party stands as an excellent example.
78. Author's interviews with party elites and observers in 1998; comments in the session on Jordan at the Middle East Studies Asssociation meeting, November 1998.
79. *Jordan Times*, October 12–13, 1995: 1. See also Robinson, "Can Islamists Be Democrats?"

80. Wickham, *Mobilizing Islam*: 32; El Bishri, "The 1952 Revolution and Democracy": 32–37.
81. Dekmejian, *Egypt Under Nasir*: 228; Cooper, *Tranformation of Egypt*: 40; Kepel, *The Prophet and the Pharaoh*: 31–35.
82. Cooper, *Transformation of Egypt*: 42–43.
83. Kepel, *The Prophet and the Pharaoh*: 130–131.
84. *al-Ahram*, February 25, 1968: 1. See also *al-Ahram*, February 28, 1968: 1.
85. Rutherford, "Struggle for Constitutionalism": 290–291.
86. Wickham, *Mobilizing Islam*: 33; Baker, *Egypt's Uncertain Revolution*: 58.
87. Brown, *Rule of Law*: 89.
88. Brown, *Rule of Law*: 86–87, 92; Rutherford, "Struggle for Constitutionalism": 283.
89. For the text of the March 30 declaration, see *al-Ahram*, March 31, 1968: 1,3. For a discussion of and reaction to the declaration, see *al-Ahram*, April 1, 1968: 1,3.
90. Rutherford, "Struggle for Constitutionalism": 258; Dekmejian, *Egypt Under Nasir*: 259–262.
91. Kepel, *The Prophet and the Pharaoh*: 132.
92. Posusney, *Labor and the State*: 85.
93. Cooper, *Transformation of Egypt*: 42.
94. Rutherford, "Struggle for Constitutionalism": 259.
95. Ibid.: 260.
96. Brown, *Rule of Law*: 92.
97. Nasir also took step to incorporate Islam into the regime, increasing the amount of religious programming on TV and radio and establishing a religious affairs committee in ASU in July 1969.
98. Cooper, *Transformation of Egypt*: 73.
99. Rutherford, "Struggle for Constitutionalism": 272.
100. Unemployment rose from 2.2 percent in 1969 to 7.7 percent in 1976. Fergany, "A Characterization of the Employment Problem in Egypt": 44.
101. In Egypt the economic and political spheres were particularly closely intertwined, given the corporatist associations established under Nasir. Thus, for instance, in 1973, Sadat responded to such pressures by purging the Communists from the ETUF board, since they were no longer needed to counter the Nasirists. See Posusney, *Labor and the State*: 100.
102. ʿAziz Sidqi was appointed Prime Minister and Sayyid Marei as First Secretary.
103. Kepel, *The Prophet and the Pharaoh*: 133.
104. Cooper, *Transformation of Egypt*: 85.
105. Sadat argued: "Democracy is political freedom, and socialism is social freedom; we cannot separate one from the other, for they are the wings of real freedom; and without them freedom cannot hover over tomorrow's anticipated horizons." Sadat, *October Working Paper*: 37–38.
106. *al-Iqtisadi*, March 15, 1974, cited in Cooper, *Transformation of Egypt*: 124.
107. Ibrahim "Egypt's Islamic Militants": 5.
108. Ibrahim, "An Islamic Alternative in Egypt": 42.
109. Hinnebusch, *Egyptian Politics Under Sadat*: 63.

110. The Economist, *Quarterly Economic Review of Egypt, Annual Supplement 1977*: 21 cited in Cooper, *Transformation of Egypt*: 118. *Al-Iqtisadi* stated that inflation was about 40 percent for 20 food items between June 1973 and June 1974 alone (January 15, 1977, cited in Cooper, *Transformation of Egypt*: 118).
111. Baker, *Egypt's Uncertain Revolution*: 144.
112. *al-Iqtisadi*, November 15, 1976, cited in Cooper, *Transformation of Egypt*: 107. See also Baker, *Egypt's Uncertain Revolution*: 149; Bianchi, *Unruly Corporatism*: 47.
113. *al-Iqtisadi*, February 15, 1975, cited in Cooper, *Transformation of Egypt*: 124.
114. Kienle, *A Grand Delusion*: 38.
115. About 4,000 militants won local offices, about 15 percent of the positions. Posusney, *Labor and the State*: 107.
116. These elites included Muhammad Abu Wafia (Social Democratic Platform, Sadat's brother-in-law and chairman of the Complaints and Proposals Committee in the People's Assembly); Khalid Muhyi al-Din (Nationalist Progressive) and Kemal Ahmad (Nasirist socialist), original Free Officers and leftist members of the ASU Central Committee; and Mustafa Kemal Murad, chairman of the Economic Committee in the People's Assembly. Cooper, *Transformation of Egypt*: 183.
117. Names of the emerging platforms included The Liberal Socialists; Egypt Nationalist; Socialist Youth of Egypt; Democratic Council; Voice of Islam; Islamic Democratic Socialist; Republican; Nasirist Socialist; Islamic Workers; Progressive Nationalist. See Cooper, *Transformation of Egypt*: 183.
118. Cooper, *Transformation of Egypt*: 186.
119. Ibid.
120. *al-Ahram*, November 21, 1975, cited in Cooper, *Transformation of Egypt*: 187. Similarly, President Sadat called upon parties to focus on their role for the nation, not individual gain or calls to the parties' parts. See speech before the Central Committee, *al-Ahram*, November 21, 1970: 1,34.
121. Cooper, *Transformation of Egypt*: 201.
122. Ibid.: 235. The Center received 82.1 percent of the ballots cast, the left .06 percent and the right 2.65 percent. Independents received the remaining votes. Marei, "Political Evolution from the One-Party to the Multi-Party System": 40.
123. *Ruz al-Yusuf*, March 14, 1976, cited in "Arab Republic of Egypt," 1976–1977: B28.
124. El-Mikawy, *The Building of Consensus*: 32–35.
125. Gavin Young, " Poor Rise Up to Rattle Egypt's Bourgeoise Teeth," *The Observer* (London), January 23, 1977: 6.
126. Ibrahim, "Egypt's Islamic Militants": 14; see also Baker, *Egypt's Uncertain Revolution*: 165.
127. Ayubi, *Political Islam*: 75.
128. Cooper, *Transformation of Egypt*: 242.
129. On Tajammuʿ linkages with the NPUP, see Posusney, *Labor and the State*: Chapter 2.

130. Hinnebusch, *Egyptian Politics Under Sadat*: 198.
131. Soltan, "Taming the Elite": 3.
132. Baker, *Egypt's Uncertain Revolution*: 154.
133. Cooper, *Transformation of Egypt*: Chapter 13; Baker, *Egypt's Uncertain Revolution*: 155.
134. On the weak, tentative nature of institutional reform, see Hinnebusch, *Egyptian Politics Under Sadat*: 254; Baker, *Egypt's Uncertain Revolution*: 242.
135. Hinnebusch *Egyptian Politics Under Sadat*: 221.
136. Ibid.: 222.
137. Cooper, *Transformation of Egypt*: 237.
138. Hinnebusch, *Egyptian Politics Under Sadat*: 197–198.
139. Shukrallah, "Political Crisis and Political Conflict": 70; Kepel, *The Prophet and the Pharaoh*: 78, 94–102.
140. *al-Ahram*, July 21, 1977: 1, 8. See also Ibrahim, "Egypt's Islamic Militants," 14, note 3.
141. Hanafi, "The Relevance of the Islamic Alternative": 63.
142. Sadat tried to balance his economic interests and his religious concerns, but his Islamist opponents were not always amused. For instance, in response to Islamists' concern that belly dancing and other raucous activities were unacceptable during Ramadan versus the regime's desire to promote tourism, the government decreed in 1979 that belly dancing could continue during Ramadan if each performance also included some religious pieces. This did not appease the Islamists. *al-Jumhuriyah*, July 15, 1979; *al-Akhbar*, August 8, 1979, cited in Ayubi, *Political Islam*: 75.
143. Law No. 40 (1977) outlawed the Muslim Brotherhood and the Nasirists in banning parties from forming if they had platforms that were similar to those of existing parties. More specifically, this law established a committee that had to be petitioned for the formation of any new party. The committee was called the "Committee for the Affairs of Political Parties." It included four members of the regime, including the Minister of Interior and three retired or senior judges appointed by the president of the committee, himself one of the four regime members.
144. Kienle, *Grand Delusion*: 20; El-Mikawy, *The Building of Consensus*: 113–114; Posusney, *Labor and State*: 111.
145. Hinnebusch, *Egyptian Politics Under Sadat*: 158–171; Wickham, *Mobilizing Islam*: 65.
146. The 1979 Law No. 36 stated that the president of a political party would be jointly responsible with the editor-in-chief of the party's newspaper for anything published in it. Boyle and Sharif, *Human Rights and Democracy*: 250.
147. The 1980 Press Law No. 48 required the press to serve the "interests of the country and its nationals." This law established the Higher Press Council, which had regulatory powers over journalists and newspapers. Bernard–Maugiron and Dupret, eds., *Egypt and Its Laws*: 346.
148. Hinnebusch, *Egyptian Politics Under Sadat*: xxxvii.
149. Ibid.: 77.

150. Notable among these was the al-Takfir wa al-Hijrah attack in 1977. Independent Islamists were also preaching against Sadat from their mosques, and from Iran, Khomeini, in the week before the assassination, called for Sadat's removal.
151. Ayubi, *Political Islam*: 76.
152. Kepel, *The Prophet and the Pharaoh*: Chapters 3, 7.
153. Wickham, *Mobilizing Islam*: 116–117; Bianchi, *Unruly Corporatism*: 195.
154. Bianchi, *Unruly Corporatism*: 196–197.
155. Ayubi, "The Political Revival of Islam": 493.
156. Ibrahim, "Egypt's Militant Islamists": 5–6.
157. Ansari, "Sectarian Conflict in Egypt": 415.
158. Meiring, *Fire of Islam*: 21.

5. Opposition Dynamics in Divided SoCs

1. Jennifer Widner makes this point as well in "Political Reform in Anglophone and Francophone African Countries."
2. It should be noted that in the case in which the moderates are uncertain about whether or not radicals will exploit their mobilization, their willingness to mobilize decreases as their expectation of the radicals entering $(1 - \lambda)$ increases. The rate at which their willingness to mobilize decreases depends upon the magnitude of the difference between their utility for Isolated Conflict and that for Joint Conflict. This utility depends in part upon the utility of the radicals' policy and the difference in the expected repression for Isolated and Joint Conflicts. The less attractive the radicals' policy preferences are to the moderates, the more an increase in $(1 - \lambda)$ leads to a decreased willingness to mobilize. The next chapter will discuss how incumbent elites might influence this factor. In addition, the greater the difference between the moderates' expected repression in Isolated and Joint Conflict, the more a change in λ influences the moderates' willingness to mobilize.
3. "Fi balagh min al-maktab al-siyasi lil-Ittihad al-Ishtiraki." *al-Ittihad al-Ishtiraki*, June 12, 1981: 2.
4. It should be noted that the UMT leadership saw this differently. They argued that the June 18th strike was successful and responsible. The official UMT paper, *l'avant garde*, announced, "18 june 1981: succès total de la grève générale à Casablanca et Mohammadia dans l'ordre, la détermination, l'enthousiasme et la responsabilité." *L'avant garde*, June 18, 1981: 1.
5. Author's interviews with party leaders and members as well as Moroccan observers.
6. The figures were 66 deaths and 11 injuries, according to the Minister of Interior. According to the opposition parties, the Association of Maroccans in France (Association des Marocains en France), and a Canadian member of the International Commission of Jurists, between 600 and 1,000 demonstrators were killed. The government allegedly stole some of the bodies in an attempt to cover up the extent of the bloodshed. *Le monde*, July 1, 1981: 6; "Few Believe Govt Version of riots," *Africa Diary*, November 19–25, 1981: 10747–10748.

7. The USFP and CDT claimed that 162 of their members were arrested. *Maroc soir*, June 28, 1981: 1; "Les procès de Casablanca: maintiens abusifs en détention," *al-Bayane*, July 16, 1981: 1.

8. Jibril, "Les événements et les problemes de fond."

9. "Government Blamed for Casablanca Violence," *Africa Diary*, October 1–7, 1981: 10684–10685. See also MAP, "Événements du 20 juin: 66 morts violentes que rien ne sauriat justifier," June 25, 1981; "M. Echiguer repond à un depute de l'USFP, a propos des événements de Casablanca: Le gouvernement ne fuit pas ses responsabilités...," *Maroc soir*, June 27, 1981: 1.

10. *Le temps*, July 10, 1981: 1.

11. Santucci, "Chroniques politiques Maroc": 904–932.

12. *Africa Diary*, October 9–15, 1983: 11621.

13. See in particular the author's interview with Dr. ʿAbd al-Majid Bouzouba (Adjoint Secretary General and Secretary of Information of CDT, Council Member of USFP), July 14, 1995, Rabat. This insight was confirmed in interviews with other party members and observers.

14. See Clément, "Les révoltes urbaines": 392–406.

15. Munson, *Religion and Power in Morocco*, reports the frustration reflected in the riots. Rioters tore up pictures and smeared excrement over them [citing Domingo del Pino, *Marruecos entre la tradicion y el modernismo* (Granada: Universidad de Granada, 1990): 156]. Graffiti appeared in the Rif Mountains warning the monarch "we are going to eat you for dessert," and protesters are said to have chanted "'Enough prisons and palaces, [we want] universities and schools,' 'One, two, three, we're going to kill the King, four, five, six, we're going to kill his son,' 'Mohammed V was our father, but you, who are you?' 'Down with Hassan II,' and 'Long live the republic' [citing Clément, "Les révoltes urbaines": 23, 30]. Clément ("Les révoltes urbaines": 396–398) and *El Pais* (January 26, 1984) estimated that over 200 were killed and 14,000 arrested. Officially, there were 29 dead and 115 injured. See also Younger, "Morocco and Western Sahara": 205–211; Majid, *Les luttes de classes au Maroc depuis l'indépendance*.

16. "King Hassan Rejects Price Hikes, Tries to Quell Riots," *Washington Post*, January 23, 1984: A12.

17. *Africa Diary*, July 1–7, 1984: 11944. For analysis of the protests, see Seddon, "Popular Protest and Political Opposition in Tunisian (sic), Morocco, and Sudan 1984–1985": 179–197.

18. King Hassan II, "Discours de S.M. le Roi à la nation," January 22, 1984.

19. *Africa Diary*, July 1–7, 1984: 11944.

20. *Africa Diary*, February 26–March 4, 1985: 12225.

21. Tessler, "Image and Reality in Moroccan Political Economy": 230–236.

22. Younger, "Morocco and Western Sahara": 205–211.

23. Among these associations are the Grand Atlas in Marakesh, Bou Regreg at Salé, Fes-Saiss in Fes, Angad Maroc Oriental in Oujda, Figuig, and Taza, and the Mediterranean in Tangier. The heads of these organizations included El Hadj Mediyuri (head of Royal Security), Muhammad ʿAwad (palace adviser), Muhammad Kebbaj (Minister of Finance), Ahmad ʿUsman (the King's brother-in-law and former Prime Minister), and Muʿti Buʿbid (former Prime Minister).

24. Zartman, "Opposition as Support of the State": 230.
25. The Constitutional Union got 24.79 percent of the votes and 83 seats. The USFP won 12.39 percent of the votes, compared to 14.63 percent in 1977, and obtained 39 seats. The Istiqlal Party won 15.33 percent of the votes, compared to 21.80 percent in 1977, and won 43 seats. See "Une nouvelle géographique politique," *Lamalif*, October 1984: 4–5. For a discussion of the elections and tactics used, see Eickelman, "Changing Perceptions of State Authority": 177–204; Claisse, "Élections communales et législatives au Maroc": 631–668.
26. Interviews with Mustapha Terrab (adviser to King Hassan II), July 12, 1995, Rabat; Dr. ʿAbd el-Majid Bouzoubaa, July 14, 1995, Rabat. Yata, "Le PPS, la question nationale et le mouvement national et progressiste."
27. For a description of events preceding and including December 14, 1990, see Hizb al-Istiqlal, *Hizb al-istiqlal bayn al-muʾtamarayn (1985–1994)* (Rabat: al-Sharakat al-maghrabia, 1995); Lijnah al-Tansiq al-Watani wa al-Dawli, *Nubir Amaoui, rajal wa qadiah* (Casablanca: Matbaʿa dar al-nashir al-maghrabi, 1993); Robert Radcliffe, "Fulbright Student Letter."
28. Interviews with Muhammad El Merghadi (USFP member), Fes, May 16, 1995; Nubir Amaoui (Secretary General of CDT, member of the USFP Central Committee), Casablanca, May 1995; Dr. ʿAbd al-Majid Bouzoubaa, Rabat, July 14, 1995.
29. Conseil national de la jeunesse et de l'avenir.
30. Rabat RTM TV, September 16, 1993, in FBIS-NES-93–179, September 17, 1993: 20.
31. Election results gave the MP 54 seats, U.C. 66 seats, and PND 22 seats. The democratic bloc obtained 53 seats for the USFP, 49 seats for the Istiqlal, 15 seats for the PPS, 2 seats for the OADP, 4 seats for the CDT, and 2 seats for the UGTM. Loyalist parties got 33 seats for the RNI, 25 for the MNP, 3 for the PDI, 3 for the UMT and 2 for independents.
32. See MAP Rabat, September 20, 1993, in FBIS-NES-93–181, September 21, 1993: 16; Munson, "International Election Monitoring"; Munson, "The Elections of 1993 and Democratization in Morocco"; Bayer, *Morocco*.
33. *Le matin du Sahara*, October 9, 1993, cited in Agnouche, "La fiction de l'alternance politique au Maroc." See also Waltz, "Interpreting Political Reform in Morocco": 282–305.
34. For example, the palace used the opposition parties' participation in local government to argue that the unions had no right to call strikes in the transportation sector in 1991. See "Recision de M. Driss Basri suite a l'appel a la grève dans les Régies autonomes de transport urbain," *Le matin du Sahara*, December 7, 1991: 1, 3.
35. In Morocco, it is the most powerful ministry. Called the "Mother of all Ministries," the Ministry of Interior has the power to veto or override decisions made in any of the other ministries. In addition, Driss Basri, the Interior Minister at that time, had a particularly long history in the office, during which he had harshly repressed his opponents. Given his level of autonomy and his past willingness to use repressive measures, opposition elites felt that taking steps toward political liberalization would be neither credible nor successful as long as he was in power. On the decision to stay out of the government, see

Middle East Economic Digest Quarterly Report, November 1993: 12; Interviews with Bouzoubaa, Amaoui, Brahim Rachidi (member of the USFP, Vice President of the Maarif commune, and member of parliament respectively), Casablanca, June 1, 1995.

36. Interview with M. Chirat (member of the UGTM leadership and Istiqlal Political Bureau), Casablanca, July 20, 1995. Party and union members from both the Istiqlal/UGTM and USFP/CDT confirmed this account.

37. The King also dismissed Prime Minister al-Lamrani, who had been hostile to the unions and traditionalist, and appointed Prime Minister al-Filali.

38. See "Dans les partis d'opposition: réformistes en difficulté, les islamistes courtisés," *La vie économique*, July 28, 1995: 3–4; "La reprise en main," *Maroc hebdo*, July 28–August 7, 1995: 6–7; Barraoui, "Vent de fronde sur les partis politiques; *La vie économique*, July 21, 1995: 3–4; Mansour, "Le coup de force de Muhammad el Yazghi" *Maroc hebdo*, July 21–27, 1995: 24–25.

39. That union and party leaders shared these concerns was widely rumored and noted in interviews with party members. A Western diplomat also confirmed this in an interview, Rabat, June 27, 1995.

40. The unions gained reimbursement of one-half of the salary for the strike period, a yearly bonus of 1,350 dirhams per worker, and the formation of a new national Advisory Council. See "al-Naqabat ta'tabir nata'ij al-majlis al-istishari," *al-Ittihad al-Ishtiraki*, June 3, 1995: 1.

41. Driss Basri served as Minister of Interior until 1999, being dismissed only when King Muhammad VI assumed the throne after his father's death. The Minister of Interior was widely considered the second most powerful man in Morocco and had a long history of brutally repressing the opposition. On the debate, see "Rabat MAP, January 10, 1995, in FBIS-NES-95–007, January 11, 1995: 19.

42. Rabat Moroccan Kingdom Radio, January 11, 1995, in FBIS-NES-95–008, January 12, 1995: 16; Rabat MAP, January 11, 1995, in FBIS-NES-95–008, January 12, 1995: 15; and Paris Radio France International, January 14, 1995, in FBIS-NES-95–010, January 17, 1995: 29.

43. The cabinet included the MP, UC, and PND, while Ahmad 'Usman's RNI and al-Mahjubi Ahardane's MNP remained outside government due to a dispute over their choice of ministers and portfolios. Negotiations with included opposition elites were unusually difficult since they objected to what they saw as privileged treatment of the opposition. Thus, the palace enlarged the cabinet from 11 to 35 members, including 15 technocrats or leading independents (13 from the previous government) and 20 positions granted to the parties (9 from the UC, 8 from the MP, and 3 from the PND). *Jeune Afrique*, March 15, 1995: 30–31, in FBIS-NES-95–035, March 22, 1995: 23.

44. *al-Hayah*, March 25, 1995: 4 in FBIS-NES-95–040, March 29, 1995: 37; MAP, December 11, 1995, in FBIS-NES-95-238, December 12, 1995: 22.

45. This was first noted in the author's interview with El Merghadi, Fes, May 16, 1995, and confirmed by other party and nonparty members.

46. USFP internal memorandum cited in Francois Soudan, "L'attente." A wide range of politically involved Moroccans voiced concerns about increasing

Islamist strength and the related threat of the military, which might intervene to restore order. These included Najib Akesbi (member of USFP, professor of economics, Agricultural Institute, Rabat, July 13, 1995); Abdelhay Moudden (professor of political science), Rabat, July 6, 1995; ʿAbdallah Saaf (professor of political science, Muhammad V University), Rabat, July 24, 1995; Aissa Elouardighi (member of Central Committee of OADP, member of SNU-Sep), Rabat, June 26, 1995. This was noted as well by the U.S. Economic Officer, Casablanca, March 8, 1995.

47. As Clement Henry Moore noted, "Time may be running out for the parties." Moore, "Political Parties": 44. Similar concerns were expressed in a meeting of PPS youth before the 1995 National Congress, Centre d'etude et de recherche ʿAziz Bellal, Rabat, July 8, 1995, and in an interview with Hafez Amiri (USFP member and former youth recruiter), Rabat, July 7, 1995. A U.S. Embassy official in Casablanca estimated that among youth, Islamists outnumber leftists by 10 to 1, interview, Casablanca, March 8, 1995.

48. "Will Morocco Go Fundamentalist?" *Foreign Report*, February 24, 1994: 1–2.

49. Examples include the Friday Islamic supplement that was added to the Istiqlal Party's newspaper and the renewed appeal of the USFP to Islamists through the return of Muhammad Basri. For a discussion of this, see also Marks, *Maghreb*.

50. This was voiced from very different perspectives. Party members noted that "now was not the time" to mobilize the masses (Brahim Rachidi, June 1, 1995). Students argued that the parties had become unwilling to challenge the palace (economic students, group interviews, April 30, 1995). Western diplomats also noted this reluctance in interviews in Rabat, 1995.

51. Interview with Abdelhay Moudden (professor of political science), Rabat, July 6, 1995. Other party members interviewed concurred, as did a U.S. Embassy official, Rabat, 1995.

52. El-Mikawy, *The Building of Consensus*: 42.

53. Ibid.: 42–43.

54. These included Law No. 40 of 1977, Law No. 33 of 1978, and Law No. 36 of 1979.

55. Zubaida, "Islam, the State and Democracy": 5.

56. The judiciary in Egypt is particularly influential and independent in comparison to other judiciaries in the Middle East. It has played an important role in determining when electoral rules are unconstitutional and in admitting parties to the political system. See al-Ahram, *The Egyptian Political System*: 14–17, 64; Brown, *Rule of Law*; Rutherford, "The Struggle for Constitutionalism." However, I take the view that at the end of the day, the government determines whether it upholds or fails to uphold the court's decision. This is shared by El-Mikawy, *The Building of Consensus*: Chapter 4.

57. Post, "Egypt's Elections": 18; see also El-Mikawy, *The Building of Consensus*: Chapter 4; Posusney, "Multi-Party Elections."

58. This alliance was in some ways more logical than the previous Wafd–Brotherhood alliance, since the Labor and Ahrar parties espoused a more Islamist platform. al-Ahram, *The Egyptian Political System*: 24–25. In their

earlier alliance, the Wafd and the Muslim Brotherhood recognized their clear differences in their positions toward Islam, experienced a struggle over who represented the "true consciousness" of the Egyptian nation, and finally came to blows in a struggle over their relative power, each considering itself more powerful than the other believed it to be. El-Mikawy, *The Building of Consensus*: 83–96.

59. El-Mikawy, *The Building of Consensus*: 83, 88–91.
60. Post, "Egypt's Elections": 18.
61. Handoussa, "Crisis and Challenge:" 4–5.
62. Fergany, "A Characterisation": 45–46.
63. Wickham, *Mobilizing Islam*: 43.
64. Assaad Ragui and Rouchdy Malat, *Poverty and Poverty Alleviation*: 29.
65. Specifically, the opposition demanded that the Ministry of Justice oversee elections, that simpler voting procedures be implemented, that they receive more media slots for campaigns, and that martial law be suspended. El-Mikawy, *The Building of Consensus*: 93.
66. The opposition parties' decisions to boycott were made easier by the fact that they expected to do poorly in the elections. The Islamic Alliance and the Wafd all experienced leadership feuds at this time, and the Islamic Alliance in particular could not expect to run candidates in all 222 districts (see El-Mikawy, *The Buildling of Consensus*: 93–94; Kienle, *A Grand Delusion*: 54.) This made the decision to boycott easier. However, it does not fully explain the decision. As we will see, the opposition parties were unwilling to boycott in 1995, despite having similarly dismal expectations.
67. *Christian Science Monitor*, November 26, 1990: 8. See also Kienle, *A Grand Delusion*: 52–54.
68. Makram-Ebeid, "Egypt's 1995 Elections": 127.
69. See El-Mikawy, *The Building of Consensus*: 93–94.
70. Tawfiq, *Majlis al-shaʿb: kursi al-muʿaradah?* 70.
71. al-Ahram, *Taqrir al-istiratizhi al-ʿarabi, 1991*.
72. Azzam, "Egypt: The Islamists and the State under Mubarak": 116–118.
73. The Muslim Brotherhood gained the majority of syndicate positions, but it did so with increasing turnout rates. See Ibrahim, "Islamic Activism in Egyptian Politics": 58.
74. Ibrahim found that less than 8 percent of those arrested for militant Islamic acts in 1970 were from shantytowns, while 36 percent arrested in the 1990s were from these sprawling slums. Ibrahim, "The Changing Face": 75; Ayubi, *Political Islam*: 83–85; Ansari, "Islamic Militants": 140–141; Abdalla, "Egypt's Islamists": 30; Fandy, "Egypt's Islamic Group": 607–625; Ibrahim, "Egypt's Islamic Militants": 13; Ibrahim, "Anatomy of Egypt's Militant Islamic Groups": 1–33.
75. Weaver, "The Novelist": 61.
76. The state had responded by distinguishing between the Muslim Brotherhood, which it allowed to continue participating in the elections, and the "terrorist" underground movements. Ayubi, *Political Islam*: 85; Bianchi, *Unruly Corporatism*: 201.

77. al-Ahram, *The Egyptian Political System:* 30; al-Ahram, *Taqrir al-istratizhi al-ʿarabi, 1990:* 341–345, 421.
78. Ibrahim, "Reform and Frustration in Egypt": 130.
79. "Charting Untrodden Ground," *al-Ahram Weekly, 201,* December 29, 1994–January 4, 1995; available at weekly.ahram.org.eg/archives/ 1994poll.yesss.htm
80. For example, the Minister of Education, Dr. Husayn Kemal Baha al-Din, reported that he transferred more than 1,000 teachers from their teaching posts to administrative jobs because they were fundamentalists; ibid.: 62, 64.
81. Zubaida, "Islam, the State and Democracy": 6.
82. Wickham, *Mobilizing Islam:* 211–212.
83. Specifically, the law required a turnout of 50 percent of the membership in the first round for elections to be valid. If this was not achieved, the syndicates were to hold a second round requiring a 33 percent turnout. If this was not achieved, control reverted to a panel of judges. An amendment passed in 1995 that ended financial sanctions for nonvoting syndicate members and expanded the latitude of judges further weakened the syndicates. Paris AFP, February 17, 1993, in FBIS-NES-93–032, February 19, 1993: 14; Kienle, *Grand Delusion:* 85; Ibrahim, Adly, and Shehata, "Civil Society and Governance in Egypt": 39–40.
84. Kienle, *Grand Delusion:* 85; Ibrahim, "Islamic Activism in Egypt": 58.
85. al-Ahram, *Taqrir al-istiratizhi al-ʿarabi, 1993:* 354.
86. Ibrahim, et al., "Civil Society and Governance in Egypt": 40.
87. Kienle, *Grand Delusion:* 73–88.
88. Cited in Wickham, *Mobilizing Islam:* 67.
89. Abdalla, "Egypt's Islamists"; *al-Musawwar,* April 7, 1995, in FBIS-NES-95–145, July 28, 1995: 20–22; Kienle, *Grand Delusion:* 89.
90. Interview with Mustafa Mashhur, Deputy General Guide, *al-Hayat,* May 7, 1995, in FBIS-NES-95–101, May 25, 1995: 16–18; El-Mikawy, *The Building of Consensus:* 88–91.
91. *al-Ahram Weekly,* January 12, 1995 in FBIS-NES-95–011, January 18, 1995: 29–30.
92. Gerges, "The End of the Islamist Insurgency": 7; Makram-Ebeid, "Egypt's 1995 Elections": 127; *al-Ahram Weekly,* January 12, 1995, in FBIS-NES-95–011, January 18, 1995: 29–30.
93. *al-Shaʿb,* May 4, 1993, in FBIS-NES-92–087, May 7, 1993: 17–18.
94. Wickham, *Mobilizing Islam:* 214.
95. In alliance with the MB, the Wafd Party got 56% of the opposition votes in the 1984 elections vs. 26.2% for the Labor Party, 2.4% for the Liberal Party, and 15.4% percent for the NPUP, In 1987, the Wafd ran alone, receiving 36.2% of the votes. The Labor–Liberal–MB alliance received 56.5%, and the NPUP got 7.3%. Fauzi Najjar, "Elections and Democracy in Egypt," *American–Arab Affairs* 29, 1989: 96–113, cited in Wickham, *Mobilizing Islam:* 91. See also Ayubi, *Political Islam:* 85.
96. Makram-Ebeid, "Democratization in Egypt": 127; Wickham, *Mobilizing Islam:* 186.

97. Abdalla, "Egypt's Islamists": 30.
98. On these charges and denials, see Ayubi, *Political Islam*: 73. Abdalla, "Egypt's Islamists": 30; interview with Ma'mun al-Hudaybi, Voice of the Islamic Republic of Iran Radio, January 8, 1995, FBIS-NES-95–005, January 9, 1995: 22–23; Mustafa Mashhur, in *al-Sha'b*, December 15, 1992, FBIS NES 992–245, December 21, 1992: 19–20; and Hamid Abu al-Nar with *al-Sha'b*, June 24–28, 1994, FBIS-NES-94–124, June 28, 1994: 21.
99. Interview with General Guide Hamid Abu al-Nasr, *al-Musawwar*, August 4, 1995, in FBIS-NES-95–151, August 7, 1995: 17–23; with spokesman Ma'mun al-Hudaybi, *al-Wafd*, January 11, 1995, in FBIS-NES-95–012, January 19, 1995: 17–18. See also Kotob, "The Accommodationists Speak": 332–335.
100. The Brotherhood denied responsibility for the demonstrations, although it controlled the association's board. *al-Arabi*, May 30, 1994, in FBIS-NES-94–106, June 2, 1994: 18–19.
101. Weaver, "The Novelist": 67. The Muslim Brotherhood responded directly to this interview in an open letter. *al-Sha'b*, January 31, 1995, in FBIS-NES-95–025, February 7, 1995: 30–32.
102. See *al-Wafd*, April 17, 1993, in FBIS-NES-93–077, April 23, 1993: 22; *al-Ahram Weekly*, June 2–8, 1994, in FBIS-NES-94–113, June 13, 1994: 14–15; *al-Sha'b*, October 15, 1993, in FBIS-NES-93–202, October 21, 1993: 19–21.
103. Cairo MENA, September 30, 1993, in FBIS-NES-93–189, October 1993: 7.
104. Arab Republic of Eygpt Radio Network, May 29, 1994, in FBIS-NES-94–104, May 31, 1994: 24–28.
105. The Muslim Brotherhood signed the letter accepting Mubarak's invitation to join the Dialogue, but the government refused to permit it. It influenced the Dialogue through its links with the SLP, but it did not sit at the table. *al-Wafd*, December 7, 1993, in FBIS NES-93–236, December 10, 1993: 18–19; MENA, June 25, 1994, cited in FBIS-NES-94–124 June 28, 1994: 17–19.
106. Makram-Ebeid, "Democratization in Egypt": 122; *al-Ahram Weekly*, May 26–June 1, 1994, in FBIS-NES-94–115, June 15, 1994: 10–11; *al-Majallah*, May 7, 1995, in FBIS-NES-95–129, July 6, 1995: 26–32; *al-Wafd*, April 22, 1994, in FBIS-NES-94–082, April 28, 1994: 23–24.
107. Karawan, "Political Parties between State Power and Islamist Opposition": 173.
108. *al-Wafd*, October 10, 1993, in FBIS-NES-93–200, October 19, 1993: 16–17; Cairo MENA, December 24, 1994, in FBIS-NES-94–248, December 27, 1994: 10.
109. The NPUP experienced a similar debate during the late 1980s. See Karawan, "Political Parties between State Power and Islamist Opposition": 170.
110. Interview with SLP leader Ibrahim Shukri in *al-Safir*, April 1, 1993, in FBIS-NES-93–066, April 8, 1993: 14–16 and in *al-Sha'b*, March 7, 1995, in FBIS-NES-95–050, March 15, 1995: 11–12.
111. Abdalla, "Egypt's Islamists and the State": 30.
112. Interview with SLP Secretary General 'Adil Husayn in *al-Ahram Weekly*, March 16–22, 1995, in FBIS-NES-95–060, March 29, 1995: 29–30.

113. *al-Shaʿb*, March 7, 1995, in FBIS-NES-95–050, March 15, 1995: 11.
114. Law No. 93 of 1995 increased penalties for "crimes of publication." See Kienle, *A Grand Delusion:* 57.
115. *al-Majallah*, May 7, 1995, in FBIS-NES-95–129, July 6, 1995: 31.
116. A straw poll by the Ibn Khaldoun Center taken six weeks before election found that 57 percent of respondents did not expect the elections to be free and fair. Ibrahim, "Reform and Frustration in Egypt": 131. See also interview with SLP leader Ibrahim Shukri, *al-Shaʿb*, March 7, 1995, in FBIS-NES-95–050, March 15, 1995: 11; *al-Majallah*, May 7, 1995, in FBIS-NES-95–129, July 6, 1995: 27.
117. Voice of Islamic Republic of Iran Radio, January 8, 1995, in FBIS-NES-95–005, January 9, 1995: 22–23.
118. The number of violent incidents instigated by various opposition forces: Independents, 304; NDP, 143; Nasirists, 42; Muslim Brotherhood, 17; SLP, 13; Liberal Party, 37; Wafd, 12. Mustafa, *al-Intikhabat al-barlimaniyah fi Misr, 1995*: 78.
119. Kienle, *A Grand Delusion*: 56.
120. Makram-Ebeid, "Democratization in Egypt"; Bellin, *Stalled Democracy*, shows similar fears at play in Tunisia.
121. Najjar, "Islamic Fundamentalism": 152–154.
122. Interview with Shaykh ʿUmar cited in Weaver, "The Novelist": 65.
123. el-Sayyid, "A Civil Society in Egypt?" 279–280.
124. *al-Ahram*, July 18, 20–25, 1993: 9 and *al-Shaʿb*, June 23, 1993, cited in ibid.: 277.
125. Kienle, *A Grand Delusion*. See also al-Sayyid, "A Civil Society in Egypt?" 284ff.

6. Formal SoCs and Informal Political Manipulation

1. In contrast to democracies, in which political entrepreneurs may choose policy positions to obtain the greatest popular support, political elites in authoritarian regimes often choose to mobilize where they have been granted political space.
2. The moderates will accept any policy for which their payoff is greater than that of the Status Quo. Thus, they want to obtain $P_M \in [0,2]$. However, if $P_R < -1$, then the largest policy position for which they are willing to mobilize remains less than 0.
3. Formally, the radicals will join in the moderates' mobilization when $(-\alpha\pi_J + \pi_M)(|P_R - 1|) + (1 - \pi_J)(-|P_R|) - C_R > 0^3$, where α is the probability that moderates' demands are met in a Joint Conflict, π_J is the probability that a Joint Conflict succeeds, π_M is the probability that the moderates succeed independently, $|P_R - 1|$ is the difference between the moderates' preferred policy and the radicals' preferred policy, and C_R are the costs to radicals of mobilizing.
4. In this case, moderates refrain if $((1 - \alpha)\pi_J)(-|P_R - 1|) + \pi_J < \beta C_M$, where $(1 - \alpha)$ is the probability that the radicals' demands are met in a Joint Conflict, π_J is the probability that a Joint Conflict succeeds, $|P_R - 1|$ is the

difference between the moderates' and the radicals' preferred policies, and βC_M is the moderates' costs of mobilizing in a joint conflict.

5. Recall that in the unified SoC, the costs of Joint Conflict (βC_M) are less than those of Isolated Conflict (C_M). In addition, π_J is greater than or equal to π_M. Consequently, the condition will hold when $((1 - \alpha) \pi_J) (-|P_R - 1|) > \beta C_M - \pi_J$. This is more likely when the radicals may succeed in gaining their demands in a Joint Conflict, i.e., the greater $((1 - \alpha) \pi_J)$ and the larger the difference between the radicals' and moderates' preferred policies, i.e., the greater $|P_R - 1|$. In this case, while the moderates may have preferred an Isolated Conflict to the Status Quo, it does not necessarily hold that they preferred a Joint Conflict to the Status Quo.

6. In terms of the model, incumbents gain when α and $(1 - \alpha)$ are nearly equal (i.e., $\alpha \to .5$) and if $P_R \to 1$.

7. This can include groups whose preferences are consistent with but much more extreme than those of the moderates (i.e., where $P_R > 2$).

8. Formally, this condition is $((1 - \alpha) \pi_J) (-|P_R - 1|) + \pi_J < \beta C_M$.

9. A third Islamist movement, the traditionalist Sunni opposition, was led by al-Faqih al-Zamzami, who died in 1989. I will not discuss this movement here, however, since it did not advocate the overthrow of the regime. Indeed, supporters of revolutionary Islamist movements have criticized al-Zamzami as being a "hidebound traditionalist unwilling to really challenge the regime of King Hassan II." In addition, some claimed that he was a government agent, focusing attention on dress and ritual rather than on the economic, social, and political transformations necessary in Morocco. Munson, *Religion and Power in Morocco*: 332–334. See also Tozy, *Monarchie et islam politique au Maroc*.

10. *Peuples Mediterraneens*, 21, October–December 1982: 57, cited in Munson, "Morocco's Fundamentalists": 340.

11. Burgat, *L'islamisme au Maghreb: la voix du sud*: 141, cited in Munson, "Morocco's Fundamentalists": 341.

12. Munson, *ibid.*: 341.

13. "Risala maftuha ila malik al-maghrib," cited in Munson, "Morocco's Fundamentalists": 337.

14. Tozy, "Islam and the State."

15. This hypothesis has been set forth most explicitly by Munson in *Religion and Power in Morocco*.

16. Ibid.: 171.

17. It should be noted that Yasin's daughter, Nadya, reportedly stated that the government made attempts to co-opt Yasin and convince him to moderate his demands.

18. Tozy, "Islam and the State."

19. Munson calls this decision to call for participation in the elections a "ploy resulting from [Yasin's] movement's inability to overthrow the regime of Hassan II." Munson, *Religion and Power in Morocco*: 168.

20. Ibid.

21. Yasin, "Iftitahiya," *al-Jama'a*, 9, 1981: 4, cited in ibid.: 168.

22. Tozy, "Islam et état au Maghreb": 38; Munson notes similar control by Yasin as well in "Morocco's Fundamentalists": 341.

23. Munson, "Morocco's fundamentalists": 342.
24. On the weakness of formal parties and revisions, see Maghraoui, "Monarchy and Political Reform in Morocco.
25. Nasir had persecuted the Muslim Brotherhood, his most formidable adversary. On October 26, 1954, a member of the Muslim Brotherhood attempted to kill Nasir during a public speech. Nasir survived, but six Brotherhood members were hanged and thousands imprisoned in retaliation. The repression of the Brotherhood also increased from the summer of 1965 through the autumn of 1966, when the regime's repression was generally high. In this period, more than 10 members of the Brotherhood were executed and hundreds were imprisoned because of an alleged plot to overthrow Nasir. Meiring, *Fire of Islam*. See also Hinnebusch, "The Formation of the Contemporary Egyptian State," for a discussion of Sadat's regime.
26. Salah Shadi, "al-Mujtama'a al-rashida," *al-Sha'b*, February 2, 1988: 5, cited in el-Sayed, "Islamic Movement in Egypt": 236.
27. Gomaa, "Islamic Fundamentalism in Egypt During the 1930s and 1970s": 143–158.
28. For a discussion of this incident, see Amin Awwad Muhanna, "Modernization: Political Stability and Instability: The Jordan Case." 'Isa Madanat confirmed this version of the period: interview, 'Isa Madanat (founding member of the Communist Party), Amman, November 1995.
29. Such Muslim Brotherhood members included Dr. Ishaq Farhan, a cabinet minister in the early 1970s; 'Abd al-Karim 'Ukur, a director in the Ministry of Awqaf and Islamic Affairs; and 'Abd al-Latif 'Arabayat, an undersecretary in the Ministry of Education. In addition, 'Abdallah al-Akayla served as the president of the most influential public university, the University of Jordan. See Milton-Edwards, "A Temporary Alliance with the Crown"; Mufti, "Elite Bargains and Political Liberalization in Jordan": 128.
30. Khoury, "The National Consultative Council of Jordan": 28.
31. The following owes much to the work of Laurie Brand, "al-Muhajirin w-al-ansar: Hashemite Strategies for Managing Communal Identity in Jordan." See also 'Adnan Abu Odeh, "al-'Aliqat al-urduniyah al-filistiniyah" *al-Siyasah al-Filastiniyah, 14*: 75–88, cited in Lynch, *State Interests and Public Spheres*: 110.
32. Carroll, *Business as Usual?* Chapter 5.
33. Brand, "al-Muhajirin w-al-ansar": 13.
34. Lynch, *State Interests and Public Spheres*.
35. Opposition statement in *Majd*, February 11, 1997, cited in FBIS-NES-97-030.
36. This concern was noted frequently in interviews with opposition elites. See Robinson, "Can Islamists Be Democrats?

Conclusion

1. Brand, "al-Muhajirin w-al-ansar."
2. Zerhouni and Maghraoui, "Between Religion and Secularism."

Bibliography

Abdalla, Ahmed. "Egypt's Islamists and the State: From Complicity to Confrontation." *Middle East Report*, July–August 1993: 28–31.

Abdallah, Radwan. Interview. Professor of Political Science University of Jordan, Amman, November 15, 1995.

Abdel-Fattah, Nabil. "Politics of Ambivalence." *al-Ahram Weekly*, October 26–November 1, 1995. Available at http://weekly.ahram.org.eg/archives/parties/labour/indians.htm.

Abidi, Aqil Hyder Hassan. *Jordan: A Political Study, 1948–1957*. New York: Asia Publishing House, 1965.

Abu Jaber, Kamel S. and Schirin H Fathi. "The 1989 Jordanian Parliamentary Elections." *Orient*, *31* (1), March 1990: 67–86.

Africa Diary. February 26–March 4, 1985: 12225; July 1–7, 1984: 11944; October 1–7, 1981: 10684–10685; October 9–15, 1983: 11621.

Agnouche, A. "La fiction de l'alternance politique au Maroc." Unpublished manuscript.

Akesbi, Najib. Interview. Professor of Economics, Mahad Ziraʿi, [Agricultural Institute] Member of USFP, Rabat, July 13, 1995.

al-Ahram. February 25, 1968: 1; February 28, 1968: 1; March 31, 1968: 1, 3; April 1, 1968: 1, 3; October 9, 1970: 1; November 20, 1970: 1; November 21, 1970: 1, 3–4; November 26, 1970: 1; December 18, 1970: 1, 3; May 1, 1971: 1, 3–4; July 21, 1977: 1, 8.

al-Ahram. *The Egyptian Political System: A View of al-Ahram's Arab Strategic Report 1989, supplemented with important comments*. Cairo: al-Ahram, 1990.

al-Ahram. *Taqrir al-istiratizhi al-ʿarabi, 1991*. Cairo: Markaz al-Dirasat al-Siyasiyah wa al-Istiratizhiyah bi al-Ahram, 1991.

al-Ahram. Taqrir al-Istiratizhi al-ʿArabi, 1993. Cairo: Markaz al-Dirasat al-Siyasiyah wa al-Istiratizhiyah bi al-Ahram, 1993.

Alam, Asadollah. *The Shah and I: The Confidential Diary of Iran's Royal Court, 1969–1977*. Trans. Alinaghi Alikhani and Nicolas Vincent. London: I. B. Tauris, 1991.

Almond, Gabriel and Sidney Verba. *Civic Culture: Political Attitudes and Democracy in Five Nations.* Princeton, NJ: Princeton University Press, 1963.

Alougili, Mazen Ahmad Sudgi. "Comparative Study of Jordan's Foreign Policy Toward Neighboring Arab States from 1967–1988." Ph.D. thesis, Boston University 1992.

Amaoui, Nubir. Secretary General of CDT, member of USFP Central Committee. Interview. Casablanca, May 1995.

Amawi, Abla. *"State and Class in Transjordan: A Study of State Autonomy."* vol. 1. Ph.D. thesis, Georgetown University, 1993.

Amawi, Abla. "Jordan" in Tachau (ed.), *Political Parties of the Middle East and North Africa*: 259–296.

Amin, Galal. *Egypt's Economic Predicament: A Study in the Interaction of External Pressure, Political Folly, and Social Tension in Egypt, 1960–1990.* New York: E. J. Brill, 1995.

Anderson, Betty. *State and the Opposition in the Hashemite Kingdom of Jordan: The First Fifty Years.* Austin: University of Texas Press, forthcoming.

Anderson, Lisa. "Lawless Government and Illegal Opposition: Reflections on the Middle East." *Journal of International Affairs, 40* (2), Spring 1987: 219–232.

Anderson, Lisa. "Political Pacts, Liberalism and Democracy: The Tunisian Pact of 1988." *Government and Opposition,* 26 (2), Spring 1991: 244–260.

Andoni, Lamis. "Jordan: Democratization in Danger." *Middle East International, 515,* December 15, 1995: 16–17.

Ansari, Hamied, "The Islamic Militants in Egyptian Politics." *International Journal of Middle East Studies,* 16 (1), Summer 1984: 123–144.

Ansari, Hamied. "Sectarian Conflict in Egypt and the Political Expediency of Religion." *Middle East Journal,* 38 (3), Summer 1984: 397–418.

el-Aoufi, Noureddine (ed.). *La societé civile au Maroc.* Rabat: Smer, 1992.

Aruri, Naseer. *Jordan: A Study in Political Development (1921–1965).* The Hague: Nijhoff, 1972.

Ashford, Douglas. *Political Change in Morocco.* Princeton, NJ: Princeton University Press, 1961.

Assaad, Ragui and Malak Rouchdy. *Poverty and Poverty Alleviation Strategies in Egypt.* Cairo: American University of Cairo, 1999.

L'avant garde June 18, 1981: 1.

Ayubi, Nazih N. "Government and the State in Egypt Today." In Tripp and Owen (eds.), *Egypt under Mubarak.* 1–20.

Ayubi, Nazih. "The Political Revival of Islam: The Case of Egypt." *International Journal of Middle East Studies,* 12 (4), Dececember 1980: 481–499.

Ayubi, Nazih. *Political Islam: Religion and Politics in the Arab World.* London: Routledge, 1991.

Azzam, Maha. "Egypt: The Islamists and the State under Mubarak." In Sidahmed and Ehteshami (eds.), *Islamic Fundamentalism*: 109–122.

Bachelani, Najma. "Mobilization and Electoral Success: Ideological Parties in Jordan, 1989–1993." Ph.D. dissertation, University of Michigan, 1999.

Baker, Raymond. *Sadat and After: Struggles for Egypt's Political Soul.* Cambridge, MA: Harvard University Press, 1990.

Baker, Raymond William. *Egypt's Uncertain Revolution under Nasser and Sadat*. Cambridge, MA: Harvard University Press, 1978.

Bailey, Clinton. "Cabinet Formation in Jordan." In Sinai and Pollack (eds.), *The Hashemite Kingdom of Jordan and the West Bank*: 102–112.

Barraclough, Steven. "Al-Azhar: Between the Government and the Islamists." *Middle East Journal*, 52 (2), May 1998: 236–249.

Barraoui, Jamal. "Vent de fronde sur les partis politiques." *La vie économique*, July, 21, 1995: 3–4.

al-Bayane. July 16, 1981: 1.

Bayat, Asef. "Revolution without Movement, Movement without Revolution: Comparing Islamic Activism in Iran and Egypt." *Comparative Studies in Society and History*, 40 (1), January 1998: 136–169.

Bayer, Thomas C. *Morocco: Direct Legislative Elections Monitoring/Observation Report*. Washington, DC: International Foundation for Electoral Systems, 1993.

Bellin, Eva Rana. *Stalled Democracy: Capital, Labor, and the Paradox of State-Sponsored Development*. Ithaca, NY: Cornell University Press, 2002.

Ben ʿAli, Driss. "Changement de pacte sociale et continuité de l'ordre politique au Maroc." In Michel Camau (ed.), *Annuaire de l'Afrique du Nord*. Paris: CNRS, 1989, 51–72.

Ben ʿAli, Driss. "Émergence de l'espace socio-politique et stratégie de l'état au Maroc." In Sedjari (ed.), *État, éspace et pouvoir locale*: 61–74.

Ben ʿAli, Driss. "La politique economique marocaine de l'indépendence a nos jours." In Ben ʿAli and Martens (eds.), *Analyses de politique économique appliúees au Maroc*: 3–26.

Ben ʿAli, Driss. Interview. Professor, Muhammad V University. July 19, 1995.

Ben ʿAli, Driss and Andre Martens (eds.). *Analyses de politique économique appliquées au Maroc*. Rabat: GREI, 1993.

Benazzou, Chaouki. *Panorama économique du Maroc 1969/1985*. Casablanca: Les editions maghrebines, 1986.

Benazzou, Chaouki and Tawfik Mouline. *Panorama économique du Maroc, 1985/1990*. Rabat: El maarif al jadida, 1993.

el-Benna, Abdelkader. "Les partis politiques au Maroc." In El-Aoufi (ed.), *La societé civile au Maroc*: 127–170.

Bermeo, Nancy (ed.). *Liberalization and Democratization: Change in the Soviet Union and Eastern Europe*. Baltimore: Johns Hopkins University Press, 1991.

Bermeo, Nancy. "Sacrifice, Sequence and Strength in Successful Dual Transitions: Lessons from Spain." *The Journal of Politics*, 56 (3), August 1994: 601–627.

Bernard-Maugiron, Nathalie and Baudouin Dupret (eds.). *Egypt and Its Laws*. London: Kluwer Law International, 2002.

Bernhard, Michael. "Civil Society and Democratic Transition in East Central Europe." *Political Science Quarterly*, 108 (2), Summer 1993: 307–326.

Berrada, Abdelkader. "Le marocanisation de 1973 éclairage rétrospectif." *Économie et socialisme*, 8, 1988: 29–69.

Berrada, Abdelkader and M. Said Saadi. "Le grand capital privé marocain." In J. C. Savtucci (ed.), *Le Maroc Actuel*. Paris: CNRS, 1992: 325–391.

Bianchi, Robert. *Unruly Corporatism: Associational Life in Twentieth-Century Egypt*. New York: Oxford University Press, 1989.

Bienen, Henry and Jeffrey Herbst. "The Relationship Between Political and Economic Reform in Africa." *Comparative Politics*, 29 (1), October 1996: 23–42.

Binder, Leonard (ed.). *Ethnic Conflict and International Politics in the Middle East*. Gainesville: University Press of Florida, 1999.

Bourqia, Rahma. "The Cultural Legacy of Power in Morocco." In Bourquia and Miller (eds.), *In the Shadow of the Sultan*: 243–258.

Bourqia, Rahma and Susan Miller (eds.). *In the Shadow of the Sultan: Culture, Power and Politics in Morocco*. Cambridge, MA: Harvard University Press, 1999.

Bouzouba, Dr. ʿAbd al-Majid. Interview. Deputy Secretary General and Secretary of Information of CDT, Council Member of USFP, Rabat, July 14, 1995.

Bova, Russell. "Political Dynamics of the Post-Communist Transition: A Comparative Perspective." *World Politics*, 44 (1), October 1991: 113–138.

Boyle, Kevin and Adel Omar Sherif (eds.). *Human Rights and Democracy: The Role of the Supreme Constitutional Court of Egypt*. London: Kluwar Law International, 1996.

Brand, Laurie. *Palestinians in the Arab World: Institution Building and the Search for the State*. New York: Columbia University Press, 1988.

Brand, Laurie A. *Jordan's Inter-Arab Relations: The Political Economy of Alliance Making*. New York: Columbia University Press, 1994.

Brand, Laurie. "'In the Beginning Was the State . . . ': The Quest for Civil Society in Jordan." In Norton (ed.), *Civil Society in the Middle East, Vol. 1*: 148–185.

Brand, Laurie. "al-Muhajirin wa-al-ansar: Hashemite Strategies for Managing Communal Identity in Jordan." In Binder (ed.), *Ethnic Conflict and International Politics in the Middle East*: 279–306.

Bratton, Michael and Nicolas van de Walle. "Popular Protest and Political Reform in Africa." *Comparative Politics*, July 1992, 24 (4): 421.

Bratton, Michael and Nicolas van de Walle. *Democratic Experiments in Africa*. New York: Cambridge University Press, 1997.

Brown, Kenneth (ed.). *État, ville et mouvements sociaux au Maghreb et au Moyen-Orient*. Paris: CNRS, 1986.

Brown, Nathan J. *The Rule of Law in the Arab World: Courts in Egypt and the Gulf*. Cambridge: Cambridge University Press, 1997.

Brynen, Rex. "The Politics of Monarchical Liberalism: Jordan." In Korany, Brynen, and Noble (eds.), *Political Liberalization and Democratization in the Arab World,* Vol 2: 71–100.

Bryen, Rex, Bahgat Korany, and Paul Noble. "Conclusion." In Korany, Bryen, and Noble, *Political Liberalization and Democratization in the Arab World: Volume 2*: 267–278.

Bryen, Rex, Bahgat Korany, and Paul Noble. *Political Liberalization and Democratization in the Arab World, Volume I*. Boulder, CO: Lynne Rienner, 1995.

Butterworth, Charles and I. William Zartman (eds.). *Between Islam and the State*. Cambridge: Cambridge University Press, 2001.

Carroll, Katherine Blue. *Business as Usual? Economic Reform in Jordan*. New York: Lexington Books, 2003.

Center for Human Rights Legal Aid (CHRLA). "Section II: Legal Restrictions Imposed on the Right to Form Political Parties in Egypt," March 9, 1999. Available at www.chrla.org/reports/poltix/poltix.html.

Center for Strategic Studies (CSS). *Public Opinion Survey on Democracy in Jordan, Preliminary Findings.* Amman: University of Jordan, March 1993.

Center for Strategic Studies (CSS). *Istitla'a li al-ra'i hawla al-dimuqratiyah fi al-Urdunn 1995: al-nita'ij al-awaliyah.* Amman: University of Jordan, March 1995.

Center for Strategic Studies (CSS). *Istatla'a al-ra'i hawl al-dimuqratiyya fi al-Urdun 1998.* Amman: Markaz al-Dirasat al-Istratijiyah, Jami'at al-Urdun, 1998.

Chai, Sun-Ki. "An Organizational Economics Theory of Antigovernment Violence." *Comparative Politics*, 26, October 1993: 99–110.

Chaudhry, Kiren Aziz. "Economic Liberalization in Oil-Exporting Countries: Iraq and Saudi Arabia." In Harik and Sullivan (eds.), *Privatisation and Liberalization in the Middle East*: 145–166.

Cheibub, Jose Antonio and Fernando Limongi. "Modes of Government Formation and the Survival of Democratic Regimes: Parliamentary and Presidential Democracies Reconsidered." Paper presented at the annual meeting of the American Political Science Association, San Francisco, August 30–September 2, 2001.

Chirat, M. Interview. Member of UGTM leadership and Istiqlal Political Bureau, Casablanca, July 20, 1995.

Chong, Dennis. *Collective Action and the Civil Rights Movement.* Chicago: University of Chicago Press, 1991.

Christian Science Monitor. May 1, 1988: 4; May 13, 1988: 9; May 1, 1989: 4; June 15, 1989: 3; November 2, 1989: 4; November 16, 1989: 4; November 26, 1990: 8; November 26, 1990: 8; June 15, 1993: 3; November 8, 1993: 2.

CHRLA. "Egyptian Politics: The Fiction of the Multiparty System," September 18, 1996. Available at www.chrla.org/releases/politics.htm.

Claisse, Alain. "Elections communales et legislatives au Maroc." *Annuaire de l'Afrique du Nord, 1985.* Paris: CNRS, 1987: 631–668.

Claisse, Alain. "Les systèmes de légitimité à l'épreuve, le cas des pays du Maghreb," in Claisse, Conac and Leca (eds.), *Le grand Maghreb*: 120–147.

Claisse, Alain, Gérard Conac, and Jean Leca (eds.). *Le grand Maghreb: donées sociopolitique et facteurs d'intégration des états du Maghreb.* Paris: Économica, 1988.

Clément, Jean-François, "Les revoltes urbaines." *Le Maroc Actual.* Paris: CNRS, 1993: 392–406.

Cohen, Amnon. *Political Parties in the West Bank Under the Jordanian Regime.* Ithaca, NY: Cornell University Press, 1982.

Coleman, James S. *Foundations of Social Theory.* Cambridge, MA: Harvard University Press, 1990.

Collier, David (ed.). *The New Authoritarianism in Latin America.* Princeton, NJ: Princeton University Press, 1979.

Combs-Schilling, M. Elaine. "Performing Monarchy, Staging Nation." In Bourqia and Miller (eds.), *In the Shadow of the Sultan*: 167–214.

Cooper, Mark N. *The Transformation of Egypt*. London: Croom Helm, 1982.

Coppedge, Michael. "District Magnitude, Economic Performance, and Party-System Fragmentation in Five Latin American Countries." *Comparative Political Studies*, 30 (2), April 1997: 156–186.

Coupe, Jeffrey A. "The Political Economy of Moroccan Adjustment." Presented at the Social Science Research Council Political Economy Workshop, University of California, Berkeley, February 1994.

Crescenzi, Mark J. C. "Violence and Uncertainty in Transition." *Journal of Conflict Resolution*, 43 (2), April 1999: 192–212.

Crowley, Stephen. "Barriers to Collective Action: Steelworkers and Mutual Dependence in the Former Soviet Union." *World Politics*, 46 (4), July 1994: 589–615.

Crystal, Jill. "Authoritarianism and Its Adversaries in the Arab World." *World Politics*, 46 (2), January 1994: 262–290.

Dagharni, Ahmad. *al-Intikhabat wa al-ahzab al-siyasiyah al-Maghribiyah*. Rabat: n.p., 1990.

Dahl, Robert. *Polyarchy: Participation and Opposition*. New Haven, CT: Yale University Press, 1971.

Dahl, Robert (ed.). *Regimes and Oppositions*. New Haven, CT: Yale University Press, 1973.

Dann, Uriel. *King Hussein and the Challenge of Arab Radicalism; Jordan 1955–1967*. New York: Oxford University Press, 1989.

Davenport, Christian. "Constitutional Promises and Repressive Reality: A Cross-National Time-Series Investigation of Why Political and Civil Liberties Are Suppressed." *Journal of Politics*, 58 (3), August 1996: 627–654.

Dawisha, Adeed and I. William Zartman (eds.). *Beyond Coercion: The Durability of the Arab State*. London: Croom Helm, 1988.

Dekmejian, Hrair. *Egypt Under Nasir: A Study in Political Development*. Albany: State University of New York Press, 1971.

DeNardo, James. *Power in Numbers: The Political Strategy of Protest and Rebellion*. Princeton, NJ: Princeton University Press, 1985.

Denoeux, Guilain. *Urban Unrest in the Middle East: A Comparative Study of Informal Networks in Egypt, Iran and Lebanon*. Albany: State University of New York Press, 1993.

Deutsch, Karl. "Social Mobilization and Political Development." *The American Political Science Review*, 55 (3), September 1961: 493–514.

Diamond, Larry and Marc Plattner (eds.). *Economic Reform and Democracy*. Baltimore: Johns Hopkins University Press, 1995.

Direction de la statistique, *Population active urbaine: résultats détailles*. Rabat: Direction de la statistique, 1990.

Direction de la statistique. *Population active urbaine: résultats détailles*. Rabat: Direction de la statistique, 1993.

Dobers, H., W. Goussous, and Y. Sara (eds.). *Democracy and the Rule of Law in Jordan*. Amman: Jordanian Printing Press, 1992.

Doumou, Abdlelali (ed.), L'*État marocain dans le durée (1850–1985)*. Mohammedia: Fedala, 1987.

Duclos, Louis-Jean. "Les élections législatives en Jordanie." *Maghreb Machrek*, *129*, July–September 1990: 47–73.

East, Roger, and Tanya Joseph. *Political Parties of Africa and the Middle East: A Reference Guide*. Harlow, Essex, United Kingdom: Longman, 1993.

Eaton, Kent. "Parliamentarism vs. Presidentialism in the Policy Arena." *Comparative Politics*, *32* (3), April 2000: 355–376.

Eckstein, Susan (ed.). *Power and Popular Protest*. Berkeley: University of Calofornia Press, 1989.

Economist Intelligence Unit. *The Economist Book of Vital World Statistics*. London: Random House Business Books, 1990.

Economist Intelligence Unit. *Country Report: Jordan*. London: The Economist Intelligence Unit, 1998.

Eickelman, Dale F. "Changing Perceptions of State Authority: Morocco, Egypt and Oman." In Salamé (ed.), *The Foundations of the Arab State*: 177–204.

Eisinger, Peter K. "The Conditions of Protest Behavior in American Cities." *The American Political Science Review*, *67* (1), March 1973: 11–28.

Elouardighi, Aissa. Interview. Member of Central Committee of Organization of Democratic and Popular Action, Member of Systeme des Nations Unies-Sep, Rabat, Morocco, June 26, 1995.

Elster, Jon and Rune Slagstad (eds.). *Constitutionalism and Democracy*. Cambridge: Cambridge University Press, 1988.

Emara, Mohamed. "Old But Also New." *al-Ahram Weekly*, October 26– November 1, 1995. Available at weekly.ahram.org.eg/archives/parties/labour/ Indians.htm.

Entelis, John P. "Introduction: State and Society in Transition." In Entelis and Naylor (eds.), *State and Society in Algeria*: 1–30.

Entelis, John P. and Phillip C. Naylor (eds.). *State and Society in Algeria*. Boulder, CO: Westview Press, 1992.

Evans, Peter, Dietrich Rueschemeyer, and Theda Skocpol (eds.). *Bringing the State Back In*. New York: Cambridge University Press, 1985.

Fandy, Mamoun. "Egypt's Islamic Group: Regional Revenge?" *Middle East Journal*, *48* (4), Autumn 1994: 607–625.

Fandy, Mamoun. *Saudi Arabia and the Politics of Dissent*. New York: St. Martin's Press, 1999.

al-Fasi, ʿAllal. *Independence Movements of Arab North Africa*. New York: Octagon Books, 1970.

Fathi, Schirin. *Jordan: An Invented Nation?* Hamburg: Deutsches Orient Institut, 1994.

Feisal, Toujan, Interview. November 1995, Amman.

Fergany, Nadir. "A Characterization of the Employment Problem in Egypt." In Handoussa and Potter (eds.), *Employment and Structural Adjustment*: 25–56.

Fischbach, Michael R. *State, Society, and Land in Jordan*. Boston: Brill, 2000.

Foreign Broadcast Information Series (FBIS-NES Series). December 21, 1992: 19–20; December 12, 1995: 22; February 19, 1993: 14; April 8, 1993: 14–16; April 23, 1993: 22; May 7, 1993: 17–18; May 19, 1993: 11–12; September 17, 1993: 20; September 21, 1993: 16; October 1, 1993: 7; October 19, 1993:

16–17; October 21, 1993: 19–21; December 10, 1993: 18–19; April 28, 1994: 23–24; May 31, 1994: 24–28; June 2, 1994: 18–19; June 13, 1994: 14–15; June 15, 1994: 10–11; June 28, 1994: 17–19; December 27, 1994: 10; January 9, 1995: 22–23; January 11, 1995: 19; January 12, 1995: 15–16; January 18, 1995: 29–30; January 19, 1995: 17–18; February 7, 1995: 30–32. March 15, 1995: 11–12; January 17, 1995: 29; March 22, 1995: 23; March 29, 1995: 29–30, 37; May 25, 1995: 16–18; July 6, 1995: 26–32; July 28, 1995: 20–22; August 7, 1995: 17–21.

Foreign Report February 24, 1994: 1.

Francisco, Ronald. "The Relationship Between Coercion and Protest." *Journal of Conflict Resolution*, 39 (2), June 1995: 263–282.

Francisco, Ronald. "Coercion and Protest: An Empirical Test in Two Democratic States." *The American Journal of Political Science*, 40 (4), November 1996: 1179–1204.

Gamson, William A and David S. Meyer. "Framing Political Opportunity." In McAdam, McCarthy, and Zald (eds.), *Comparative Perspectives on Social Movements*: 275–290.

Gamson, William. *The Strategy of Protest*. Homewood, IL: Dorsey, 1975.

Gandhi, Jennifer and Adam Przeworski, "Dictatorial Institutions and the Survival of Dictators." Presented at the annual meeting of the American Political Science Association, San Francisco, August–September 2001.

Gavin, Maxwell. *Lords of the Atlas: The Rise and Fall of the House of Glaoua, 1893–1956*. London: Longmans, 1966.

Gavious, Arich and Shlomo Mizrahi. "Two-Level Collective Action and Group Identity." *Journal of Theoretical Politics*, 11 (4), 1999: 497–517.

Geddes, Barbara. "Economic Reform and Democracy: Challenging the Conventional Wisdom." *Journal of Democracy*, 5 (4), October 1994: 104–118.

Geddes, Barbara. "The Breakdown of Authoritarian Regimes: Empirical Tests and Game Theoretic Arguments." Presented at the Center for Comparative Research, Yale University, fall 2000.

Geller, Daniel. "The Impact of Political System Structure on Probability Patterns of Internal Disorder." *American Journal of Political Science*, 31 (2), May 1987: 217–235.

Gellner, Ernest. "Patterns of Rural Rebellion in Morocco." *Archives Européenes de Sociologie*, 3, 1962: 297–311.

Gellner, Ernest and Jean-Claude Vatin (eds.). *Islam et politique au Maroc*. Paris: Centre nationale de la recherche scientifique (CNRS), 1981.

Gerges, Fawaz. "The End of the Islamist Insurgency in Egypt? Costs and Prospects." *Middle East Journal*, 54 (4), Autumn 2000: 592.

Gersovitz, Mark and Henry Bienen. "Economic Stabilization, Conditionality and Political Stability." *International Organization*, 29, Autumn 1985: 729–754.

Ghadbian, Najib. *Democratization and the Islamist Challenge in the Arab World*. Boulder, CO: Westview Press, 1997.

Ginkel, John and Alastair Smith. "So You Say You Want a Revolution: A Game Theoretic Explanation of Revolution in Repressive Regimes." *Journal of Conflict Resolution*, 43 (3), June 1999: 291–316.

Glenn, John. "Competing Challengers and Contested Outcomes to State Breakdown." *Social Forces*, 78 (1), September 1999: 187–212.

Glubb, Sir John Bagot. *A Soldier with the Arabs*. London: Hodder and Stoughton, 1957.

Goldberg, Ellis, Resat Kasaba, and Joel Migdal (eds.). *Rules and Rights in the Middle East: Society, Law and Democracy*. Seattle: University of Washington Press, 1993.

Goldberg, Harvey. *The Life of Jean Jaures*. Madison: University of Wisconsin Press, 1962.

Goldstone, Jack and Bert Useem. "Prison Riots as Microrevolutions: An Extension of State-Centered Theories of Revolution." *American Journal of Sociology*, 104 (4), January 1999: 985–1029.

Gomaa, Ahmed. "Islamic Fundamentalism in Egypt during the 1930s and 1970s: Comparative Notes." In Gabriel R. Warburg and Uri M. Kupferschmidt (eds.), *Islam, Nationalism, and Radicalism in Egypt and the Sudan*. New York: Praeger, 143–158.

Goodson, Larry and Soha Radwan. "Democratization in Egypt in the 1990s: Stagnant, or Merely Stalled?" *Arab Studies Quarterly*, 19 (1), Winter 1997: 1–21.

Goodwin, Jeff and James M. Jasper. "Caught in a Winding, Snarling Vine: The Structural Bias of Political Process Theory." *Sociological Forum*, 14 (1), 1999: 29–54.

Greenwood, Scott. "Business Regime Loyalties in the Arab World: Jordan and Morocco in Comparative Perspective." Ph.D. thesis, University of Michigan, 1998.

Guerraoui, Driss (ed.). *Ajustement et developpement*. Belvedere-Casablanca: Toubkal, 1993.

Gurr, Ted Robert. "On the Political Consequences of Scarcity." *International Studies Quarterly*, 29, 1985: 51–75.

Gurr, Ted Robert. "War, Revolution and the Growth of the Coercive State." *Comparative Political Studies*, 21 (1), 1988: 45–65.

Gurr, Ted Robert, *Why Men Rebel*. Princeton, NJ: Princeton University Press, 1970.

Gupta, Dipak, Harinder Singh, and Tom Sprague. "Government Coercion of Dissidents: Deterrence or Provocation?" *Journal of Conflict Resolution*, 37 (2), June 1993: 301–339.

Haddadine, Khalil. Interview. MP, Jordanian Arab Ba'ath Socialist Party, August 15, 1998.

Haggard, Stephan and Robert R. Kaufman (eds.). *The Political Economy of Democratic Transitions*. Princeton, NJ: Princeton University Press, 1995.

Haggard, Stephan and Robert Kaufman. "The Politics of Stabilisation and Structural Adjustment." In Sachs (ed.), *Developing Country Debt and Economic Performance, Vol. I*.

Haggard, Stephan and Robert Kaufman. "Economic Adjustment in New Democracies." In Nelson (ed.), *Fragile Coalitions*: 57–78.

Hamarnah, Mustafa. *al-Urdunn* (Cairo: Markaz ibn Khaldun, 1995).

Hanafi, Hassan. "The Relevance of the Islamic Alternative." Presented at Centre for Development Studies, University of Bremen, 1992.

Handoussa, Heba. "Crisis and Challenge: Prospects for the 1990s." In Handoussa and Potter (eds.), *Employment and Structural Adjustment: Egypt in the 1990s*: 3–21.

Handoussa, Heba and Gillian Potter (eds.). *Employment and Structural Adjustment: Egypt in the 1990s*. Cairo: American University of Cairo Press, 1991.

Harbeson, John, Donald Rothchild, and Naomi Chazan, *Civil Society and the State in Africa*. Boulder, CO: Lynne Rienner, 1994.

Hardin, Russell. *Collective Action*. Baltimore: Johns Hopkins University Press, 1982.

Hardin, Russell. *One for All: The Logic of Group Conflict*. Princeton, NJ: Princeton University Press, 1995.

Harik, Illiya. "The Single Party as a Subordinate Movement." *World Politics*, 26, October 1973: 80–105.

Harik, Iliya and Denis J. Sullivan (eds.). *Privatization and Liberalization in the Middle East*. Bloomington: Indiana University Press, 1992.

Hart, David (ed.). *Tribe and Society in Rural Morocco*. London: Frank Cass, 2000.

Hart, David. "Rural and Tribal Uprisings in Post-Colonial Morocco, 1957–60: An Overview and a Reappraisal." In Hart (ed.), *Tribe and Society in Rural Morocco*: 84–104.

Hashemite Kingdom of Jordan. *Political Parties Law No. 32 for the Year 1992*. Amman: Press and Publications Department, January 1994.

Hassan II, King of Morocco. *The Challenge: The Memoirs of King Hassan II of Morocco*. Trans. Anthony Rhodes. London: Macmillan, 1978.

Hassan II, King. "Discours de S.M. le Roi a la nation." In Ministère de l'Information (ed.), *Discours et interviews de S.M. le Roi Hassan II, Tome VIII*.

Hawatmeh, George. "The Changing Role of the Press." In Hawatmeh (ed.), *Jordanian Experience since 1989*: 3–9.

Hawatmeh, George. *Jordanian Experience since 1989: The Role of the Press*. Amman: University of Jordan Press,

Hefner, Robert. *Civil Islam: Muslims and Democratization in Indonesia*. Princeton, NJ: Princeton University Press, 2000.

Hendriks, Bertus. "Egypt's New Political Map." *Middle East Report*, 17, July-August 1987: 23–30.

Hermassi, Elbaki and Dirk Vanderwalle. "The Second Stage of State Building." In Zartman and Habeeb (eds.), *Polity and Society in Contemporary North Africa*: 19–41.

Heydemann, S. "Taxation without Representation: Authoritarianism and Economic Liberalization in Syria." In Goldberg, Kasaba and Migdal (eds.), *Rules and Rights in the Middle East*: 69–102.

Hinnebusch, Raymond A. "The Reemergence of the Wafd Party: Glimpses of the Liberal Opposition in Egypt." *International Journal of Middle East Studies*, 16 (1), March 1984: 99–121.

Hinnebusch, Raymond A. *Egyptian Politics Under Sadat*. Cambridge: Cambridge University Press, 1985.

Hinnebusch, Raymond A. "The Formation of the Contemporary Egyptian State from Nasser and Sadat to Mubarak." In Owiess (ed.), *The Political Economy of Contemporary Egypt*: 188–221.

Hizb al-Istiqlal. *Hizb al-Istiqlal bayna al-mu'tamarayn (1985–1994)*. Rabat: Al Sharakat al-Maghrabia, 1995.

Hodgkin, Thomas. *African Political Parties*. London 1961.

Hoffman, Eleanor. *Realm of the Evening Star: A History of Morocco and the Land of the Moors*. Philadelphia: Chilton, 1965.

Hourani, Hani. Interviews, Director, al-Urdunn al-Jadid Center, November 1995 and August 1998.

Huntington, Samuel. *Political Order in Changing Societies*. New Haven, CT: Yale University Press, 1968.

Huntington, Samuel. *The Third Wave: Democratization in the Late Twentieth Century*. Norman: University of Oklahoma Press, 1991.

Hurani, Hani (ed.). *al-Ahzab al-siyasiyah al-Urduniyah*. Amman: Markaz al-Urdun al-Jadid lil-Dirasat: 1997.

al-Husayn, ʿAbdallah ibn. *My Memoirs Completed*, Trans. Harold Glidden. New York: Longman, 1951.

Ibrahim, Saad Eddin. "Egypt's Islamic Militants." *Middle East Research and Information Project, 12*, February 1982: 5–14.

Ibrahim, Saad Eddin. "The Changing Face of Egypt's Islamism Activism." In Ibrahim (ed.), *Egypt, Islam and Democracy*: 69–81.

Ibrahim, Saad Eddin. "An Islamic Alternative in Egypt: The Muslim Brotherhood and Sadat." In Ibrahim (ed.), *Egypt, Islam and Democracy*: 35–52.

Ibrahim, Saad Eddin. "Anatomy of Egypt's Militant Islamic Groups: Methodological Notes and Preliminary Findings." In Ibrahim (ed.), *Egypt, Islam and Democracy*: 1–34.

Ibrahim, Saad Eddin. "Reform and Frustration in Egypt." *Journal of Democracy*, 7 (4), 1996: 125–135.

Ibrahim, Saad Eddin (ed.). *Egypt, Islam, and Democracy: Critical Essays*. Cairo: American University in Cairo Press, 2002.

Ibrahim, Saad Eddin, Huwaida Adly, and Dina Shehata. "Civil Society and Governance in Egypt." Presented at the Second International Conference of the Civil Society and Governance Programme, Institute of Development Studies, University of Sussex, held in Cape Town, South Africa, February 18–21, 1999. Available at http://nt1.ids.ac.uk/ids/civsoc/docs/Egypt.doc.

Ihrai, Said. *Pouvoir et influence: état, partis, et politique étrangère au Maroc*. Rabat: El Maarif al-jadida, 1986, 226.

"Islamism's Melting Pot." *al-Ahram Weekly*, October 26–November 1, 1995. Available at weekly.ahram.org.eg/archives/parties/labour/shukri.htm.

Ismal, Tarek Y. and Jacqueline S. Ismael (eds.), *Politics and Government in the Middle East and North Africa*. Miami: Florida International Press, 1991.

al-Ittihad al-ʿAmm lil-Shaghalin. *Tadakhal al-akh ʿAbd al-Razzaq Faylali al-katib al-ʿamm lil-ittihad al-ʿamm lil-shaghalin fi munaqish barnamij hakuma al-Sayyid ʿAbd al-Latif al-Filali al-Thaniya*. Casablanca: Manshurat al-Ittihad al-'Amm lil-Shagalin, March 1995.

al-Ittihad al-Ishtiraki June 12, 1981: 2; June 3, 1995: 1.

al-Ittihad al-Maghrebi lil-Shaghal. *Min ajli rif ʿa tahadi al-taghir al-dimuqrati*. Casablanca: n.p., June 1992.

al-Ittihad al-Maghrebi lil-Shaghal. *Min ajli rifaʿa al-dimuqratiyya: haquq al-'insan wa al-haquq al-niqabiya*. Casablanca: n.p., February 1994.

Jamal, ʿAbd al-Sami. *Kitab al-aswad li-ahzab Misr*. Cairo: n.p., 1989.

Jenkins, J. Craig and Bert Klandermans (eds.). *The Politics of Social Protest: Comparative Perspectives on the State and Social Movements*. Minneapolis: University of Minnesota Press, 1995.

Jennings, M. Kent and Ellen Ann Anderson. "Support for Confrontational Tactics Among AIDS Activists: A Study of Intra-Movement Divisions." *American Journal of Political Science*, 40 (2), May 1996: 311–334.

Jeune Afrique. June 22–28, 1995: 16–17.

Jibril, Muhammad. "Les événements et les problèmes de Fond." *Lamalif*, 127, July–August 1981: 28–31.

Jordan Media Group. *Jordan: Keys to the Kingdom*. Amman: Jordan Media Group, 1995.

Jordan Times. November 11, 1985: 1; January 20, 1992: 3; September 2, 1992: 3; September 25, 1992: 1; July 27, 1993: 1; May 29, 1995: 1; October 1, 1995: 1; October 12–13, 1995: 1; October 26–27, 1995: 6; November 15, 1995: 1; November 19, 1995: 1; November 20, 1995: 1; December 2, 1995: 3; December 10, 1995: 3; December 11, 1995: 1; August 5, 1998: 3.

Jordanian Engineers Association. "La li al-tatbiʿa." Amman, n.p.: November 1995.

Jureidini, P. A. and R. D. McLaurin. *Jordan: The Impact of Social Change on the Role of the Tribes*. New York: Praeger, 1984.

al-Kabariti, ʿAbd al-Karim. Minister for Foreign Affairs. "Opening Remarks" at the Seminar on Democracy and the Rule of Law. Amman: Royal Cultural Center, November 19, 1995.

Kamrava, Mehran. "Revolution Revisited: The Structuralist–Voluntarist Debate." *Canadian Journal of Political Science*, 32 (2), June 1999: 317–345.

Karawan, Ibrahim. "Political Parties Between State Power and Islamist Opposition." In Butterworth and Zartman (eds.), *Between Islam and the State*: 158–183.

Karl, Terry Lynn. "Dilemmas of Democratization in Latin America." *Comparative Politics*, 23, October 1990: 1–21.

Karmeshu, V. P. Jain and A. K. Mahajan. "A Dynamic Model of Domestic Political Conflict Process." *Journal of Conflict Resolution*, 34 (2), June 1990: 252–269.

Kassem, Maye. *Egyptian Politics: The Dynamics of Authoritarian Rule*. Boulder, CO: Lynne Rienner, 2004.

Kepel, Gilles. *The Prophet and the Pharaoh: Muslim Extremism in Egypt*. Trans. Jon Rothschild. London: al-Saqi Books, 1985.

Khadir, ʿAzmah. Interventions at the Seminar on Democracy and the Rule of Law – Assessment and Outlook. Amman: Royal Cultural Center, November 19, 1995.

Khalil, Muhammad. *The Arab States and the Arab League*. Bayrut: Khayat, 1962.

Khassawneh, Anis. "The Social Setting of Administrative Behavior in Jordan." Ph.D. thesis, Claremont Graduate School, 1987.

Khouri, N. A. "The National Consultative Council of Jordan: A Study in Legislative Development." *International Journal of Middle East Studies*, 13 (4), 1981: 435–447.

Khrouz, Driss. *L'Économie marocaine: Les raisons de la crise*. Casablanca: Les éditions maghrebines, 1988.

Khrouz, Driss. "De l'endettement a l'ajustement." In Guerraoui (ed.), *Ajustement et developpement*: 80.

Kilani, Sa'eda. Interview. Journalist for *Jordan Times*, December 1, 1995.

Kienle, Eberhard (ed.). *Contemporary Syria: Liberalization between Cold War and Cold Peace*. London; British Academic Press, 1994.

Kienle, Eberhard. "More Than a Response to Islamism: The Political Deliberalization of Egypt in the 1990s." *Middle East Journal*, 51, Spring 1998: 219–235.

Kienle, Eberhard. *A Grand Delusion: Democracy and Economic Reform in Egypt*. London: I. B. Tauris, 2001.

Kirkbride, Alec. *From the Wings: Amman Memoirs 1947–1951*. London: Frank Cass, 1976.

Kitschelt, Herbert. "Political Opportunity Structures and Political Protest: Anti-Nuclear Movements in Four Democracies." *British Journal of Political Science*, 16, 1986: 57–85.

Klandermans, Bert, Hanspeter Kriesi, and Sidney Tarrow (eds.). *From Structure to Action: Comparing Social Movement Research Across Cultures*. Greenwich, CT: JAI Press, 1988.

Koopmans, Ruud. "The Dynamics of Protest Waves: West Germany, 1965 to 1989." *American Sociological Review*, 58, October 1993: 637–658.

Korany, Bahgat. "The Magreb." In Ismael and Ismael (eds.), *Politics and Government in the Middle East and North Africa*: 513–536.

Korany, Bahgat, Rex Bryen, and Paul Noble (eds.). *Political Liberalization and Democratization in the Arab World: Volume 2*. Boulder: Lynne Rienner, 1998.

Korany, Bahgat. "Monarchical Islam with a Democratic Veneer: Morocco." In Korany, Brynen, and Noble (eds.), *Political Liberalization and Democratization in the Arab World, Volume 2*: 157–184.

Kornbluth, Danishai. "Jordan and the Anti-Normalization Campaign, 1994–2001." *Terrorism and Political Violence*, 14 (3), Autumn 2002: 80–108.

Kostiner, Joseph (ed.). *Middle East Monarchies: The Challenge of Modernity*. Boulder, CO: Lynne Rienner, 2000.

Kotob, Sana Abed. "The Accommodationists Speak: Goals and Strategies of the Muslim Brotherhood of Egypt." *International Journal of Middle East Studies*, 27 (3), August 1995: 321–339.

Kowalewski, David and Dean Hoover. *Dynamic Models of Conflict and Pacification: Dissenters, Officials and Peacemakers*. Westport, CT: Praeger, 1995.

Kramer, Gudrun. "Good Counsel to the King." in Kostiner (ed.), *Middle East Monarchies*: 257–287.

Krane, Dale. "Opposition Strategy and Survival in Praetorian Brazil, 1964–79." *Journal of Politics,* 45 February 1983: 28–63.

Kriesi, Hanspeter. "The Political Opportunity Structure of New Social Movements: Its Impact on Their Mobilization." In Jenkins and Klandermans (eds.), *The Politics of Social Protest*: 167–198.

Kuran, Timar. "Now Out of Never: The Element of Surprise in the East European Revolution of 1989." In Bermeo (ed.), *Liberalization and Democratization: Change in the Soviet Union and Eastern Europe*: 7–48.

Lamchichi, Abderrahim. *Islam et contestation au Maghreb*. Paris: L'harmattan, 1989.

Landau, Rom. *Moroccan Drama, 1900–1955*. San Francisco: American Academy of Asian Studies, 1956.

Langohr, Vickie. "Tentative Propositions on NGOs and Democratization in the Arab World." Presented at the annual meeting of the American Political Science Association, San Francisco, August–September 2001.

Langohr, Vickie. "Too Much Civil Society, Too Little Politics: Egypt and Liberalizing Arab Regimes." *Comparative Politics*, 36, January 2004: 181–204.

Larbi, Hanane and Rachid Sbihi. *Économie marocaine: une radioscope*. Rabat: Al maarif al jadida, 1986.

Lawson, Fred. "Divergent Modes of Economic Liberalization in Syria and Iraq." In Harik and Sullivan (eds.), *Privatization and Liberalization in the Middle East*: 123–144.

Leca, Jean. "Opposition in the Middle East and North Africa." *Government and Opposition*, 32 (4), 1997: 557–577.

Leites, Nathan and Charles Wolf, Jr. *Rebellion and Authority*. Chicago: Markham, 1970.

Lerner, Daniel. *The Passing of Traditional Society: Modernizing the Middle East*. New York: Free Press, 1966.

Leveau, Remy. "Religion et état: Islam et contrôle politique au Maroc." In Gellner and Vatin (eds.), *Islam et politique au Maroc*: 271–279.

Leymarie, Serge and Jean Tripier. *Maroc: Le prochain dragon?* Paris: Editions EDDIF, 1992.

Lichbach, Mark Irving. "Deterrence or Escalation? The Puzzle of Aggregate Studies of Repression and Dissent." *Journal of Conflict Resolution*, 31 (2), June 1987: 266–297.

Lichbach, Mark Irving. *The Rebel's Dilemma*. Ann Arbor: University of Michigan Press, 1995.

Lichbach, Mark Irving and Alan S. Zuckerman. *Comparative Politics*. Cambridge: Cambridge University Press, 1997.

Lijnah al-Tansiq al-Watani wa-al-Dawli. *Nubir Amaoui, rajal wa qadiya*. Casablanca: Matba'a Dar al-Nashir al-Maghrabi, 1993.

Ling, Dwight. *Morocco and Tunisia: A Comparative History*. Washington, DC: University Press of America, 1979.

Linz, Juan. "Opposition to and Under an Authoritarian Regime." In Dahl (ed.), *Regimes and Oppositions*: 171–259

Linz, Juan and Arturo Valenzuela, (eds.). *The Failure of Presidential Democracy*. Baltimore: Johns Hopkins University Press, 1994.

Linz, Juan. "Presidential or Parliamentary Democracy: Does It Make a Difference?" In Linz and Valenzuela (eds.), *The Failure of Presidential Democracy*.

Linz, Juan and Alfred Stepan. *Problems of Democratic Transition and Consolidation: Southern Europe, South America and Post-Communist Europe.* Baltimore: Johns Hopkins University Press, 1996.

Lohmann, Susanne. "The Dynamics of Informational Cascades: The Monday Demonstrations in Leipzig, East Germany, 1989–1991." *World Politics, 47* (1), October 1994: 42–101.

Loveman, Mara. "High-Risk Collective Action: Defending Human Rights in Chile, Uruguay and Argentina." *American Journal of Sociology, 104* (2), September 1998: 477–525.

Lucas, Russell. "Institutions and Regime Survival Strategies." Ph.D. dissertation, Georgetown University, 2000.

Lust-Okar, Ellen. "The Decline of Jordanian Political Parties: Myth or Reality?" *International Journal of Middle East Studies, 33* (3), November 2001: 545–569.

Lust-Okar, Ellen and Amaney Jamal. "Rulers and Rules: Reassessing Electoral Laws and Political Liberalization in the Middle East." *Comparative Political Studies 35* (3), April 2002: 337–366.

Lynch, Marc. *State Interests and Public Spheres: The International Politics of Jordan's Identity.* New York: Columbia University Press, 1999.

Madanat, ʿIsa. Member, National Charter Committee. Interventions at the Seminar on Democracy and the Rule of Law – Assessment and Outlook. Amman: Royal Cultural Center, November 19, 1995.

Madanat, ʿIsa. Interview. Founding Member of the Jordanian Communist Party, Amman November 20, 1995.

Maghraoui, Abdeslam. "Monarchy and Political Reform in Morocco." *Journal of Democracy, 12*, (1), January 2001: 73–86.

Maghreb Arab Press (MAP). June 25, 1981.

Mahawin, Mawafiq. *al-ʿAhzab wa al-quwwa al-siyasiyah fi al-Urdunn: 1927–1987: bibliografiyah.* Beirut: Dar al-Sadiq li al-Tibaʿah wa al-Nashr, 1988.

Mainwaring, Scott. "Presidentialism, Multipartism, and Democracy: The Difficult Combination," *Comparative Political Studies, 26* (2), July 1993: 198–228.

Mainwaring, Scott and Matt Shugart, "Juan Linz, Presidentialism and Democracy." *Comparative Politics, 29*, July 1997: 449–471.

Majid, Majdi. *Les luttes de classes au Maroc depuis l'Indépendance.* Rotterdam: Editions hiwar, 1987.

Makram-Ebeid, Mona. "Democratization in Egypt: The 'Algeria Complex.'" *Middle East Policy, 3* (3), 1994; 119–124.

Makram-Ebeid, Mona. "The Role of the Official Opposition." In Tripp and Owen (eds.), *Egypt under Mubarak*: 21–52.

Makram-Ebeid, Mona. "Egypt's 1995 Elections: One Step Forward, Two Steps Back?" *Middle East Policy, 4* (3), 1996: 119–136.

el-Malki, Habib. "L'endettement international du Maroc: Un fait de longue durée?" in Doumou (Ed.), l'*Etat Marocain dans le durée (1850–1985)*: 153–172.

el-Malki, Habib. *Trente ans d'économie marocaine 1960–1990*. Paris: CNRS, 1989.

Malloy, James M. (ed.), *Authoritarianism and Corporatism in Latin America*. Pittsburgh: University of Pittsburgh Press, 1977.

Mamoun Fandy. "Egypt's Islamic Group: Regional Revenge?" *Middle East Journal*, 48 (4), Autumn 1994: 607–625.

Mansour, Abdellatif. "Le coup de force de Muhammad el Yazghi." *Maroc hebdo*, July 21–27, 1995: 24–25.

Marks, Jon. *Maghreb: MEED Quarterly Report*. London: MEED, November 1993.

Maroc hebdo. July 21–27, 1995: 24–25; July 28–August 7, 1995: 6–7.

Maroc soir. June 27, 1981: 1.

Mason, T. David. "Modernization and Its Discontents Revisited: The Political Economy of Urban Unrest in the People's Republic of China." *Journal of Politics*, 56 (2), May 1994: 400–424.

Massad, Joseph A. *Colonial Effects: The Making of National Identity in Jordan*. New York: Columbia University Press, 2001.

Le matin du Sahara. December 7, 1991: 1, 3.

Maxwell, Gerald and Pamela Oliver. *The Critical Mass in Collective Action*. Cambridge: Cambridge University Press, 1993.

McAdam, Doug, "Conceptual origins, current problems, Future Directions." In McAdam, McCarthy, and Zald (eds.), *Comparative Perspectives on Social Movements*: 23–40.

McAdam, Doug. "Gender as a Mediator of the Activist Experience: The Case of Freedom Summer." *American Journal of Sociology*, 97, March 1992: 1211–1240.

McAdam, Doug, John D. McCarthy, and Mayer N. Zald (eds.). *Comparative Perspectives on Social Movements: Political Opportunities, Mobilizing Structures and Cultural Framings*. Cambridge: Cambridge University Press, 1996.

McAdam, Doug, Sidney Tarrow, and Charles Tilly. "Toward an Integrated Perspective on Social Movements and Revolution." In Lichbach and Zuckerman, (eds.), *Comparative Politics*: 142–173.

McCarthy, John D. and Mayer N. Zald. "Resource Mobilization and Social Movements: A Partial Theory." *American Journal of Sociology*, 82 (6), May 1977: 1212–1241.

McFaul, Michael. "State Power, Institutional Change and the Politics of Privatization in Russia." *World Politics*, 47 (2), January 1995: 210–243.

Meiring, Desmond. *Fire of Islam*. London: Wildwood, 1982.

el Merghadi, Muhammad. Interview. Member of USFP Fes, Morocco, May 16, 1995.

Meyer, David and Suzanne Staggenborg. "Movements, Countermovements, and the Structure of Political Opportunity." *American Journal of Sociology*, 101 (6), May 1996: 1628–1660.

Middle East Economic Digest. May 8, 1981: 22.

Middle East International. November 17, 1989: 17–19; December 15, 1995: 16–17; August 2, 1996: 11; December 5, 1997: 12–13; February 27, 1998: 8.

Middle East Watch. *Behind Closed Doors: Torture and Detention in Egypt*. New York: Human Rights Watch, 1992.

Midlarsky, Manus and Kenneth Roberts. "Class, State and Revolution in Central America: Nicaragua and El Salvador Compared." *Journal of Conflict Resolution, 29* (2), June 1985: 163–193.

Migdal, Joel. *Peasants, Politics and Revolutions*. Princeton, NJ: Princeton University Press, 1974.

Migdal, Joel S., Atul Kohli, and Vivienne Shue. *State Power and Social Forces: Domination and Transformation in the Third World*. Cambridge: Cambridge University Press, 1994.

El-Mikawy, Noha. *The Building of Consensus in Egypt's Transition Process*. Cairo: American University in Cairo Press, 1999.

El-Mikawy, Noha. "State/Society and Executive/Legislative Relations." In El-Mikawy and Handoussa (eds.), *Institutional Reform and Economic Development in Egypt*: 79–86.

El-Mikawy, Noha and Heba Handoussa (eds.) *Institutional Reform and Economic Development in Egypt*. Cairo: American University in Cairo Press, 2002.

Milton-Edwards, Beverly. "A Temporary Alliance with the Crown: The Islamic Response in Jordan." In Piscatori (ed.), *Islamic Fundamentalism and the Gulf Crisis*: 88–108.

"Mini Symposium: Social Movements." *Sociological Forum, 14* (1), 1999: 54–136.

Mishal, Shaul. *West Bank/East Bank: Palestinians in Jordan 1947–1967*. New Haven, CT: Yale University Press, 1978.

Le monde. July 1, 1981: 6.

Ministère de l'Information (ed.). *Discours et interviews de S.M. le Roi Hassan II, Tome VIII*. Rabat: Ministère de l'information, 1991.

Moore, Clement Henry. "Political Parties." In Zartman and Habeeb (eds.), *Polity and Society in Contemporary North Africa*: 42–67.

Moore, Will H. "Rational Rebels: Overcoming the Free Rider Problem." *Political Research Quarterly, 48* (2), June 1995: 417–454.

Moore, Will H. "Dissent and Repression: Substitution Effects in Violent Political Conflict Behavior." July 1998. Unpublished manuscript. Available at http://garnet.acns.fsu.edu/~whmoore/researchpapers.html.

Moore, Will H. "The Repression of Dissent: A Substitution Model of Government Coercion." *Journal of Conflict Resolution, 44* (1), February 2000: 107–127.

Morrisson, Christian. *Equity and Adjustment in Morocco*. Washington, DC: Organization for Cooperation and Development, 1991.

El-Mossadeq, Rkia. "Political Parties and Power-sharing." In Zartman (ed.), *The Political Economy of Morocco*: 59–83.

Moudden, Abdelhay. Interview. Professor of Political Science, Rabat, Morocco, July 6, 1995.

Mufti, Malik. "Elite Bargains and the Onset of Political Liberalization in Jordan." *Comparative Political Studies, 32*, February 1999: 100–129.

Muhanna, Amin Awwad. "Modernization: Political Stability and Instability: The Jordan Case." Ph.D. thesis, University of Southern California at Los Angeles, August 1986.

Muhsin, ʿAziz. Interview. Chambre de commerce and d'industrie de la wilaya du grand Casablanca, Casablanca, May 30, 1995.

Munson, Henry, Jr. "Morocco's Fundamentalists." *Government and Opposition*, 26 (3), Summer 1991: 331–345.

Munson, Henry, Jr. "International Election Monitoring: A Critique Based on One Monitor's Experience in Morocco." *Middle East Report*, 209, Winter 1998: 37–39.

Munson, Henry, Jr. *Religion and Power in Morocco*. New Haven, CT: Yale University Press, 1993.

Munson, Henry, Jr. "The Elections of 1993 and Democratization in Morocco." In Bourqia and Miller (eds.), *In the Shadow of the Sultan*: 259–281.

Musa, Sulayman and Munib al-Madi. *Tarikh al-Urdun fi al-qurn al-ʿashrin: 1900–1959*. Amman: Maktaba al-madatasib, 1988.

Mustafa, Halat. *al-Intikhabat al-barlimaniyah fi Misr, 1995*. Cairo: Al-Ahram Center for Political and Strategic Studies, 1996.

Mustafa, Halah. *Intikhabat al-barlamaniyah fi Misr 1995*. Cairo: Markaz al-Dirasat al-Siyasiyah wa-al-Istiratijiyah, al-Ahram, 1997.

Mutawi, S. A. *Jordan in the 1967 War*. New York: Cambridge University Press, 1987.

Najjar, Fauzi M. "Islamic Fundamentalism and the Intellectuals: The Case of Naguib Mahfouz." *25 (1), British Journal of Middle Eastern Studies*, 1998: 139–168.

Nedelcovych, Mima Sava. "Determinants of Political Participation: A Survey Analysis of Moroccan University Students." Ph.D. thesis, Florida State University, 1980.

Nelson, Joan (ed.). *Fragile Coalitions: The Politics of Economic Adjustment*. Washington, DC: Overseas Development Council, 1989.

Nelson, Joan. "Linkages Between Politics and Economics." In Diamond and Plattner (eds.), *Economic Reform and Democracy*: 45–58.

Neto, Octavio Amorim and Gary W. Cox. "Electoral Institutions, Cleavage Structures and the Number of Parties." *The American Journal of Political Science*, 41 (1), January 1997: 149–174.

Nevo, Joseph. *King Abdallah and Palestine: A Territorial Ambition*. New York: St. Martin's Press, 1996.

Niblock, Tim and Emma Murphy. *Economic and Political Liberalization in the Middle East*. London: British Academic Press, 1993.

Njadat, Muhammad. Interview. Member of National Assembly and Jordanian National Alliance Party, Amman, August 20, 1998.

Norton, Augustus Richard (Ed.). *Civil Society in the Middle East*, Vols. I and II. London: E. J. Brill, 1995, 1996.

O'Donnell, Guillermo. *Modernization and Bureaucratic-Authoritarianism: Studies in South American Politics*. Berkeley: University of California Press, 1973.

O'Donnell, Guillermo and Philippe C. Schmitter. *Transitions from Authoritarian Rule: Tentative Conclusions about Uncertain Democracies*. Baltimore: Johns Hopkins University Press, 1986.

O'Donnell, G., Philippe C. Schmitter, and Laurence Whitehead (eds.). *Transitions from Authoritarian Rule: Comparative Perspectives*. Baltimore: Johns Hopkins University Press, 1986.

Obeidat, Ahmad. "Democracy in Jordan and Judicial Control: The Actual Situation." In Dobers, Goussous, and Sara (eds.), *Democracy and the Rule of Law in Jordan*: 39–47.

Opp, Karl-Dieter and Wolfgang Roehl. "Repression, Micromobilization, and Political Protest." *Social Forces*, 69 (2), December 1990: 521–547.

Ordeshook, Peter and Olga Shvetsova. "Ethnic Heterogeneity, District Magnitude, and the Number of Parties." *American Journal of Political Science*, 38 (1), February 1994: 100–123.

Oweiss, Ibrahim M. *The Political Economy of Contemporary Egypt*. Washington, DC: Center for Contemporary Arab Studies, 1990.

Paige, Jeffrey. *Coffee and Power: Revolution and the Rise of Democracy in Central America*. Cambridge, MA: Harvard University Press, 1997.

Payne, Rhys. "Economic Crisis and Policy Reform." In Zartman (eds.), *Polity and Society in Contemporary North Africa*: 139–167.

Paz, Reuven. "The Global Jihad Brotherhood: Egyptian Islamic Jihad and the Islamic Movement of Uzbekistan," *PolicyWatch*, 561, September 24, 2001. Available at http://www.ciaonet.org/pbei/winep/policy_2001/par03.html

Perrault, Gilles. *Notre ami Le Roi*. Paris: Gallimard, 1990.

Perthes, Volker. "States of Economic and Political Liberalization." In Kienle (ed.), *Contemporary Syria*: 44–71.

Piscatori, James (ed.). *Islamic Fundamentalism and the Gulf Crisis*. American Academy of Arts and Sciences, 1991.

Piven, Frances and Richard Cloward. *Poor People's Movements: Why They Succeed, How They Fail*. New York: Pantheon Books, 1977.

Plascov, Avi. *The Palestinian Refugees in Jordan, 1948–1957*. London: Frank Cass, 1981.

Pool, David. "The Links Between Economic and Political Liberalization." In Niblock and Murphy (eds.), *Economic and Political Liberalization in the Middle East*: 40–54.

Popkin, Samuel. *The Rational Peasant*. Berkeley: University of California Press, 1979.

Popkin, Samuel. *Political Entrepreneurs and Peasant Movements in Vietnam: Rationality and Revolution*. Berkeley: University of California Press, 1979.

Post, Erika. "Egypt's Elections." *Middle East Report 147*, July–August 1987: 17–22.

Posusney, Marsha Pripstein. *Labor and the State in Egypt: Workers, Unions, and Economic Restructuring*. New York: Columbia University Press, 1997.

Posusney, Marsha Pripstein, "Multi-Party Elections in the Arab World: Institutional Engineering and Oppositional Strategies." *Studies in Comparative International Development*, 36, Winter 2002: 34–62.

Przeworski, Adam. "Some Problems in the Study of the Transition to Democracy." In O'Donnell, Schmitter, and Whitehead (eds.), *Transitions from Authoritarian Rule*: 47–63.

Przeworski, Adam. "Democracy as a Contingent Outcome of Conflicts." In Elster and Slagstad (eds.), *Constitutionalism and Democracy*: 74–75.

Przeworski, Adam. *Democracy and the Market: Political and Economic Reforms in Eastern Europe and Latin America*. Cambridge: Cambridge University Press, 1991.

Przeworkski, Adam, Michael Alvarez, Jose Cheibub, and Fernando Limongi. *Democracy and Development: Political Institutions and Well-Being in the World, 1950–1990*. Cambridge: Cambridge University Press, 2000.

Przeworski, Adam and Jennifer Gandhi, "An Institutional Theory of Development." Presented at the annual meeting of the American Political Science Association, San Francisco, August–September 2001.

Pye, Lucian W. "Political Science and the Crisis of Authoritarianism." *American Political Science Review*, 84 (1), March 1990: 3–19.

Rachidi, Brahim. Interview. Member of the USFP, Vice President of Maarif Commune and Member of Parliament, Casablanca, June 1, 1995.

Radcliffe, Robert. "Fulbright Student Letter, Fez, Morocco; December 20, 1990," unpublished manuscript.

Radwan, ʿAbdallah. Interview. Independent, Professor of Political Science, Amman, November 19, 1995.

al-Raʾi. January 14, 1995: 1.

Reising, Uwe. "United in Opposition? A Cross-National Time-Series Analysis of European Protest in Three Selected Countries, 1980–1995." *Journal of Conflict Resolution*, 43 (3), June 1999: 317–342.

Remmer, Karen L. "The Politics of Economic Stabilization: IMF Standby Programs in Latin America, 1954–1984." *Comparative Politics*, 19 (1), October 1986: 1–24.

Rhodes, Anthony (trans.). *The Challenge: The Memoirs of King Hassan II of Morocco*. London: Macmillan, 1978.

Richards, Alan. "The Political Economy of Dilatory Reform: Egypt in the 1980s." *World Development*, 19, December 1991: 1721–1730.

Richards, Alan and John Waterbury. *A Political Economy of the Middle East: State, Class, and Economic Development*. Boulder, CO: Westview Press, 1990.

Riker, William. *The Theory of Political Coalitions*. New Haven, CT: Yale University Press, 1962.

Robinson, Glenn. "Can Islamists Be Democrats? The Case of Jordan." *Middle East Journal*, 51 (3), Summer 1997: 373–387.

Robinson, Glenn. "Defensive Democratization in Jordan." *International Journal of Middle East Studies*, 30 (3), August 1998: 387–410.

Rousset, Michel. "Le système politique du Maroc," in Claisse, Conac, and Leca (eds.), *Le grand Maghreb*: 52–72.

Rousset, Michel. "La difficile conciliation entre l'idéologie unanimitaire et l'idéologie démocratique: la cas du Maroc." *Maghreb Review*, 10 (1), 1985: 11.

Roussillon, Alain. "Islam, islamisme, et démocratie: recomposition du champ politique." *Peuples Mediterraneens*, 41–42 October 1987–March 1988: 303–339.

Royaume du Maroc, Ministère du plan. *Annuaire statistique du Maroc.* Rabat: Direction de la statistique, 1979–1994.

Rubin, Barry. *Islamic Fundamentalism in Egyptian Politics.* New York: St. Martins Press, 1990.

Rutherford, Bruce K. "The Struggle for Constitutionalism in Egypt: Understanding the Obstacles to Democratization in the Arab World." Ph.D Dissertation, Yale University, 1999.

Ryan, Curtis. "Peace, Bread and Riots: Jordan and the International Monetary Fund." *Middle East Policy,* 6 (2), October 1998: 54–66.

Saaf, Abdallah. *Chroniques des jours de reflux.* Paris, Harmattan, 1993.

Sachs, J.D. (ed.). *Developing Country Debt and Economic Performance, Vol. I: The International Financial System.* Chicago: University of Chicago Press, 1989.

El-Sadat, Anwar. *The October Working Paper, April 1974.* Cairo, Ministry of Information: April 1974.

Sagiv, David. "Judge Ashmawi and Militant Islam in Egypt." *Middle Eastern Studies, 28* (3), July 1992: 531–547.

Salamé, Ghassan. *The Foundations of the Arab State.* New York: Croom Helm, 1987.

Santucci, J. C. "Chroniques politiques Maroc." *Annuaire de l'Afrique du Nord 1984.* Paris: CNRS, 1986, 904–932.

Santucci, Jean-Claude (ed.). *Le Maroc actuel: Une modernisation au miroir de la tradition.* Paris: CNRS, 1992.

Sarah, Fayiz. *Ahzab wa-al-quwwa al-siyasiyah fi al-Maghreb.* London: Riyad al-Rayyis lil-kutub wa-al-nashr, 1990.

Satloff, Robert B. *Troubles on the East Bank: Challenges to the Domestic Stability of Jordan.* Washington, DC: Center for Strategic and International Studies, Georgetown University, 1986.

el-Sayed, Moustapha K. "The Islamic Movement in Egypt: Social and Political Implications." In Oweiss (eds.), *The Political Economy of Contemporary Egypt*: 222–240.

el-Sayyid, Mustapha Kamel. "A Civil Society in Egypt?" In Norton (ed.), *Civil Society in the Middle East, Vol. I*: 269–293.

el-Sayyid, Zahra. *Ahzab al-muʿaradah wa siyasat al-infitah al-iqtisad fi misr.* Cairo: Jumhuriyat Misr al-arabiyah: Dar al-mawqif al-arabiyah, 1986.

Schwedler, Jillian. "Framing Political Islam in Jordan and Yemen." Ph.D. thesis, New York University, 2000.

Schwedler, Jillian. *Faith in Moderation: Islamist Parties in Jordan and Yemen.* Cambridge: Cambridge University Press, in press.

Scott, James. *The Moral Economy of the Peasant: Rebellion and Subsistence in Southeast Asia.* New Haven, CT: Yale University Press, 1976.

Scott, James. *Weapons of the Weak: Everyday Forms of Peasant Resistance.* New Haven, CT: Yale University Press, 1985.

Seddon, David. "Popular Protest and Political Opposition in Tunisian (sic), Morocco, and Sudan 1984–1985." In Brown (ed.), *Etat, ville et mouvements sociaux au Maghreb et au Moyen-Orient*: 179–197.

Sedjari, Ali (ed.), *État, éspace et pouvoir locale*. Rabat: Les éditions guessous, 1991.

Sehimi, Mustapha. "Les elites ministerielles au Maroc: constantes et variables." In Santucci (ed.), *Le Maroc actuel*: 209–231.

Shami, Majed Khalil. "A Study of Marketing Practices and Financial Performances of the Banking Industry in Jordan." Ph.D. Thesis, San U.S. International University, 1991.

Shukrallah, Hani. "Political Crisis and Political Conflict in Post-1967 Egypt." In Tripp and Owen (eds.), *Egypt under Mubarak*: 53–101.

Shwadran, Benjamin. *Jordan: A State of Tension*. New York: Council for Middle Eastern Affairs Press, 1959.

Siavelis, Peter. "Continuity and Change in the Chilean Party System: On the Transformational Effects of Electoral Reform." *Comparative Political Studies*, *30* (6), December 1997: 651–674.

Sidahmed, Salam and Anoush Ehteshami (eds.). *Islamic Fundamentalism*. Boulder, CO: Westview Press, 1996.

Silawi, Saʿad. Interview. Journalist, *al-Raʾi*, November 20, 1995.

Sinai, Anne and Allen Pollack (eds.). *The Hashemite Kingdom of Jordan and the West Bank*. New York: American Academic Association for Peace in the Middle East, 1977.

Sinclair, Stuart. *Middle East Economic Handbook*. London: Euromonitor Publications, 1986.

Singerman, Diane. *Avenues of Participation: Family, Politics, and Networks in Urban Quarters of Cairo*. Princeton, NJ: Princeton University Press, 1995.

Singerman, Diane. "The Politics of Emergency Rule in Egypt." *Current History*, *101*, January 2002: 29–36.

Skidmore, Thomas E. "The Politics of Economic Stabilization in Postwar Latin America." In Malloy (ed.), *Authoritarianism and Corporatism in Latin America*: 149–190.

Skocpol, Theda. *States and Social Revolutions*. Cambridge: Cambridge University Press, 1979.

Skocpol, Theda and Jeff Goodwin. "Rentier State and Shiʾa Islam in the Iranian Revolution." *Theory and Society*, *11*, May 1982: 265–283.

Smadi, M. A. *The Unemployment Problem in Jordan: Characteristics and Prospects*. Amman: Royal Scientific Society, 1987.

Snow, Peter. *Hussein: A Biography*. London: Barrie and Jenkins, 1972.

Soltan, Gamal Abdel Gawad. "Taming the Elite: The Politics of Late Authoritarianism in Egypt." Presented at the annual conference of the Middle East Studies Association, Orlando, FL, November 2000.

Soudan, François, "L'attente." *Jeune Afrique*, June 22–28, 1995: 16–17.

Springborg, Robert. "Professional Syndicates in Egyptian Politics, 1952–1970." *International Journal of Middle East Studies*, *9* (3), October 1978: 275–295.

Stepan, Alfred. *Rethinking Military Politics: Brazil and the Southern Cone*. Princeton, NJ: Princeton University Press, 1988.

Stepan, Alfred and Cindy Skach. "Constitutional Frameworks and Democratic Consolidation: Parliamentarianism versus Presidentialism." *World Politics*, *46* (1), October 1993: 1–22.

Suleiman, Michael W. "Socialization to Politics in Morocco: Sex and Regional Factors." *International Journal of Middle East Studies*, 17 (3), August 1985: 313–327.

Suleiman, Michael W. "Attitudes, Values and Political Process in Morocco." In Zartman (ed.), *The Political Economy of Morocco*: 98–116.

Sullivan, Denis J. and Sana Abed-Kotob. *Islam in Contemporary Egypt: Civil Society vs. the State*. Boulder, CO: Lynne Rienner, 1999.

Suraqiya. May 1, 1989: 8–9.

Swearingen, Will D. *Moroccan Mirages: Agrarian Dreams and Deceptions*. Princeton, NJ: Princeton University Press, 1987.

Taagepera, Rein. "The Number of Parties as a Function of Heterogeneity and Electoral System." *Comparative Political Studies*, 32 (5), August 1999: 531–548.

Tachau, Frank (ed.). *Political Parties of the Middle East and North Africa*. Westport, CT: Greenwood Press, 1994.

Taji-Farouki, Suha. *A Fundamental Quest: Hizb al-Tahrir and the Search for the Islamic Caliphate*. London: Grey Seal, 1996.

al-Tall, Murawayd. Interview. Amman, November 1995.

Tamimi, Azzam (ed.). *Power-Sharing Islam?* London: Liberty for Muslim World Publications, 1993.

Tarrow, Sidney. *Power in Movement: Social Movements, Collective Action and Contentious Politics*, 2nd ed. Cambridge: Cambridge University Press, 1998.

Tawfiq, Ashraf Mustafa. *Majlis at-Shaʿb: Kursi al-Muʿaradah?* Cairo: al-Sharq al-Awsat lil ʿAlam al-ʿArabi: 1990.

Le temps. July 10, 1981: 1.

Terrab, Mustapha. Interview. Adviser to King Hassan II, Rabat, July 12, 1995.

Tessler, Mark. "Alienation of Urban Youth." In Zartman (ed.), *Polity and Society in Contemporary North Africa*: 71–101.

Tessler, Mark. "Image and Reality in Moroccan Political Economy." In Zartman (ed.), *The Political Economy of Morocco*: 212–242.

"Thalathin ʿamann ʿala nashu al-harakah al-naqabiyah al-ʿamaliyah al-urdunniyah: 1946–1970." *al-Urdunn al-Jadid*, July 1984: 19–33.

"Thalathin ʿamann ʿala nashu al-harakah al-naqabiyah al-ʿamaliyah al-urdunniyah: 1971–1976." *al-Urdun al-Jadid*, December 1984: 17–54.

Tilly, Charles. *From Mobilization to Revolution*. Reading, MA: Addison-Wesley, 1978.

Tozy, Mohammed. "Islam et état au Maghreb." *Maghreb Machrek*, 126, October–December 1989: 38.

Tozy, Mohammed. "Islam and the State." In Zartman and Habeeb (eds.), *Polity and Society in Contemporary North Africa*: 102–122.

Tozy, Mohammad. *Monarchie et islam politique au Maroc*. Paris: Presses de sciences politiques, 1999.

Treisman, Daniel. "Political Decentralization and Economic Reform: A Game-Theoretic Analysis." *The American Journal of Political Science*, 43 (2), April 1999: 488–517.

Tripp, Charles and Roger Owen (eds.). *Egypt under Mubarak*. London: Routledge, 1989.

Tutunji, Janab. "Planning a Workforce for the Future." *Middle East Economic Digest* (MEED), May 8, 1981: 22.

al-Urdunn al-Jadid Research Center. *Post-Election Seminar: A Discussion of Jordan's 1993 Parliamentary Election*. Amman, Jordan: al-Urdunn al-Jadid, 1995.

U.S. State Department. "Jordan Human Rights Practices, 1995," March 1996. Available online at http://dosfan.lib.uic.edu/ERC/democracy/1995_hrp_report/ashrp_report-nea/Jordan.html.

U.S. State Department, "Morocco Human Rights Practices." March 1996. Available at http://www.state.gov/www/global/human-rights/1996_hrp_report/morocco.html.

La vie économique. July 21, 1995: 3–4; July 28, 1995: 3–4.

Walker, Jack. *Mobilizing Interest Groups in America: Patrons, Professions and Social Movements*. Ann Arbor: University of Michigan Press, 1991.

Wallerstein, Immanuel. *Modern World-System*. New York: Academic Press, 1974.

Walton, John. "Debt, Protest and the State in Latin America." In Eckstein (ed.), *Power and Popular Protest*: 299–328.

Walton, John and Charles Ragin. "Global and National Sources of Political Protest: Third World Responses to the Debt Crisis." *American Sociological Review*, 55 (6), December 1990: 876–890.

Waltz, Susan. "Interpreting Political Reform in Morocco." In Bourqia and Miller (eds.), *In the Shadow of the Sultan*: 282–305.

Waltz, Susan. *Human Rights and Reform: Changing the Face of North African Politics*. Berkeley: University of California Press, 1995.

Washington Post. January 10, 1984: A10; January 23, 1984: A12; December 27, 1985: A1, 21; March 14, 1989: A21; April 20, 1989: A28, 31; April 21, 1989: A22. April 22, 1989: A1, 20; April 24, 1989: A11; April 25, 1989: A11; October 3, 1989: A25.

Waterbury, John. *The Commander of the Faithful: The Moroccan Political Elite, A Study in Segmented Politics*. London: Weidenfeld & Nicolson, 1970.

Waterbury, John. "The Political Management of Economic Adjustment and Reform." In Nelson (ed.), *Fragile Coalitions*: 39–56.

Waterbury, John. *The Egypt of Nasser and Sadat: The Political Economy of Two Regimes*. Princeton, NJ: Princeton University Press: 1983.

Weaver, Mary Anne. "The Novelist and the Sheikh," *The New Yorker*, 70, January 1995: 52–68.

Wickham, Carrie Rosefsky. *Mobilizing Islam: Religion, Activism and Political Change in Egypt*. New York: Columbia University Press, 2003.

Widner, Jennifer (ed.). *Economic Change and Political Liberalization in Sub-Saharan Africa*. Baltimore: Johns Hopkins University Press, 1994.

Widner, Jennifer. "Political Reform in Anglophone and Francophone African Countries." In Widner (ed.), *Economic Change and Political Liberalization in Sub-Saharan Africa*: 49–79.

Wiktorowicz, Quintan. *The Management of Islamic Activism: Salafis, the Muslim Brotherhood, and State Power in Jordan*. Albany: SUNY Press, 2001.

Wiktorowicz, Quintan (ed.). *Islamic Activism: A Social Movement Theory Approach*. Bloomington: Indiana University Press, 2004.

Wintrobe, Ronald. "The Tinpot and the Totalitarian: An Economic Theory of Dictatorship." *American Political Science Review*, *84* (3), September 1990: 849–872.

Yata, ʿAli, "Le PPS, la question nationale et le mouvement national et progressiste." *Economie et socialisme*, *11*, January 1992: 87–114.

Younger, Sam. "Morocco and Western Sahara." *Africa Review*, *9*, 1985: 205–211.

Zaki, Moheb. *Egyptian Business Elites: Their Visions and Investment Behavior*. Cairo: Arab Center for Development and Future Research, 1999.

Zald, Mayer N. and Michael A. Berger. "Social Movements in Organizations: Coup d'Etat, Insurgency and Mass Movements." *American Journal of Sociology*, *83*, (4), January 1978: 823–861.

Zartman, I. William, "Opposition as Support of the State." In Dawisha and Zartman (eds.), *Beyond Coercion*: 61–87.

Zartman, I. William. *Man, State and Society in Contemporary Maghrib*. New York: Praeger, 1973.

Zartman, I. William (ed.). *The Political Economy of Morocco*. New York: Praeger, 1987.

Zartman, I. William. "King Hassan's New Morocco." In Zartman (ed.), *The Political Economy of Morocco*: 1–33.

Zartman, William I. and Charles E. Butterworth (eds.). *Between the State and Islam*. Cambridge: Cambridge University Press, 2000.

Zartman, I. William and Mark Habeeb (eds.). *Polity and Society in Contemporary North Africa*. Boulder, CO: Westview Press, 1993.

Zerhouni, Saloua and Driss Maghraoui. "Between Religion and Secularism: The Debates on Cultural Identity and Politics in Morocco." Presented at the Middle East Seminar Series, Yale University, April 2004.

Zielinski, Jakub. "Transitions from Authoritarian Rule and the Problem of Violence." *Journal of Conflict Resolution*, *43* (2), April 1999: 213–228.

al-Zouby, Salim, Dr. Ahmad al-Momany, and Dr. Mahmoud Kilani. "Discussion to the Report of the Committee or Formulation of Conclusions." In Dobers, Goussous, and Sara, (eds.), *Democracy and the Rule of Law*: 92–121.

Zubaida, Sami. "Islam, the State and Democracy: Contrasting Conceptions of Society in Egypt." *Middle East Report*, *179*, November–December 1992: 2–10.

Index